Daniel Leese and Puck Engman (Eds.)
Victims, Perpetrators, and the Role of Law in Maoist China

Transformations
of Modern China

Edited by
Daniel Leese, Eugenia Lean, Alexander C. Cook,
Nicola Spakowski, and Dong Guoqiang

Volume 1

Victims, Perpetrators, and the Role of Law in Maoist China

A Case-Study Approach

Edited by
Daniel Leese and Puck Engman

ISBN 978-3-11-070778-6
e-ISBN (PDF) 978-3-11-053365-1
e-ISBN (EPUB) 978-3-11-053109-1

Library of Congress Cataloging-in-Publication Data
Names: Engman, Puck, editor. | Leese, Daniel, editor.
Title: Victims, perpetrators, and the role of law in Maoist China : a
  case-study approach / edited by Daniel Leese and Puck Engman
Description: Berlin ; Boston : Walter de Gruyter GmbH, 2018 | Includes
  bibliographical references and index.
Identifiers: LCCN 2018010534 (print) | LCCN 2018012282 (ebook) | ISBN
  9783110533651 | ISBN 9783110531046 (hardcover : alk. paper)
Subjects: LCSH: Law–China–History–20th century. |
  Law–China–History–Cases. | China–Politics and government–1949-1976. |
  China–History–1949-1976.
Classification: LCC KNQ120 (ebook) | LCC KNQ120 .V538 2018 (print) | DDC
  349.5109/045–dc23
LC record available at https://lccn.loc.gov/2018010534

Bibliographic information published by the Deutsche Nationalbibliothek
The Deutsche Nationalbibliothek lists this publication in the Deutsche Nationalbibliografie;
detailed bibliographic data are available on the Internet at http://dnb.dnb.de.

© 2020 Walter de Gruyter GmbH, Berlin/Boston
This volume is text- and page-identical with the hardback published in 2018.
Cover image: Street demonstration in Guilin celebrating the rehabilitation of Zhang Xiongfei,
1983 © Zhang Xiongfei
Typesetting: Integra Software Services Pvt. Ltd.
Printing and binding: CPI books GmbH, Leck

www.degruyter.com

Acknowledgements

Several chapters of this volume were first presented as draft versions at a workshop entitled "Digital Humanities and the Maoist Legacy: Challenges and Opportunities," held at the University of Freiburg, Germany, from 19 to 21 February 2015. Given that the workshop covered a broad range of topics, from particular digital methods to historical case studies, only part of the presentations have been collected in this volume. We would like to thank Gao Tianding, Konrad Lawson, Song Yongyi, Andrew Walder, Wu Yiching, Xu Bin, and Zhou Zunyou for their contributions, some of which have already been published elsewhere, as well as for their helpful comments. We extend special thanks to Albin Eser, former director of the Max Planck Institute for Foreign and International Criminal Law in Freiburg, for graciously accepting the invitation as keynote speaker.

The presentations and discussions on questions of digital methods have shaped our ongoing research on how China dealt with the legacies of Maoist era injustices, which under the title of "The Maoist Legacy: Party Dictatorship, Transitional Justice, and the Politic of Truth" has received generous support from the European Research Council (ERC) under the European Union's Seventh Framework Programme (FP7/2007-2013) / ERC grant agreement n° 336202].

We gratefully acknowledge additional support by the Freiburg Institute for Advanced Studies (FRIAS) for hosting the workshop. We also express appreciation for the support of the Max Planck Institute for Foreign and International Criminal Law in Freiburg, not least for their outstanding library that has been an ideal location to prepare this book. We would like to thank Rabea Rittgerodt, our editor at De Gruyter, as well as Anett Rehner for guiding the manuscript smoothly through all stages of production. Tim Löfstedt provided excellent assistance with the editing of several chapters. Finally, special thanks go to Amanda Shuman, not only for her careful translation of one of the chapters in this volume, but also for her continuous support throughout the editing process.

Contents

Acknowledgements —— V

    Daniel Leese and Puck Engman
    Introduction: Politics and Law in the Early People's Republic of China —— 1

    Xu Lizhi
1   Beyond "Destruction" and "Lawlessness": The Legal System during the Cultural Revolution —— 25

    Michael Schoenhals
2   The Intelligence Sleeper Who Never Was: Han Fuying and Case 5004 —— 52

    Wang Haiguang
3   A Different Category of Life: The Counterrevolutionary Case of a Rural Schoolteacher —— 75

    Puck Engman
4   Vetting the People's Servant: On the Principles of Revolutionary Integrity —— 98

    Jeremy Brown
5   A Policeman, His Gun, and an Alleged Rape: Competing Appeals for Justice in Tianjin, 1966–1979 —— 127

    Zhang Man
6   From Denial to Apology: Narrative Strategies of a "Perpetrator" after the Cultural Revolution —— 150

    Song Guoqing
7   The Floating Fate of a Rebel Leader in Guangxi, 1966–1984 —— 174

Contributors —— 201

Index —— 203

Daniel Leese and Puck Engman
Introduction

Politics and Law in the Early People's Republic of China

In the fall of 1957, as the Anti-Rightist campaign gained momentum in the People's Republic of China (PRC), representatives of the nascent legal system came under heavy attack. By December, internal campaign documents listed 1,140 members of the judiciary or of university law departments who had been recently purged on grounds of having attacked the socialist system or for having tried to subvert the dictatorship of the proletariat.[1] Among these were the leaders of eight provincial-level justice departments and six high people's courts, as well as some of China's most prominent law scholars.[2] Particularly hard hit was the criminal adjudication tribunal of the country's highest legal organ, the Supreme People's Court. Most of its members were singled out as "rightists" and lost their positions and Party membership. These included the chair of the tribunal, Jia Qian, who just one year earlier had been selected by Mao Zedong personally to head the special military courts in Shenyang and Taiyuan tasked with sentencing the remaining Japanese war criminals.[3] His two deputies, Zhu Yaotang and Lin Hengyuan, as well as the heads of the three criminal sentencing groups, judges Yang Xianzhi, Zhang Xiangqian, and Liu Yinxia, were all expelled from their offices, along with judge He Shao'an, legal advisor Yu Zhongluo, and others.[4] Unlike former Nationalist Party judges, who had been able to stay on in their positions after the founding of the People's Republic due to the lack of qualified communist personnel but then been removed from their offices as part of the Judicial Reform (*sifa gaizao*) campaign in 1952, most of the accused had joined the Chinese Communist Party (CCP) during the Yan'an period in the late 1930s.[5]

Why was this group at the apex of the Chinese criminal sentencing system purged and socially ostracized for more than twenty years, that is, until the late 1970s, when its surviving members were finally rehabilitated?[6] Internal case verdicts and materials from the relevant organization departments reveal strong tensions between some of the judges mentioned above and Party stalwarts, such as the contemporary vice president of the Supreme People's Court, Gao Wanlin, regarding the role of law. The conflict mainly centered on the question of "administrating justice independently" (*shenpan duli*), as stipulated by Article 78 of the 1954 Constitution. Were cases to be handled according to existing laws and regulations or should the ultimate decision rest with the respective Party committees? Although most of the accused were Party members, they had stressed the importance of independent legal procedure without political interference and the need for clear standards of adjudication as part of a comprehensive "science of law" (*falü kexue*). Given the absence of both a criminal law and a criminal procedure law, many members of the tribunal were troubled by the problem of arbitrary case sentencing due to shifting political tides, the resulting miscarriages of justice, and the lack of defining the precise nature of different types of crime.

A main point of contention was a secret directive by the CCP Center from October 18, 1954, entitled "Renewed Regulations on the Approval Procedure of Death Sentence Cases."[7] It lowered the standard for the approval of "regular" death sentences—those sentences not involving members of the Party, the government, the army, or "well-known" personalities—by stipulating that the CCP Center no longer needed to approve every decision. Instead, Party committees at the municipal or provincial level were granted authority to do so. The directive, in effect, required the Supreme People's Court to get permission from these Party committees in order to overturn a lower-level court's death penalty ruling. Jia Qian was quoted as saying: "If Party committees govern everything, what are courts supposed to do? Lodging appeals against death sentences with the Supreme People's Court thus equals a mere formality."[8] Jia even resisted implementing the directive, leading to further trouble with parts of the court leadership. Judge Zhang Xiangqian complained that even the few existing regulations, for example on economic crime or the punishment of counterrevolutionaries, had seldom been relied on in sentencing work at the Supreme People's Court: "If the original sentence did not mention specific articles, neither did we. If years were added to a sentence, this was done in chaotic fashion."[9] Jia Qian and his deputy Zhu Yaotang traced the origins of this problem to what they termed "accommodationist thinking" (*qianjiu sixiang*).[10] Judges had all too often given in to the political directives of Party committees and discarded legal principles. Especially during political campaigns, wrongful sentences had been handed out in large numbers.[11] The only countermeasure at the disposal of the judges had been to return the case to the lower instances and to advocate retrial. Once political passions calmed down, the same case would often be handled in a completely different manner.

The debates on the arbitrariness of criminal case sentencing that came to the fore in the mid-1950s harked back to a contentious issue that had characterized CCP history for a long time: the relationship between politics and law. While ruling by political fiat allowed for the greatest possible discretion, it necessarily resulted in excesses, as Mao himself stated back in 1926: "To right a wrong, it is necessary to exceed the proper limits; the wrong cannot be righted without doing so."[12] Once political campaigns and revolutionary warfare gave way to state building in local base areas, however, general rules and principles were set up to ease governance. To "operate in campaign mode" meant forgoing top-leadership control over regional developments and eroded social stability.[13] The relationship between politics and law was therefore characterized by a constant ebb and flow of attempts to carve out professional standards of adjudication and the (partial) overruling of the former in times of political campaigns.[14]

By the time the PRC was founded in 1949, substantial laws and detailed procedures with regard to criminal law were still not in place. Besides the legacies of decades of violent conflicts and ongoing consolidation efforts to suppress enemies of the socialist state, the lack of codified laws was due to differing ideas regarding the role of law in socialist society. Most Party leaders shared an instrumental view of law as a weapon of class struggle and as an expression of class interest. Yet, in order to symbolically strengthen the break with the past, many top leaders rejected any semblance of the "bourgeois" laws passed by the Nationalist Party, even for a period of transition. Already in February 1949, the CCP Center abrogated the Six Codes of the Nationalist Party and instructed the courts in the communist-held territories to rely on CCP norms and the study of Marxism-Leninism and Mao Zedong Thought instead, while preparing for the "systematic promulgation" of the "new laws of the people."[15] However, both in practice and theory, the break with the past was less clear.[16] Jia Qian, among others, had argued for a selective appropriation of older criminal adjudication principles, until new laws had been drafted. He referred to it as a "bricks and tiles theory" (*zhuanwa lun*),[17] which likened using inherited laws to the re-use of construction materials for new purposes after the scrapping of an old building. This issue was not necessarily bound to become contentious given that Dong Biwu, president of the Supreme People's Court from 1954 to 1959 and the leading legal authority of Maoist era China, as well as Stalin's main legal advisor, Andrey Vyshinsky, had voiced similar views on inheriting older laws.[18] Ultimately, the problem rested less with the concept of inheriting previous laws than with Jia's failure to display personal loyalty to the Party leadership on several issues. With the start of the Anti-Rightist campaign, he was publicly criticized for negating the class nature of socialist law, for expounding an "old law standpoint," and for failing to understand the importance of previous sentencing work as judicial precedent.

While the CCP leadership subscribed to the Leninist concept of an ultimate withering away of state and law, opinions on when and how this stage would be achieved differed. Was the solution to be found in maximizing political power through special legal and public security organs executing clearly defined laws and procedures, or was the inherently "bourgeois" nature of law and legal thinking as such the major obstacle for realizing social justice? The Bolshevik's answer in the years after 1917 tended toward the latter. Lenin and the so-called legal nihilists that led the judiciary at the time only accepted law as a temporary concession and as an instrument of politics that would eventually be replaced by planification and administrative-technical rules.[19] However, by the mid-1930s, Stalin and Vyshinsky had come to argue in favor of a strong state and judiciary to suppress domestic and international enemies as well as to aid socialist construction. As Stalin put it several times: "The withering away of the state will come not through a weakening of the state authority but through its maximum intensification."[20] Capitalist encirclement and the continued need to accustom the populace to the fundamental rules of community life were cited as reasons for the continued need of law in socialist society.[21]

The Soviet Union after 1936 presented one possible model to follow, which displayed a strong emphasis on legal codification and institutionalization, commonly termed "socialist legality." Soviet experts were invited to the People's Republic in order to help with the building of the legal system and Chinese legal officials visited the Soviet Union to see first-hand how the model worked.[22] Up to the Anti-Rightist campaign, it looked like the CCP would follow the path toward a Stalinist legal system, as advocated by the invited experts.[23] Considerable steps in this direction had been taken with the passing of the 1954 Constitution and several important laws, for example on the organization of courts and procuratorates. Criminal adjudication and criminal procedure did not receive similar codification until 1979.[24] It is in this context that we should view the criticism on arbitrary sentencing by the Supreme People's Court judges, as well as the larger debate on the role of law in socialism, which (re-) emerged in the mid-1950s in legal journals, including *Faxue* and *Zhengfa yanjiu*.[25] Calls for legal professionalization, unified standards of adjudication, and non-interference in judicial decision-making processes were, in most cases, not meant to destabilize the Party dictatorship but to strengthen it. Nevertheless, the debates also mirrored the fact that main protagonists of the discussion had come to hold varying views on what constituted "socialist legality."[26]

Given the increasingly leader-centric Chinese political system, Mao Zedong's views on the relation of law and politics carried supreme importance. Carving out a field of special legal expertise did not rest lightly with Mao, who was always weary of potential threats to Party rule and his personal power. Not only was the proclaimed goal of "administrating justice independently" bound to restrict political flexibility, it would also lead to a bureaucratization of judicial affairs and to discarding the principle of "putting politics first." At the Nanning Conference in early January 1958, Mao explicitly referred to the discussions in the legal sphere: "Some people in political-legal institutions have stated that Party and state are not separated. Should not each get one half? This will not work. There should be no division at first, later they can be divided."[27] His perception was well in line with his previous views on the continuing threats posed by enemies inside and outside the People's Republic that could only be dealt with effectively by concentrating power.²⁸ For Mao, law and courts constituted a weapon that, along with the procuratorates and the public security apparatus, fulfilled the fundamental function of detecting, investigating, and sentencing individuals or groups posing a threat or inflicting harm on society. This siege mentality, born from decades of warfare and internecine struggle, remained dominant and led Mao to ultimately prioritize flexibility over legal institutionalization, as was to become particularly clear during the Great Leap Forward and the Cultural Revolution. This attitude would lead domestic and international critics to claim arbitrary dictatorship or "legal nihilism" as Mao's preferred mode of governance.²⁹

Dossiers, File-Selves, and Practices of Law in Maoist Era China

There can be little doubt that with the Anti-Rightist campaign broader debates about the relationship between politics and law were suppressed for a period lasting until Mao's death. While some individuals continued to voice concerns or even questioned the legality of the system as such, the debates between different groups within the Chinese judiciary were muted. However, the weakening of legal debate did not equal a destruction of the legal system as such. In most parts of the country, courts came to be replaced by military control committees in the late 1960s (they were reopened by 1973), but they were only part of a much larger body of institutions involved in administrating justice. Our knowledge about how the changes in elite debates on the function and future of socialist law influenced legal practice is still rudimentary at best. What was the impact of the Anti-Rightist campaign's attack upon China's most prominent legal scholars on the enforcement of norms in a largely rural country where trained legal professionals were few and far between? Did the abrupt end to critical discussion of law in 1957 translate into an equally marked break in terms of local practice? Questions such as these can only be answered once our knowledge of legal practice matches that of judicial debates.

When Jerome Cohen published his monumental *The Criminal Process in the People's Republic of China* in 1968, he cited a discussion with a former PRC trial court judge, who advised him to combine the study of normative documents with an analysis of the concrete application of these regulations in day-to-day legal work: "You should never accept at face value the published policies and statutory documents. Instead, you ought to try to understand the essence of Communist law from living examples while studying the statutes and decrees published in each period. If you depart from this, it will not be possible to achieve anything."[30] Despite the lack of access to sources in the early 1960s, Cohen was able to include a sizable number of case examples in his volume, mostly taken from contemporary newspapers. In similar fashion, William Alford, in his classic study of the "unjust" case of Yang Naiwu and Xiao Baicai from the late Qing dynasty, demonstrated the problems of generalizing from codified texts rather than actual legal practice.[31] In recent legal histories on late imperial and Republican era China, questions related to the application, enforcement, and mobilization of legal and political norms accordingly have assumed greater prominence.[32] The same holds true for works by social scientists on the role of law in today's China.[33] In the field of PRC history, on the other hand, research seems to suffer from some of the afflictions identified by Peter Perdue with regard to the representation of Chinese property rights in the West, including an "excessively high level of abstraction" and a "lack of concern with how institutional orders and legal statutes affected social practice."[34]

While this volume touches upon the larger debates on the relationship between politics and law, it is primarily devoted to examining the local dynamics of socialist legal practice in the first thirty years of the PRC and the immediate post-Mao era. Like Cohen and Alford, the contributors aim to "char[t] in meaningful and explicated detail" the "full course" of cases.[35] In this, we follow researchers who have eschewed a purely text-centric approach to Chinese law and have come to advocate a law-and-society perspective, or what Philip Huang has called a "historical-social" method.[36] The emphasis of this volume is therefore on analyzing how law was understood, contested, and adapted by local actors in diverse settings and at different times.

In the case of the People's Republic, limited accessibility of archival records poses a serious obstacle to historical research that seeks to go beyond the declared intent of the law. Due to the ongoing sensitivity of historical court records and public security documentation from the early PRC, these files are rarely available in archives.[37] Even where judicial materials have been made accessible to researchers, they consist mainly of meeting minutes, directives, and formal reports of a kind that do not, in and of themselves, allow for close reading of investigative and adjudicatory practices. To pursue the tension between principle and practice in the application of political and legal rules, the following chapters rely on a wide range of sources, including normative documents, policy implementation reports, and oral histories. Crucial for most of the chapters, however, are personal dossiers and case files of various types. These grassroots sources are mostly documents from work units or judicial organs. They were never meant to be stored in regular archives but marked to be discarded or destroyed at some point, quite often during the "great cleansing" of archives after 1978.[38] As factories or even local Party-state organs attempted to derive at least some profit from these seemingly worthless relics of the Maoist past, the documents found their way into private collections, secondhand bookstores, and flea markets.

The characteristics of the respective files vary considerably. Michael Schoenhals bases his study, which centers on a targeted investigation in the early 1950s that never developed into a court matter, on an investigation file of a public security case examination group in Northeastern China, while Jeremy Brown uses a criminal case file of a suspected rape case adjudicated by public security agencies to analyze contesting narratives about the event. Several chapters rely on personnel dossiers, administrative files held and regularly updated by the respective work unit. These allow us to see how the criteria for investigation changed over time, as in Puck Engman's chapter on the repeated evaluations of a low-level cadre's questionable past. During periods of mass mobilization, in particular, large numbers of quasi-legal documents were added to such dossiers, including investigation reports, corroborating evidence, and official decisions regarding the status of the individual or administrative sanctions applied. Wang Haiguang's study of a rural schoolteacher, accused of being a counterrevolutionary during the One Strike, Three Antis campaign, makes strong use of such a file. In another chapter, Zhang Man relies on the files of a factory archive to demonstrate how the end of the Cultural Revolution cast the actions of a rebel leader turned cadre in a new light. In her analysis of the strategies he employed to defend himself against accusations of having driven a person to suicide, she refers to Leigh Payne's notion of "confessional scripts"[39] to show how the factory cadre reshaped his account, initially stressing his adherence to the political norms of the time but ultimately shifting to expressing guilt and showing remorse.

None of the above-mentioned files were ever intended to be returned to the individuals in question, but to remain within state or Party archives. During the great archival cleansing after the Cultural Revolution, outdated self-criticisms would occasionally be returned or, more often, weeded out for destruction. But most people had to spend enormous efforts to gain some insight into how they had been represented in case files and dossiers; in other words, to get to know their archival "file-selves."[40] The decisions made by Party committees and legal authorities were inscribed directly onto these file-selves, serving in turn to guide further state action toward the associated individuals. In this light, the case of Zhang Xiongfei, chronicled by Song Guoqing in this volume, appears as an account of a former rebel leader's uphill battle to challenge the fallacious representation of him in Guangxi administration's archives, not least by means of building a counter-archive to document and contest such official labeling.

By organizing their studies around dossiers representing specific individuals, contributors to this volume are connected by their methodological approach. The chapters also share a common concern with disaggregating criminal and administrative justice, whether the overarching historical framework is the policing of a new state in the early years of CCP rule, the campaign justice of the long 1960s, or the policies of rehabilitation and reconciliation in the 1970s. By providing accounts of how norms were implemented and contested in local settings, they pose questions transcending current descriptions of how the political-legal system was supposed to have functioned. Of course, there are dangers with regard to an excessively narrow focus on individual life stories and grassroots sources.[41] As Fudan historian Dong Guoqiang has warned, social historians are well advised not to treat their objects of study as isolated phenomena that derive their momentum solely from their own inherent logic.[42] The case studies therefore are less intended as self-contained micro-histories than as building blocks toward a new understanding of the political-legal system in the first thirty years of the PRC.

Political-Legal Administration at the Grassroots

A case-study approach to the enactment of law in the Mao period and its immediate aftermath, as adopted in this volume, does not immediately solve the problem of misrepresenting the realities of former legal practice. Quite to the contrary, there is a danger of either overgeneralizing the findings from grassroots files or of rendering them unique and beyond comparison. The social historian can control for this in several ways. In-depth empirical knowledge about one's sources is crucial in order to be aware of methodological problems and the relevance of the case in question. Equally important, however, is an understanding of how these individual case studies relate to larger questions in the field of PRC history. While the contributions to this volume touch upon many subjects, they are bound together by two common themes. First, they question the prevalent assumption that the Cultural Revolution constitutes a radical break in adjudication practices and that with the arrest of the "Gang of Four" China returned from "lawlessness" to the path of socialist legality. This assumption is rooted in the notion that the budgetary constraints and political radicalism of the 1960s disrupted legal construction. We do not reject this view altogether, but we maintain that it needs a great deal of qualification. We propose that a predictable pattern of violent excess followed by remedial measures conditioned legal practice and administrative justice over an extended period, even across the 1978 divide, leading to cyclical debates and conflicts about the relationship of procedural and distributive justice. A related proposition, further discussed in the next section, is that the CCP developed a distinctive strategy to retroactively address the foreseeable miscarriages of justice generated through this process.

The volume begins with a case study by legal historian Xu Lizhi on the role of law during the Cultural Revolution, which systematically analyzes the continuities and divergences from previous practice at the level of normative rule making. Against this background, the subsequent chapters provide a kaleidoscopic view of how state laws and Party norms were enforced and mobilized on the ground. The case studies break down the macro-concepts of retributive and restorative justice to their most basic social operations: the identification and penalization of perpetrators, on the one hand, and the recognition and assuagement of victims, on the other. Most of the chapters focus on investigation and adjudication by the *zhengfa* or *gong-jian-fa* sector (which joined together the procuratorate and courts with the public security apparatus). The volume also looks at how law was practiced in a period, roughly between 1968 and 1972, when military control committees replaced these institutions and took over their different functions. Moreover, we discuss the role of institutions never considered part of the judiciary, but that nevertheless had the power to investigate, arrest, and punish rule-breakers. In the absence of codified law and trained legal professionals, Party cadres, and *gong-jian-fa* functionaries adopted a holistic approach to dealing with "problems" involving criminal and political offenses.[43] Thus, decisions on what appear to be criminal matters were subsumed into the broader administration of conflict-resolution and social control. Although some early laws and decrees contained relatively clear instructions on how to punish offenders, many Party documents simply instructed local authorities to deal with political errors and crimes at their own discretion (*zhuoqing*), based on the principle of analogy.[44]

In the opening chapter, Xu Lizhi calls for a reconsideration of the legal system's role during the Cultural Revolution, arguing for a greater deal of continuity than previous scholarship has allowed for. To be sure, there was little constructive debate around the development and future of the socialist legal system. Indeed, the authors of the Li Yizhe manifesto "On Socialist Democracy and the Legal System" were branded as reactionaries and detained in 1975 after having called for a system not too different from what had been promised twenty years earlier.[45] However, Xu convincingly argues that during the Cultural Revolution there was a bifurcation between the rhetoric about law and the actual criminal process. Because previous scholarship has focused primarily on the former aspect, it has overestimated the singularity of the Cultural Revolution's "lawlessness" and overemphasized discontinuities and contraction of the legal sphere. The theoretical debates touched upon above shed light on legal alternatives envisioned by the political elite and judicial professionals, but they cannot tell us much about how law was enforced, adapted, and contested in everyday life.[46] As Xu Lizhi points out, a view of law in the Cultural Revolution informed by the debates of the 1950s and late 1970s is partial at best. In stressing the peculiarity of the Cultural Revolution, this view furthermore obscures the fact that the Party was unable or unwilling to develop a comprehensive alternative to "bourgeois" law for most of its first thirty years in power, notwithstanding the legislative push in the years leading up to 1958. The CCP came to govern with a bare minimum of laws and without a clear normative hierarchy to determine the relationship between Party rules and state decrees; even political speeches and newspaper editorials could have the force of law. Throughout the period in question, the authority of a "law" was less dependent on the lawmakers' expertise or the legitimacy of procedure, than it was on its adherence to the current Party line. Cohen's interlocutor phrased it the following way: "When I was receiving my special judicial training, I was repeatedly told that in the execution of law, the interest of the various political movements is imperative. Law is flexible. Any mechanical application of legal provisions will result in the error of dogmatism."[47]

The studies in this volume demonstrate the extent to which both state functionaries and the public were attuned to the rapid changes of this "flexible" normative framework. Cadres would treat comparable acts in highly different fashion depending on political imperatives, which could appear as formal rules, secret investigation quotas, and as nationwide calls for leniency or for increased vigilance against the class enemy. This volume documents how individuals made use of inconsistencies in the patchwork of principles to defend past behavior or to affirm themselves as norm-abiding citizens. Especially productive were contradictions arising from the dual set of norms at the center of the polity, in other words, from the unstable synthesis of the Party's revolutionary principles and state laws. Both accusers and accused evoked a set of common references pertaining to the rights and duties sketched out in the Constitution and other laws of the socialist state.[48] The response, however, could very well be taken from Party regulations or with reference to the overarching principles of the communist movement. Moreover, the relative importance of secret Party regulations sustained an asymmetrical relationship between Party cadres and outsiders, as the latter were limited in their ability to defend themselves simply because they did not have access to all the relevant information.

Lacking insight into specific provisions, people outside of the Party bureaucracy tended to rely on general principles and public statements made by political leaders. Mao Zedong, whose instructions were ubiquitous, was the ultimate source of contradictory authority. One single sentence by the Chairman could be used either to justify harsh punishment ("counterrevolutionaries must be eliminated wherever found…") or to reverse unjust verdicts ("…mistakes must be corrected whenever discovered").[49] With regard to law, this particular dialectical approach allowed him to state in 1958: "We no longer need to draw up a criminal law, a civil law, or a [criminal] procedure law."[50] Just four years later, in 1962, Mao would claim the opposite: "We not only need a criminal law, we also need a civil law. Currently we are in a state of lawlessness. It does not work without laws; we definitely should make [*gao*] a criminal law and a civil law."[51] Contradicting the Chairman with his own quotes, however, would not have been an advisable strategy at the time, even if these quotes had been publicly known.

As noted above, the courts were far from the only institutions with the power to assess responsibility or mete out punishment. While only two of the case studies in this volume feature direct involvement by a court (see Song Guoqing's chapter) or a corresponding body (see Wang Haiguang's chapter), most of them document convictions and punishments. Even without taking the matter to court, Party committees and public security organs had a wide repertoire of sanctions at their disposal, including demotion, public shaming, deprivation of political rights, restriction of movement, and re-education through labor. They also had the power to banish people to the countryside, a space that officials treated, in the words of Jeremy Brown, as "part prison, part garbage dump." Brown's chapter describes a contentious but conscientious investigation that led to the punishment, out of court, of a Tianjin police officer accused of rape. There was never any formal conviction specifying a particular criminal act. Instead, the rape was interpreted as part of a pattern of conduct that led the military control committee in charge of public security in 1969 to brand the officer as a "bad element" and deport him to his native village for supervision by the masses.

Several chapters in this volume stress the persistent importance of written confessions and testimonies at the cost of material evidence. Wang Haiguang's chapter details how an accused counterrevolutionary and his family were required to write and rewrite testimonies until the investigators deemed the narrative of his "crimes" sufficient in conforming to the current political discourse. According to the paternalist logic behind this exercise, the state employed coercive measures to promote education and individual reform, which required active participation by the wrongdoer. Just as the convicted were required to engage in labor and study, the accused had to testify and confess. Beyond the rehabilitative ideal, however, "education" could also serve as a euphemism for sanctions aiming to brand or isolate individuals. Particularly infamous were the "study classes" of the late 1960s and early 1970s, which feature prominently in Zhang Man's chapter. Here, to "study" could entail going through the torturous ordeal of "conveyor belt" (*chelun zhan*) interrogations until one was prepared to give a confession that tallied with the suspected crimes. Similarly, class status and political labels, which ostensibly aided personal transformation, actually became sources of exclusion and suspicion, as Puck Engman and Wang Haiguang show in their chapters. From two different perspectives, they describe how, in the 1960s, the growing suspicion that those with a "reactionary" class background posed a counterrevolutionary threat made entire strata of people into targets of surveillance and persecution. Seemingly insignificant events, when exacerbated by a "bad" class background, were taken as evidence of reactionary attitudes or even counterrevolutionary crime.

In sharp contrast to the examination of routine transgressions, Michael Schoenhals renders the early PRC as a national security state in his study of a highly sensitive and secretive investigation of a suspected enemy asset. His account brings to mind what David Shearer has dubbed the "martial law socialism" under Stalin, but Schoenhals invites us to consider other possible points of comparison.[52] By introducing a vocabulary unfamiliar to research on Mao's China, he highlights the relevance of the topic for political developments today and warns the reader that what may now seem like a "terroristic socio-political order" was not necessarily perceived as such by the people who lived in it. His study of a provincial-level public security investigation that failed to yield any results reveals the person-hours and other resources spent to meet the quotas of the Internal Elimination of Counterrevolution. The great number of campaign investigations that never led to any conviction serves as a useful reminder that there could be affinity and fluidity between "regular" police work and nationwide "terror."

The chapters of this volume fit the image of a system where the investigation of political crimes depended on the political environment and in which the ebbs and flows of state violence followed the rhythm of political campaigns. Yet equally strong is the impression that political campaigns did not lead to the abandonment of procedure, however flawed. Instead, we can identify a continuity of a set of basic principles that facilitated and expedited the criminal process in the absence of codified laws and legally trained officials, including the oft-repeated promise of leniency to those who confessed, reliance on testimonies, and a preference for "handling" situations and people rather than punishing individual acts. While it is clear that these principles lent themselves to abuse, they could also serve to limit bureaucratic exercise of violence. Although the CCP repeatedly demonstrated its willingness to violently suppress internal enemies and crime, coordination of these efforts was fiscally taxing and organizationally complex. More research is needed on the constraints of state repression, not least to further our understanding of regional and temporal differences in the human toll of nationwide campaigns. In this, qualitative and quantitative methods will need to be combined to counter what Michael Schoenhals refers to as "politically motivated massaging" of facts. Any analysis that aims to use available statistics to make claims beyond the discursive realities of violence must first consider the possibility that such data may have been distorted not only to cover up excess, but also to promote the image that local leaders were able to meet and even surpass the targets.

Rehabilitation and Retroactive Justice

The second unifying theme of this collection relates to how the CCP handled past injustices. While the program for reviewing historical cases after Mao Zedong's death was unprecedented, the process itself continued a pattern that had already emerged in the revolutionary base areas in the 1930s.[53] Simply put, each instance of large-scale repression was followed by reconciliatory measures. This strategy is epitomized in a decision issued by the CCP Center in August 1943, during the later stages of the Yan'an Rectification movement, which stated that "overly leftist action" and mistakes of judgment were inevitable and necessary byproducts of political campaigns. Such "leftist" excesses, the decision specified, had to be amended, but not prematurely: "Neither premature revision [*jiuzheng*] nor overdue revision is any good. [To revise] too early is to take a shot in the dark, it hinders the development of the movement; [to revise] too late produces mistakes [and] damages the spirit. Hence, the principle is to pay close attention and to revise when the time is due."[54] This unmistakably dialectical strategy for policing the revolution—where periods of mass mobilization, when the Party leadership was prepared to accept "leftist" excesses, were followed by periods of retroactive and reconciliatory policies, accompanied by increased vigilance against "rightist" deviation—remained in place after the founding of the PRC. In the former phase, the *gong-jian-fa* organs can be understood as instruments of "campaign justice," a term used by Peter Solomon to describe how arrests, prosecution, and trials were used to expedite grain collection and collectivization in the Soviet Union.[55] After the movement had concluded, however, law served social reconciliation and restorative justice instead. Thus, mass mobilizations in the PRC were followed by efforts to address the premeditated "excesses" that they had engendered.

After the end of the Civil War, the Suppress Counterrevolutionaries campaign confirmed that the public security sector and the people's courts would continue to function as instruments of campaign justice. The campaign served as a test run for the judiciary, during which the courts would prove, in the words of Dong Biwu, that they could be "the sharpest weapon of the people's democratic dictatorship."[56] In 1951, at the height of the campaign, the Central People's Government adopted the "Regulations for the Punishment of Counterrevolution," one of the few pieces of criminal legislation produced in the Mao Zedong era.[57] Thereafter, with the shift toward economic reconstruction around the time of the first five-year plan, the main tasks of the judiciary switched to a reconciliatory mode. In 1953, there were requests for a "change in trial work style" as the CCP Center instructed the courts to review cases and exonerate the victims of "wrongful arrests, wrongful detentions, wrongful convictions, and wrongful killings."[58] Dong Biwu now called for a review of many of the roughly six million cases that had been handled by Chinese courts since 1949 in order to check for "three wrongs" (wrongful arrests, wrongful detentions, and wrongful convictions). He estimated that, on average, ten percent of all cases had been handled incorrectly and would have to be remedied one way or another.[59] There were even attempts at regulating this process. In March 1957, the Central Case Correction Group (*Zhongyang qing'an xiaozu*) circulated provisions allowing for economic compensation "to a small number that have suffered serious personal or economic harm as the result of wrongful imprisonment."[60] Further initiatives at retroactive justice took place in the early 1960s in an attempt to correct the verdicts handed out by a zealous judiciary during the Great Leap Forward and the Anti-Rightist campaign.[61]

The death of Mao Zedong in September 1976 set in motion events that would develop into a sustained effort of retroactive justice, which was both quantitatively and qualitatively incomparable with earlier dynamics. In fact, there is only one example of redressing injustice committed under Communist Party rule that comes close: the "thaw" that followed Stalin's death on March 5, 1953, during which cadres and citizens across the Eastern Bloc benefited from a range of reconciliatory measures.[62] In both the Chinese and Soviet case the process began in familiar fashion: with purges of political rivals. The arrest of Mao's widow, Jiang Qing, together with the other members of what now became known as the Gang of Four, was followed by a nationwide hunt for local collaborators of an alleged counterrevolutionary conspiracy to seize power. Meanwhile, the CCP Center issued a call to reverse the cases of all those who had been wrongly arrested, prosecuted, investigated, imprisoned, or penalized for their opposition to the Gang.[63] Neither of these measures were particularly new, as there had been similar initiatives in the wake of Lin Biao's death in 1971 and under Deng Xiaoping in 1975, but the scope is noteworthy. To give one local example: In March 1978, Xinhua news agency reported that Shanghai had so far rehabilitated over 10,000 people who had faced persecution because of such charges.[64] Over the next few years, the figure grew exponentially as the total number of "unjust, false, and mistaken verdicts" identified by the city reached 310,000.[65]

A change in the evaluation of the Cultural Revolution and, indirectly, the historical contribution of Mao Zedong were necessary conditions for the high tide of reversing "unjust, false, and mistaken verdicts" in the spring of 1979, directly following the Third Plenum of the Eleventh CCP Central Committee. Across the country, administrative and judicial bodies were tasked with revising an ever-increasing number of cases, dating not only from the Cultural Revolution but also from the first seventeen years of the PRC and even the early stages of the Chinese communist movement. Especially in late 1978 and early 1979, the movement for historical justice became a platform for voicing grievances and occasionally even criticism of the political system. People wrote petitions, put up big-character posters (*dazibao*), made contact with highly placed cadres, or tried to get media exposure.[66] Song Guoqing's study underlines the centrality of the big-character poster as one of the "weapons of the weak" of the Cultural Revolution.[67] Rather than serving as a safe way to launch groundless accusations, as *dazibao* have come to be represented, he shows how they could be used to document and publicize atrocities condoned by the state. At the same time, the big-character posters became instrumental in generating a community of victims. Song further shows how someone who had been imprisoned as a "counterrevolutionary" relied on friends and relatives to persistently petition for a review of his case, not only to local authorities but also to Beijing. Without a comparable network, the Tianjin police officer in Jeremy Brown's chapter was no less persistent (but ultimately less successful) in appealing to the local public security bureau responsible for his case. The need to accommodate petitioners became a political priority. In 1982, appeals to have political labels and criminal verdicts revised accounted for eighty percent of the petitioners. By 1986, the proportion had decreased to less than a third.[68]

The chapters in this volume give an idea of how retroactive justice could play out at the individual level. Wang Haiguang's study conveys the sense of a routine matter: the case of the framed schoolteacher had come up for reinvestigation during the Cultural Revolution, leading to an inconclusive if lenient decision in 1971. In February 1979, at the high tide of reversals, he was formally rehabilitated. Much more complicated was the reversal of the high-profile case of the Guangxi rebel leader depicted in Song Guoqing's chapter. Song shows how the fate of a vocal and influential rebel was inversely tied to that of the regional leadership; rehabilitation became possible only after the Party Center got directly involved in the matter and replaced key officials in Guangxi. Not only those charged for political reasons tried to have their cases reviewed. Jeremy Brown's study shows how the discourse of reversing injustices was appropriated to overturn a decision on a criminal matter. Crucially, the reinvestigation of the police officer's case in 1978 led to a removal of the officer's label as a "bad element," but the investigators found that the rape charges held and rejected his attempts to link his case to the political environment.

Without a doubt, public encouragement to expose official misconduct led to wrongful charges and the persecution of already vulnerable groups, as the chapters by Wang Haiguang and Puck Engman illustrate. However, there is no reason to believe that this environment did not also bring to light real abuse of power and position. Brown accordingly suggests that the credible accusations of rape against a police officer would not have come to light without the Cultural Revolution. On a related note, Song Guoqing points out that the nationwide criticism of Lin Biao and Confucius in the mid-1970s gave a platform to former rebel leaders in Guilin to hold former Guangxi strongman Wei Guoqing responsible for those massacred during the violent repression of rebels in 1968.

The courts and adjudication groups of the Mao Zedong era convicted many more common criminals than counterrevolutionaries, but corresponding institutions were less prone to reverse these verdicts after 1978. Although common criminal cases were reviewed, the policy on reversals was stricter, with predictable consequences. A 1979 report by the Supreme People's Court Party Group stated that while fifty-four percent of the reviewed counterrevolutionary cases in the whole country had been reversed, the figure for ordinary crimes was only seven percent.[69] According to Xu Lizhi, the sharp discrepancy suggests that the legal system of the Cultural Revolution was judged (in practice if not in words) to have been relatively successful in handling common crimes and reveals a far greater amount of continuity than previous research has allowed for.

The most famous expression of historical justice in the wake of Mao's death was surely the trial against the Lin Biao and Jiang Qing Counterrevolutionary Cliques in the winter of 1980–81, colloquially referred to as the Gang of Four trial.[70] It was denounced as a show trial in the tradition of the Moscow Trials by its critics, while Chinese propaganda hailed it as comparable to the post-war trials in Nuremberg and Tokyo.[71] What is often overlooked is that it was only the most prominent among hundreds of trials held all over the country to convict former Party officials and rebel leaders for counterrevolutionary crimes committed during the Cultural Revolution. Still, the number of recognized victims greatly exceeded the list of convicted perpetrators. For both old cadres who had committed "serious mistakes" and students guilty of violence, an acceptable defense was claiming to have acted under the influence of an erroneous political line.[72] Punishment frequently took the form of disciplinary action. Zhang Man shows in her chapter that the model of accountability sanctioned by the CCP provided individuals with ample opportunities to escape meaningful punishment, as a detailed confession and promises of bettering oneself often sufficed. Responsibility was shifted upwards and the vast majority of cadres and the masses could claim to have been duped by the Gang of Four. As Deng Xiaoping and other CCP leaders decided to deal with past atrocities in "broad strokes," to "look forward," and to focus on socialist modernization,[73] all but an isolated few came to be collectively recognized as victims of the Cultural Revolution.

By offering detailed accounts of the workings of law and the different procedures that authoritatively defined victims and perpetrators, this volume provides insight into the messy reality of political justice during the first decades of the People's Republic. The outcome of individual cases not only depended on central-level policies, but also on local circumstances, persistence, the skillful employment of rhetoric, and personal relations. The case studies illustrate the intricacies of administrating justice in the Maoist period, yet they should also lead us to critically rethink the relationship of law and politics in the People's Republic of China.

Notes

1 "Qingkuang jianbao (zhengfeng zhuanji) huibian" [Collection of Situation Reports, Special Rectification Issue], no. 41, in *Fanyou juemi wenjian* [Top-Secret Documents from the Anti-Rightist Campaign], vol. 8, ed. and comp. Song Yongyi (Hong Kong: Mirror Books, 2015), 145.
2 The most prominent example is Yang Zhaolong of Fudan University in Shanghai, who was accused of negating the class nature of law and became the most prominent criticism target in the judicial realm, see Zhonggong zhongyang xuanchuanbu, ed., *Xuanjiao dongtai* [Propaganda Trends], no. 371 (March 24, 1958), 5–8.
3 Liu Qinxue, "Mao Zedong zhiling Jia Qian shen Riben zhanfan" [Mao Zedong Ordered Jia Qian to Try Japanese War Criminals], *Dangshi bolan*, no. 5 (2005), 39–42.
4 See "Quanguo renmin daibiao dahui changwu weiyuanhui chezhi renyuan" [Personnel Removed from the Standing Committee of the National People's Congress] (June 3, 1958), accessed August 30, 2017, http://www.npc.gov.cn/wxzl/gongbao/2000-12/06/content_5000530.htm.
5 On the prevalence of Nationalist legal personnel continuing to serve after 1949, see Glenn Tiffert, "The Chinese Judge: From Literatus to Cadre, 1906–1949," in *Knowledge Acts in Modern China: Ideas, Institutions, and Identities*, eds. Robert Joseph Culp, Eddy U, and Wen-Hsin Yeh (Berkeley: University of California Institute of East Asian Studies, 2016), 147.
6 A report on the first rehabilitations at the Supreme People's Court may be found in "Zhongyang yixie bumen yi gaizheng yi pi cuohua youpai" [Some Central Departments Have Already Corrected the Verdicts of Several Wrongly Labeled Rightists], *Renmin Ribao*, January 2, 1979, 1.
7 "Zhonggong zhongyang guanyu sixing anjian pizhun chengxu de chongxin guiding" [Renewed Regulation by the CCP Center on the Approval Procedures for Death Penalty Cases], *Gongan jianshe*, no. 108 (November 28, 1954), 1.
8 See the administrative conclusion on Jia Qian reprinted in Song Yongyi, ed., *Qian ming Zhongguo youpai chuli jielun he geren dang'an* [Administrative Conclusions and Personal Dossiers of One Thousand Chinese Rightists], vol. 3 (Hong Kong: Mirror Books, 2015), 25.
9 Song, *Qian ming* 6, 113.
10 Song, *Qian ming* 6, 221.
11 According to Wu Jiazhen, dismissed from his position as vice-president of the Zhejiang High People's Court during the Anti-Rightist campaign, twenty percent of the criminal verdicts

handed out during the early stages of the campaign to Eliminate Counterrevolutionaries in Zhejiang Province had been wrongful, see Song, *Qian ming* 5, 170. Internal statistics render the total for "all types of counterrevolutionary elements, criminal elements, and other reactionary elements" (*ge zhong fangeming fenzi, xingshi fanzui fenzi he qita fandong fenzi*) discovered during four rounds of investigation in Zhejiang Province between 1955 and 1958 as 13,521 individuals, compare *Quanguo sufan yundong tongjibiao* [Nationwide Statistics from the Campaign to Eliminate Counterrevolutionaries] (Beijing: Zhongyang shiren xiaozu bangongshi, September 1, 1958), table 1. The national total is given at 33,814,094 investigation targets and 449,083 convictions, with some ten percent of the investigations still ongoing, *ibid.* For statistics on the investigation targets during the first three rounds of the campaign, see the chapter by Michael Schoenhals.
12 Mao Zedong, *Selected Works of Mao Tse-Tung*, vol. 1 (Beijing: Foreign Languages Press, 1967), 28.
13 This "mode" is described in similar terms in Arch Getty's article on Stalinist mass operations, "'Excesses Are Not Permitted': Mass Terror and Stalinist Governance in the Late 1930s," *The Russian Review* 61, no. 1 (2002): 117.
14 On Mao's preference for political movements "shattering all standards" (*dapo changgui*) to generate momentum within the socialist polity, see Michael Schoenhals, "Political Movements, Change and Stability: The Chinese Communist Party in Power," *The China Quarterly* 159 (1999): 595–605. For a similar observation with regard to police work, see Michael Dutton, *Policing Chinese Politics: A History* (Durham: Duke University Press, 2005).
15 "Zhonggong zhongyang guanyu feichu Guomindang de liufa quanshu yu queding jiefangqu de sifa yuanze de zhishi" [Instruction of the CCP Central Committee on Abrogating the Six Codes of the Guomindang and Establishing the Principles for the Administration of Justice in Liberated Areas], February 1949, in *Zhongguo fazhi shi ziliao xuanbian* [Selection of Materials on the History of the Chinese Legal System], vol. 2, ed. Zhongguo fazhi shi ziliao xuanbian bianxiezu (Beijing: Qunzhong chubanshe, 1988), 1187–89.
16 Glenn D. Tiffert, "Abrogation and Its Discontents: Towards New Paradigms of PRC Law and the 1949 Revolution" (unpublished paper, AAS 2016).
17 Song, *Qian ming* 3, 25. Compare Zhang Shangzhuo and Min Sheng, "Jianguo chuqi dui suowei 'jiu fa guandian' de pipan," [Criticism of the So-Called "Old Law Viewpoint" in the Early PRC], in *Zhongguo dangdai faxue zhengming shilu* [Records of Contentious Issues in Modern Chinese Law Studies], eds. Guo Daohui, Li Buyun, and Hao Tiechuan, (Changsha: Hunan renmin chubanshe, 1998), 31–32. Yang Zhaolong supplemented the emphasis on inheriting parts of the old Criminal Law theoretically by claiming that the class character of law was never as straightforward as commonly believed, since people of various class backgrounds had taken part in its formulation, see Yang, "Falü de jiejixing he jichengxing" [The Class Character and Inheritability of Law], *Huadong zhengfa xuebao*, no. 3 (1956), 26–34.
18 Compare Jiang Yanling and Liu Jingyao, "Lun Dong Biwu lifa sixiang dui dangdai Zhongguo fazhi jianshe de qishi" [On the Revelations of Dong Biwu's Legislative Thought for Legal Construction in Contemporary China], *Shehui kexue*, no. 5 (2009): 71–73.
19 On the evolution of Lenin's thinking on law, see Jane Burbank, "Lenin and the Law in Revolutionary Russia," *Slavic Review* 54, no. 1 (1995): 23–44. While all major legal scholars and judicial functionaries of the time subscribed to a similar line of thinking, Evgeny Pashukanis was arguably the one who did the most to advance it theoretically, arguing that Marx' critique of the political economy could be extended to the legal sphere because the legal form was analogous to the commodity form. As a victim of Stalin's Great Purge,

however, his theory was suppressed and had no direct impact on the development of legal thought in China.
20 The phrase was widely quoted at the time and was elaborated upon in the most authoritative treatise on legal theory under Stalin, see Andrei Vyshinsky, ed., *The Law of the Soviet State*, trans. Hugh W. Babb (New York: Macmillan, 1948), 62.
21 For the Soviet case see Peter Solomon, *Soviet Criminal Justice under Stalin* (Cambridge: Cambridge University Press, 1996).
22 Arguably the most important such delegation was invited to visit the Soviet Union between March 11 and July 10, 1955. Headed by Minister of Justice Shi Liang, it was divided into three groups that visited courts, procuratorates, and law faculties. Each group compiled their observations in collections and translated documents to advance knowledge about the Soviet legal system within the Chinese bureaucracy, see Tang Shichun, "1955 nian Zhongguo sifa gongzuo fang Su daibiaotuan yu Sulian fazhi xingxiang de suzao" [The 1955 Chinese Judicial Work Delegation Visit to the Soviet Union and the Portrayal of the Soviet Legal System], *Zhongguo shehui kexueyuan jindaishi yanjiusuo qingnian xueshu luntan* (2008): 475–490.
23 For the influence of Soviet experts on the early development of Chinese law, see Shen Zhihua, *Sulian zhuanjia zai Zhongguo (1948–1960)* [Soviet Experts in China: 1948–1960] (Beijing: Zhongguo guoji chubanshe, 2003); Douglas Stiffler, "'Three Blows of the Shoulder Pole': Soviet Experts at Chinese People's University," 1950–1957," in *China Learns from the Soviet Union* (1949-Present), eds. Thomas Bernstein and Hua-Yu Li (Lanham: Lexington Books, 2010), 303–336. The theoretical influence of Andrei Vyshinsky, state prosecutor under Stalin, is particularly noteworthy. His argument for developing law under socialism dominated the translated textbooks and essays used in Chinese legal education in the 1950s. He remained a major reference during the re-engagement with the theoretical foundations of socialist legality in the 1980s. For an illustrative example of Vyshinsky's lasting influence, see Sun Guohua and Zeng Bing, *Ping Weixinsiji guanyu fa de dingyi* [On the Definition of Law by Vyshinsky], *Faxuejia*, no. 2 (1996): 38.
24 Although it would not be adopted for decades, the Central Government completed a first draft of the Criminal Law in July 1950. Drafting work continued under the Law Office of the National People's Congress up until 1957 and was resumed during a brief spurt of activity in 1962–63, after which it was interrupted for over fifteen years. As legal experts were being rehabilitated, the Criminal Law was finally passed in 1979; its swift adoption was a clear indicator of just how advanced earlier drafts had been, compare Wang Mingxuan and Zhao Bingzhi, eds., *Xin Zhongguo xingfa lifa wenxian ziliao zonglan* [Survey of Documents on Criminal Justice Legislation in New China], 3 vols. (Beijing: Zhongguo gongan daxue chubanshe, 1998).
25 On current censorship of these debates in PRC databases, see Glenn Tiffert, "Peering Down the Memory Hole: History, Censorship and the Digital Turn," *Washington Post*, August 21, 2017, https://www.washingtonpost.com/r/2010-2019/WashingtonPost/2017/08/23/Editorial-Opinion/Graphics/Tiffert-Peering_down_the_memory_hole_2017.pdf.
26 For an overview of the Yan'an era debates on the role of law and the emergence of a "hybrid" legal system, see Xiaoping Cong, *Marriage, Law, and Gender in Revolutionary China, 1940–1960* (Cambridge: Cambridge University Press, 2016), chapter 2.
27 "Zai Nanning huiyi shang de jianghua" [Talk at the Nanning Conference], January 11, 1958, in *Xuexi wenxuan* [Study Selections], vol. 2 (n.p.: 1967), 42.
28 On the institutional consequences of Mao Zedong's continuing siege mentality see the superb overview by Liu Zhong, "'Dang guan zhengfa' sixiang de zuzhi shi shengcheng

(1949–1958)" [An Organizational History of the Emergence of the Concept "The Party Controls Politics and Law"], *Faxuejia*, no. 2 (2013): 16–32.

29 Following de-Stalinization and the Soviet-Sino split, socialist legal scholars joined in with the international criticism against Chinese jurisprudence, maintaining that Mao had embraced the "cult of the individual" just like Stalin before him, see John N. Hazard, *Communists and Their Law: A Search for the Common Core of the Legal Systems of the Marxian Socialist States* (Chicago: University of Chicago Press, 1969), 25.

30 Jerome Alan Cohen, *The Criminal Process in the People's Republic of China, 1949–1963: An Introduction* (Cambridge, Mass.: Harvard University Press, 1968), 60.

31 William P. Alford, "Of Arsenic and Old Laws: Looking Anew at Criminal Justice in Late Imperial China," *California Law Review* 72, no. 6 (1984): 1190. On a related note, see his "On the Limits of Grand Theory in Comparative Law," *Washington Law Review*, no. 61 (1986): 945–56.

32 One can mention, for example, the Brill series *The Social Science of Practice*, edited by Philip C.C. Huang, which publishes monographs and edited volumes with the goal of emphasizing "actual economic and legal, and historical and social practices, and the theoretical logics evidenced therein." Another recent initiative explores the relationship between law and space, how law defines territories, and how it adapts to local conditions, see Jérôme Bourgon, ed., *Legalizing Space in Imperial China* (Saint-Denis: Presses Universitaire de Vincennes, 2016).

33 Neil J. Diamant, Stanley B. Lubman, and Kevin J. O'Brien, eds., *Engaging the Law in China: State, Society, and Possibilities for Justice* (Stanford: Stanford University Press, 2010).

34 Peter Perdue, "Constructing Chinese Property Rights: East and West," in *Constituting Modernity: Private Property in the East and West*, ed. Huri Islamoglu (London: I.B. Tauris, 2004), 42. See also Alford, "Limits of Grand Theory," 945.

35 Alford, "Arsenic," 1888–89.

36 Diamant, Lubman, and O'Brien, *Engaging the Law*; Philip C.C. Huang and Kathryn Bernhardt, eds., *The History and Theory of Legal Practice in China: Toward a Historical-Social Jurisprudence* (Leiden: Brill, 2014).

37 Daniel Leese, "Case Files as a Source of Alternative Memories from the Maoist Past," in *Popular Memories of the Mao Era: From Critical Debate to Reassessing History*, ed. Sebastian Veg (Hong Kong: Hong Kong University Press, 2018), chapter 10.

38 On the regulations of the archives see *ibid*.

39 Payne argues that confessional scripts "allow perpetrators to reinvent their past through narrative" to fit political or personal needs, see *Unsettling Accounts: Neither Truth nor Reconciliation in Confessions of State Violence* (Durham: Duke University Press, 2008), 19.

40 The term "file-self" was coined by psychologist Rom Harré in his study on *Personal Being: A Theory for Individual Psychology* (Cambridge, Mass.: Harvard University Press, 1984) and transferred to the realm of communist file-keeping practice by Sheila Fitzpatrick, see *Tear off the Masks! Identity and Imposture in Twentieth-Century Russia* (Princeton: Princeton University Press, 2005), 14–18. A fascinating account of a researcher's confrontation with her archival "file-self" can be found in Katherine Verdery, *Secrets and Truth: Ethnography in the Archive of Romania's Secret Police* (Budapest: Central European University Press, 2014).

41 For a critical view on grassroots historians who "grub for diversity in the dustbins of history," see Elizabeth J. Perry, "The Promise of PRC History," *Journal of Modern Chinese History* 10, no. 1 (2016): 113–117.

42 Dong Guoqiang, "Shehui shi shiye xia de 'wenhua da geming' yanjiu" [Research on the 'Cultural Revolution' from the Perspective of Social History], *Dangshi yanjiu*, no. 2 (2012). Dong is careful to note that his words of caution against a "one-sided" social history approach are not to be read as an expression of doubt over the possible contributions of a local and social perspective to the overall understanding of the development of the Cultural Revolution.
43 Peter Solomon's characterization of local legal officials in the early Soviet Union as "ordinary people performing strange and wonderful new roles" seems apt also for the Chinese case, *Soviet Criminal Justice*, 38. Klaus Mühlhahn makes a similar point in his general overview of the Chinese situation, *Criminal Justice in China: A History* (Cambridge, Mass.: Harvard University Press, 2009), 176–236.
44 Such early laws include the "Regulations for the Punishment of Counterrevolutionaries" (1951) and "Regulations for the Punishment of Corruption" (1952).
45 Anita Chan, Stanley Rosen, and Jonathan Unger, eds., *On Socialist Democracy and the Chinese Legal System: The Li Yizhe Debates* (New York: M.E. Sharpe, 1985).
46 The discursive aspect remains important to our perspective to the extent that it gave shape to legal consciousness among the population. In this respect, it is important to note that these debates were not exclusively of an elite character but took place in public and that mass participation was, at times, encouraged. Neil J. Diamant and Xiaocai Feng, "The PRC's First National Critique: The 1954 Campaign to 'Discuss the Draft Constitution,'" *The China Journal*, no. 73 (January, 2015): 1–37; Eddy U, "Intellectuals and Alternative Socialist Paths in the Early Mao Years," *The China Journal*, no. 70 (2013): 1–23.
47 Cohen, *Criminal Process*, 60.
48 Diamant and Feng, "The PRC's First National Critique," 5; Yiching Wu, "The Great Retreat and Its Discontents: Re-Examining the Shengwulian Episode in the Cultural Revolution," *The China Journal*, no. 72 (July 2014): 16.
49 "On the Correct Handling of Contradictions Among the People," February 27, 1957, in *Selected Works of Mao Tse-Tung*, vol. 5 (Beijing: Foreign Languages Press, 1977), 397.
50 Quoted from Peng Zhen zhuan bianxiezu, ed., *Peng Zhen zhuan* [Biography of Peng Zhen], vol. 4 (Beijing: Zhongyang wenxian chubanshe, 2014), 1332.
51 Ibid.
52 David R. Shearer, *Policing Stalin's Socialism: Repression and Social Order in the Soviet Union, 1924–1953* (New Haven: Yale University Press, 2009), 8.
53 The decision of the enlarged Sixth Plenum of the Sixth CCP Central Committee, which convened in November 1938, urged local Party organs to revise mistakenly labeled "'leftist' rightist opportunists" during the purge of Zhang Guotao's allies, see Zhonggong zhongyang wenxian yanjiushi and Zhongyang dang'anguan, eds., *Jiandang yilai zhongyao wenxian xuanbian* [Selection of Important Documents Since the Founding of the Party], vol. 15 (Beijing: Zhongyang wenxian chubanshe, 2011), 764. Even earlier was the "Resolution of the Northwest Central Bureau to Examine the Work to Eliminate Counterrevolutionaries" (Xibei zhongyangju shencha sufan gongzuo de jueding), November 26, 1935, which led to the rehabilitation of wrongly accused Party members, such as Liu Zhidan and Gao Gang. The resolution can be found in Zhongguo renmin jiefangjun zhengzhi xueyuan dangshi jiaoyanshi, ed., *Zhonggong dangshi cankao ziliao* [CCP Party History Reference Materials], vol. 7 (n.p.: n.d.), 229–230; the campaign and rehabilitation process is described in Song Jinshou, "Wo liaojie de Xibei geming genjudi sufan" [My View on the Elimination of Counterrevolutionaries in the Northwest Revolutionary Base Area], *Yanhuang chunqiu*, no. 10 (2012), 47–55.

54 Zhonggong zhongyang, "Guanyu shencha ganbu de jueding" [Decision on Cadre Examination], in *Jiandang yilai zhongyao wenxian* 20, 534. Gao Hua, *How the Red Sun Rose: The Origin and Development of the Yan'an Rectification Movement, 1930–1945*, trans. Stacey Mosher and Guo Jian (Hong Kong: The Chinese University Press, 2018).

55 Solomon, *Soviet Criminal Justice*, 88–90.

56 From Dong's speech on July 26, 1950, at the First National Judicial Conference, in which he advocated legal repression as an addition to, and eventually a substitute for, military force, see Gong Yuxiang, "Dong Biwu sifa sixiang shuyao" [Outline of Dong Biwu's Legal Thought], *Fazhi yu shehui fazhan*, no. 1 (2006). Similarly, scholar Wang Zhongfang judged the suppression of counterrevolutionaries a success; it had helped Chinese public security develop beyond the restriction of the Soviet model and raised the prestige of the judiciary, quoted in Dutton, *Policing Chinese Politics*, 162, 169.

57 The regulations differ from many other provisions in that they clearly define various counterrevolutionary acts and provide standards for their punishment. Equally noteworthy is the fact that the regulations were made public immediately after their adoption and even openly discussed in the Party press, in contrast to later directives, which would typically circulate solely within the Party organization.

58 The CCP Center issued these instructions (*zhishi*), which had been drafted by Peng Zhen and approved by Mao Zedong, on April 7, see *Peng Zhen nianpu* [Chronological Biography of Peng Zhen], vol. 2 (Beijing: Zhongyang wenxian chubanshe, 2012), 349. For an overview of Peng Zhen's contribution to the development of the legal system, see Pitman B. Potter, *From Leninist Discipline to Socialist Legalism: Peng Zhen on Law and Political Authority in the PRC* (Stanford: Stanford University Press, 2003).

59 Compare Dong Biwu, *Lun jiaqiang renmin sifa gongzuo* [On Strengthening the People's Judicial Work] (Beijing: Falü chubanshe, 2001), 152–53.

60 The Central Case Correction Group was set up to coordinate the work by local groups (made up by public security, procuratorate, and court personnel) to re-examine and reverse verdicts on counterrevolutionary crimes. The March 1957 notice, which carried a joint report by the Zhejiang Provincial Case Correction Group, Financial Office, and Civil Affairs Office, is quoted in Zhang Jing, "Shilun xingshi susong guocheng zhong qinquan xingwei yinqi de peichang wenti" [Tentative Discussion on Compensation Issues Resulting from Tortious Acts in the Criminal Procedure Process], *Zhongguo faxue*, no. 1 (1987): 11.

61 Dangdai Zhongguo congshu bianji weiyuanhui, ed., *Dangdai Zhongguo de shenpan gongzuo* [Adjudication in Contemporary China], vol. 1 (Beijing: Dangdai Zhongguo chubanshe, 1993), 98–101; Shao Wenjie, ed., *Henan shengzhi* [Henan Provincial Chronicle] (Zhengzhou: Henan renmin chubanshe, 1993), 101.

62 Daniel Leese, "Defining Right from Wrong: The Role of Law in the Repudiation of the Cultural Revolution" (unpublished paper, AAS 2016). Several recent studies have dealt with the social and political consequences of the Soviet "thaw," see Miriam Dobson, *Khrushchev's Cold Summer: Gulag Returnees, Crime, and the Fate of Reform after Stalin* (Ithaca: Cornell University Press, 2009); Polly Jones, *Myth, Memory, Trauma: Rethinking the Stalinist Past in the Soviet Union, 1953–70* (New Haven: Yale University Press, 2013); Kevin McDermott and Matthew Stibbe, eds., *De-Stalinising Eastern Europe: The Rehabilitation of Stalin's Victims after 1953* (New York: Palgrave Macmillan, 2014).

63 Zhonggong zhongyang, "Guanyu chongxin chuli chunshu fandui 'sirenbang' anjian de tongzhi" [Notice on Reopening Cases of Opposition Exclusively Against the 'Gang of Four'],

Zhongfa (1976) no. 23, December 5, 1976, quoted from Maoist Legacy Database (MLD), item no. 1998.

64 Xinhua Domestic Service, "Shanghai CCP committee exonerates over 10,000 people," March 12, 1978, FBIS-CHI-78.

65 Shanghai tongzhi bianzuan weiyuanhui, ed., "Zongshu" [Summary], in *Shanghai tongzhi* (Shanghai: Shanghai shehui kexue chubanshe, 2005), accessed January 17, 2018, http://www.shtong.gov.cn/Newsite/node2/node2247/node4560/index.html.

66 During an interview with Daniel Leese in 2015, the late Dai Huang recollected how as a Xinhua journalist writing on political injustices, he would get swamped with petitions from ordinary citizens, even while on his bicycle on his way to work. For his overview about the process of reversing verdicts and case examples, see Dai Huang, *Hu Yaobang yu pingfan yuan jia cuo an* [Hu Yaobang and the Reversal of Unjust, False, and Mistaken Cases] (Beijing: Zhongguo wenlian chuban gongsi, 1998). On the great number of people petitioning to have their cases reversed, see Xiao Donglian, *Lishi de zhuangui: cong boluan fanzheng dao gaige kaifang, 1979–1981* [Turning Point in History: From Restoring Order from Chaos to the Reform and Opening up, 1979–1981] (Hong Kong: Chinese University Press, 2008), 107–10; Isabelle Thireau and Linshan Hua, *Les ruses de la démocratie: protester en Chine* (Paris: Seuil, 2010), 179–212.

67 James Scott, *Weapons of the Weak: Everyday Forms of Peasant Resistance* (New Haven: Yale University Press, 1987).

68 Zhonggong Jiangxi shengwei bangongting xinfangchu, Jiangxi sheng renmin zhengfu bangongting xinfangchu, eds., *Xinfang gongzuo ziliao xuan (1980–1987)* [Selected Materials on Letters and Visits Work], vol. 1 (n.p.: 1989), 37, cited in Thireau and Hua, *Les ruses de la démocratie*, 192.

69 Zhonggong zhongyang, "Pizhuan zuigao renmin fayuan dangzu guanyu shanshi shanzhong de wancheng fucha jiuzheng yuan jia cuo an gongzuo ji ge wenti de qingshi baogao" [Transmission of the Supreme People's Court Party Group's Report with Request for Instructions on a Few Issues Related to Carrying Through the Work to Re-examine and Revise Unjust, False, and Mistaken Verdicts to the End], *Zhongfa* (1979) no. 96, January 25, 1983, in MLD, item no. 72.

70 On the trial as text, see Alexander C. Cook, *The Cultural Revolution on Trial: Mao and the Gang of Four* (Cambridge: Cambridge University Press, 2016).

71 Fei Xiaotong, the famous sociologist who served as one of the judges at the trial, evoked the post-war trial analogy in a *People's Daily* article reprinted as the introduction to *A Great Trial in Chinese History* (Beijing: New World Press, 1981), 1–11. Zhang Sizhi, who was part of the legal defense, notes a fundamental affinity between the trials in Moscow, Nuremberg, and Beijing, Judith Bout, *Les confessions de Maître Zhang* (Paris: Francois Bourin, 2013), 287.

72 Zhonggong zhongyang zuzhibu, "Guanyu jiaqiang lao ganbu gongzuo de ji dian yijian" [A Few Opinions on the Strengthening of Old Cadre Work], December 29, 1978, in MLD, item no. 217; Zhonggong zhongyang, "Guanyu qingli 'san zhong ren' ruogan wenti de buchong tongzhi" [Additional Notice on Some Problems with Clearing Out the "Three Types of People"], *Zhongfa* (1984) no. 17, July 31, 1984, in MLD, item no. 74; Liu Zhenhua, "Zhengque duidai ganbu zai 'wenge' zhong de cuowu" [Correctly Treating Mistakes Committed by Cadres in the "Cultural Revolution"], *People's Daily,* June 21, 1985.

73 Deng Xiaoping used this metaphor on various occasions, most famously in his speech at the Third Plenum of the Eleventh Central Committee, see "Jiefang sixiang, shishi qiushi, tuanjie yizhi xiang qian kan" [Emancipate the Mind, Seek Truth from Facts, and Unite as One in Looking to the Future], December 13, 1978, in Zhonggong zhongyang wenxian yanjiushi, ed., *Sanzhong quanhui yilai zhongyao wenxian huibian* [Collection of Important Documents since the Third Plenum], vol. 1 (Beijing: Renmin chubanshe, 1982), 20–21.

Xu Lizhi
1 Beyond "Destruction" and "Lawlessness"
The Legal System during the Cultural Revolution

Chinese domestic interest in the question of the Cultural Revolutionary legal system and related research has been going on for over forty years, at least if one takes the appearance of the big-character poster "On Socialist Democracy and the Socialist Legal System"[1] in Guangzhou back in 1974 as a starting point. Since then, there have been two periods of increased public and scholarly attention. The first phase began immediately after the end of the Cultural Revolution when, in the process of contemplating the lessons to be drawn from the movement, a discussion emerged on the question of the legal system during the Cultural Revolution. Many writings on this period still contain elements of this discussion.[2] The second phase commenced in the late 1990s when the legal system during the Cultural Revolution became a subject of special interest in the field of legal history. Key publications of this period all contain special sections on the development of the legal system during the Cultural Revolution.[3] Since the turn of the millennium, a few more articles on the subject have been published.[4] There have also been several debates regarding the question of crime during these years,[5] yet overall, there has been no substantial new research on this subject.

There is a fairly obvious tendency in current debates and research on the Cultural Revolutionary legal system. Most participants analyze the period from the angle of "negating" the Cultural Revolution and therefore emphasize the destruction of the legal system. The aforementioned big-character poster by the Li Yizhe group is a case in point. The authors take the standpoint that, by the summer of 1968, the socialist legal system was destroyed through the perversion of the existing structures by the Lin Biao Clique. The result is described as a situation of "lawlessness" (*wufa wutian*). Research after the Cultural Revolution has basically followed this line of reasoning and has taken the destruction of the legal system as the dominant model of explanation. The situation of the legal system during this period has accordingly been characterized as "complete destruction" or "extreme destruction."[6] Others have used phrases such as the "complete erosion of the legal system," the "legal system's demolition" or have described it as "unworthy of being mentioned" because "democracy and the legal system were completely ruined."[7] Finally, some scholars have analyzed the period from the angle of "rule of man" vs. "rule of law." During the Cultural Revolution, the CCP accordingly

---
Translated and edited by Daniel Leese

displayed a "legal nihilism" that emphasized "rule of man" and neglected "rule of law." The terms are used both as analytical categories to explain a major reason for the emergence of the Cultural Revolution as well as a description of frequently witnessed phenomena during this period.[8]

This trope of "destruction," which these writings employ, is built on the assumption that the socialist legal system built after 1949 was abandoned, ceased to function, or at least came to be fundamentally altered during the Cultural Revolution. Phenomena of turmoil doubtlessly existed at the time and current scholarly literature has mostly focused on an analysis of these instances. The resulting discursive framework and scholarly agenda has accordingly been primarily focused on revealing the destruction of the legal system. This research tendency is closely related to the peculiar nature of the object of analysis. Chinese society during the period of the Cultural Revolution was special in so far as appearance and reality were often bifurcated. Developments on the surface and internal working procedures differed enormously. The destruction of the legal system took place mostly on the surface and thus quickly garnered scholarly attention, not least because it is comparatively easy to describe.

The emergence of this research trend is also related to the official evaluation of the period. After the end of the Cultural Revolution, the official negation of the movement, as well as the emphasis on showcasing its destructive impact on existing structures and the public order, has had a major influence on scholarship. This tendency has also had a positive aspect. By revealing the destruction wrought by the Cultural Revolution, contemporary experiences could be summarized as a warning for later generations. Yet to describe this period solely in terms of destruction raises suspicions of partiality. The Cultural Revolution was a movement conducted under CCP control and built on the premise of keeping the foundations of state and society in place. The aim of the movement was to stabilize the dictatorship of the proletariat and to hinder a "capitalist restoration." It was not a revolution aimed at overturning the system as such. Within Party theory and institutions, the post-1949 legal system was always closely entwined with the people's democratic dictatorship and the dictatorship of the proletariat. Thus, why would Cultural Revolutionary authorities have aimed at completely discarding the legal system with its close relation to the dictatorship of the proletariat which was, after all, massively strengthened during the Cultural Revolution? According to our current understanding, the legal system built up before the Cultural Revolution suffered attacks and even partial destruction during the late 1960s. But from a macroscopic point of view, it was nowhere as serious as a collapse or near breakdown of the legal system. While destruction did take place, other parts of the legal system continued working within certain limits and some functions of the system were even strengthened.

Basic Characteristics of the Legal System and the Question of Continuity

The Chinese "socialist legal system," prior to the Cultural Revolution, was a fairly special type of legal system. Scholars were previously of the opinion that it should be classified as part of the continental civil law tradition and not as a distinctive type of legal system. This viewpoint has some truth to it. Formally speaking, the Chinese "socialist legal system" is a system that puts existing laws into practice. It therefore definitely shares some characteristics with the civil law tradition. But if one analyzes some of its essential features, significant differences come to the fore. The Chinese "socialist legal system" clearly has some special characteristics that set it apart from other legal systems. First, the legal system operates within the limits of political restrictions, as it was formed and developed under the rules and guidance of political principles. Second, the legal system was founded on the precondition of disbanding China's previous legal system and setting one up anew in accordance with revolutionary theories. From the previous legal order, only a few parts were kept that did not touch upon questions of ideology. Third, the laws were painstakingly drawn up by the Party-state upon coming to power; the organically grown part is minor. Private law has therefore been overshadowed by public law. Fourth, the legal system is of relational character. Laws only have absolute authority within a predefined range. Fifth, the system's changeability has been considerable. Conflicts between the legal system's "socialist" attributes and its "regular" or "professional" components were bound to appear. The constant tug of war between these two different sets of components led to numerous changes over time.

Due to these special characteristics of the "socialist legal system," it is legitimate to view it as a distinct type of legal system that differs from its modern Western counterparts. This legal system, just like the socialist system and the dictatorship of the proletariat, was a product of the international communist movement and appeared in all socialist countries. The system emerged in embryonic form in the base areas controlled by the CCP prior to 1949.[9] By the mid-1950s, it had developed into a basic framework, encompassing the following four parts: legal principles, a system of legal sources, a judiciary, and a legal order. This framework experienced some setbacks, such as when some "professional" principles that had been written into the 1954 Constitution came to be criticized in the late 1950s. Although this led to some disorder in the establishment of legal institutions, the basic structure and main pillars of the system continued to exist.

During the Cultural Revolution period, the legal system experienced severe shocks. Major changes took place with regard to nearly every aspect of the legal system, yet the basic structure was by no means destroyed. The Cultural Revolutionary leadership circles did not reject the former legal system outright. The 1954 Constitution was fully confirmed[10] and the elements that had previously constituted the legal system, i.e. the legal principles, legal sources, the judiciary, and the legal order, still remained in place. There were no essential changes in any of these four areas. Only with regard to parts of the legal system's structures, its role and function, and implementation, did there appear some variations from previous practice. The main characteristics of the pre-Cultural Revolution legal system, such as the interference of politics in legal affairs, the fact that law obtained absolute authority only within predefined spaces, and the volatile character of the legal system were all upheld during this period. Several of these traits were even strengthened, as will be shown in the following sections of this chapter by looking at the four parts of the legal system in closer detail.

The Continuation of Legal Principles

Within the Chinese "socialist legal system," legal principles assume a highly important role. Principles of political character especially play both a regulatory and guiding function, touching upon all aspects of the legal system. Among the political principles, the most important ones are the guiding role of Marxism-Leninism and Mao Zedong Thought, the leadership of the CCP, the dictatorship of the proletariat, and the socialist path. These later coalesced into the "four cardinal principles."[11] They still represent the fundamental principles that the CCP has uniformly upheld in assuming power and governing the country. The principles emerged in the process of establishing a "socialist" legal system and came to assume a fundamental guiding role with regard to the creation of every part of the legal system, as well as during the implementation of all types of legal measures. Every measure with legal relevance that the CCP adopted before and after coming to power was decided on, carried out, and completed according to the guiding function of these principles. This applied, for example, to the abolishment of the Republican legal system and the cleansing and reeducation of remaining judicial personnel, and to setting up Party groups within courts and procuratorates. The importance of politics was also visible in having to implement judicial work in accordance with the Party's guiding principles and policies, as well as in adhering to the Party's concrete decisions and instructions. Furthermore, the adoption of the Constitution and other laws and regulations followed the overarching necessity of carrying out socialist transformation and exercising class dictatorship. The influence of these principles was further visible in the naming practices of judicial institutions: the word "people's" was added to the names of courts and procuratorates in order to symbolically demonstrate that they followed the basic principle of being instruments of the people's democratic dictatorship, even beyond the actual act of establishing these institutions. Simultaneously, it also reflected the guiding function of the Marxist theory of "sovereignty of the people."[12]

In addition to the four cardinal principles, two other relatively important political principles deserve mention. One is the principle of the mass line, which demands that judicial work serve the masses and rely on the masses.[13] The masses should be drawn into legal activities by way of taking part in case investigations, adjudication, and the actual implementation of sentences. The other principle is the distinction between two different types of contradictions.[14] Within judicial work, a distinction had to be drawn between friend/enemy contradictions and contradictions among the people. Cases were to be dealt with based on the respective nature of the contradiction. Friend/enemy cases accordingly were to adopt the method of dictatorship, while cases of contradictions among the people were to be handled through critical education. Legal sanctions were perceived only as a supplementary measure.

Of course, within China's "socialist legal system" there also existed several professional principles. Among these was the principle laid down in the 1954 "Organic Law of the People's Courts" and the "Organic Law of the People's Procuratorates" stating that judicial organs should apply laws equally to all parties. They further included the principle laid down in the 1954 Constitution and related organic laws that judicial organs "administer justice independently" (Article 78), and the principle that gradually emerged after 1949 that public security organs, courts, and procuratorates divide their work responsibilities and mutually constrain each other. Professional principles also stated that in criminal adjudication punishment and leniency should work in tandem and that in civil suits mediation be emphasized. Yet, unlike the above-mentioned principles of political character, all of these principles belonged to the realm of the judicial organs' working principles. Professional principles only became effective within a predefined range and only under the precondition that they would not stand in conflict with political principles.

Some of these professional principles were discarded following the change in the CCP's political line and the general trend towards anti-professionalism in the national legal system after 1957. During the Anti-Rightist campaign, the principles of "equality before the law" (Article 85) and independent administration of justice received criticism. Equality before the law was perceived as "obliterating the class character of law" and thus as "talking about equality with counterrevolutionaries." Judicial independence was described as the "attempt to set up the judiciary and the people's democratic dictatorship in opposition to each other."[15] At the same time, political principles were gradually strengthened. This holds especially true with regard to Party leadership, as a more systematic system of Party control over the judiciary was established. The CCP Center, as well as all kinds of Party committees above county-level, established political-legal commissions tasked with drawing up guiding principles and policies for judicial work, thus coordinating the relations between public security organs, courts, and procuratorates. Local judicial institutions were made responsible to local Party committees. Not only did they have to adhere to the Party's guiding principles and policies but they also had to follow instructions and concede supervision through the Party organization regarding case sentencing. Verdicts on important criminal cases were first commented on and then approved by Party committees at the same level. The principles of the mass line and of distinguishing between two different kinds of contradictions gained a more important place. There was even a specific debate on how to distinguish and handle the problem of two different types of contradictions in judicial work among legal scholars at the time.[16]

Up to the Cultural Revolution, this general trend became more pronounced. Professional principles were gradually eroded and political principles assumed extreme importance. This can be seen in five trends.

First and most conspicuously, the guiding role of Marxism was strengthened and the propagation of Marxism-Leninism and Mao Zedong Thought became even more prominent. Likewise, criticism of every idea or expression considered in opposition to this ideology was heightened. In 1975, the guiding function of Marxism-Leninism and Mao Zedong Thought was written into the Constitution and it was stipulated that "state organizations and state personnel must earnestly study Marxism-Leninism-Mao-Zedong-Thought."[17] All segments of state and society, including the legal system, now fell under the constraints of accepting the guiding role of this ideology. At that time "Mao Zedong Thought" had been transformed into the theory of "continuing revolution under the dictatorship of the proletariat."[18] This theory was officially negated after 1978. However, this was only a change in content with regard to "Mao Zedong Thought" and did not affect the strengthening of the principle of the "guiding role of Marxism-Leninism-Mao-Zedong-Thought" as such. Many of the changes within the legal system during this period were closely related to this ongoing process of strengthening the importance of ideology. Even the "smashing of the public security organs, procuratorates, and courts,"[19] which is commonly perceived as a destruction of the legal system, could ideologically be justified with the decision-maker's understanding of Marxism.[20]

Second, the "dictatorship of the proletariat" was pushed to extremes. Not only did the level of strengthening surpass any previous period, the meaning of "dictatorship" was also broadened, giving rise to the theory of "exercising all-round dictatorship over the bourgeoisie in the superstructure, including all spheres of culture."[21] Because the basic function of the political-legal sector, as part of the administrative system, was to serve as instrument of dictatorship, it had for a long time been referred to as a "sword," which makes the strengthening of the "dictatorial" principle with regard to the legal system abundantly clear. The majority of laws to appear within this ten-year period, as well as those normative documents with legal validity all related to "strengthening the dictatorship of the proletariat." The "Six Articles on Public Security" (*gongan liu tiao*),[22] which came to have an enormous impact on criminal adjudication during the Cultural Revolution, were drawn up according to the principle of "strengthening the dictatorship of the proletariat." The guiding principle of prioritizing attacks against "counterrevolution," as well as the practice of not having the organs of dictatorship handle civil cases, are all expressions of this underlying principle.

Third, the leadership of the CCP was gradually strengthened. Although during the Cultural Revolution alleged "capitalist roaders" were purged from the Party and especially local institutions were attacked, this did not shake the fundamental principle that the Party was to assume overall leadership. The Party Constitutions passed at the Ninth Party Congress in 1969 and at the Tenth Party Congress in 1973 both clearly stipulated that all organs of the dictatorship of the proletariat, the PLA, the people's militias, the Communist Youth League, the trade unions, the poor and lower middle peasant associations, the Red Guards, and other revolutionary mass organizations, "need to accept the leadership of the Party."[23] The 1975 Constitution also made clear that the National People's Congress should be considered a power structure under the leadership of the CCP,[24] thereby indicating the ultimate superiority of the Party over state institutions. With regard to the legal system, Party control over legislation was preserved. The Constitution and other documents with legal validity that emerged within the ten-year period were quite often drafted on behalf of the CCP Center or even directly drawn-up and proclaimed in its name. The principle of Party leadership over the judiciary remained unchanged as well. Only when the local Party leadership was paralyzed were some changes made. Leadership power over local judicial organs in these circumstances was exercised either by Party committees within the PLA or by local revolutionary committees under the leadership of the Party Center. Once lower-level Party organizations had been reestablished, the old system remained in effect. Local Party committees guided the respective judiciary. Decisions regarding arrests and verdicts in criminal cases were commented on and approved by the local Party committee.

Fourth, the principle of socialism was continuously upheld. Concerning activities deemed to be destructive to the socialist economy, such as engaging in "speculation and profiteering," harsh counter-policies were implemented throughout the Cultural Revolution.[25] In 1968 and 1970 specific campaigns sought to target illicit economic behavior. In related documents, the CCP Center made it abundantly clear that fighting economic crimes such as "speculation and profiteering" should be regarded as being of "equal importance to fighting active counterrevolution."[26] When circumstances were particularly grave, these types of crimes were to be punished more harshly, and even led to the execution of a small number of convicts accused of the most severe economic crimes. The severity of punishment thus exceeded the pre-Cultural Revolution period.

Fifth, the principles of the mass line and the distinction between two types of contradictions were left in place. Especially with regard to the mass line, the emphasis on implementing "mass dictatorship" was strengthened. The range of mass involvement in judicial affairs was accordingly widened. It was increasingly common to hold discussions with members of the masses before deciding on a criminal case verdict.[27] During the Cultural Revolution, legal principles were not completely rejected. Previously existing political principles remained, some of which were even reinforced as a result of the overall political situation.

The Continuity of Legal Sources

The question of legal sources in the post-1949 Chinese legal system is complex. Besides state legislation, which has been treated as a legal source in different types of legal systems, there were many other types of official documents that came to assume legal validity. In February 1949, the CCP Center clearly stipulated in its "Instruction to Abolish the Guomindang's Six Codes and to Define the Judicial Principles for the Liberated Areas": "Under the present circumstances, where the people's law has not yet been fully established, the working principles of the judicial organs shall be based on the following. In cases where rules have been enshrined in manifestos, laws, orders, regulations, or decisions, these rules in the manifestos, laws, orders, regulations, or decisions should be followed. In cases where there are no rules enshrined in manifestos, laws, orders, regulations, or decisions, the policies of new democracy should be followed."[28] Although this principle was adopted in the context of sparse legal sources, it foreshadowed the trend that the CCP would adopt after coming to power. Not only did what are commonly termed "laws" come to constitute important legal sources, but policies and decisions drafted by the ruling Party and state institutions also assumed this function. CCP leaders later confirmed this viewpoint several times. Mao Zedong, for example, claimed: "Every decision of ours is law; holding a meeting is also law,"²⁹ and Liu Shaoqi stated: "Law can only serve a referential purpose when getting things done" (*falü zhi neng zuo wei banshi de cankao*).³⁰

It has never been completely clarified which sources of law the judiciary should ultimately rely upon, or in what hierarchical relation the different legal sources should be placed. In pre-Cultural Revolution practice, the legal system's sources consisted of the following five components. (1) Policies of the ruling Party. These usually took the form of requests or regulations of principal character that enforced a guiding role over legislation and the judiciary. They most often appeared in documents circulated by Party and state organs or in speeches by Party leaders. Examples include the "Instruction of the CCP Center on Punishing Private Businessmen who Violated the Law and Resolutely Fight Off the Mad Attacks of the Bourgeoisie during the 'Three Antis' Struggle,"³¹ which was passed in January 1952, or the principle of "killing none and capturing few." Mao Zedong had coined this phrase during the Yan'an period in the struggle against "spies" and re-emphasized it in a 1956 speech when outlining how to deal with counterrevolutionaries in administrative units.³² (2) Laws, regulations, administrative statutes, and decisions of truly national legislative character drawn up by the state legislative organs or central government, such as the "Constitution of the People's Republic of China" passed in 1954, the well-known "Regulations for the Punishment of Counterrevolutionaries" decreed in 1951, the 1952 "Regulations for the Punishment of Corruption," or the "Decision that all Death Penalty Cases need to be Decided on or Approved by the Supreme People's Court" issued by the National People's Congress in 1957.³³ (3) Documents of normative character issued by the CCP Center or the Central Government. These include the "Draft Regulations on the Policy Limits of Arresting Counterrevolutionaries and other Criminal Elements" issued by the CCP Center in 1956 and the "Additional Explanations of the CCP Center's Ten Person Small Group" on the above document passed the following year.³⁴ Other examples include the "Report on Resolutely Preventing the Problem of Free Movement of the Population" put forward by the Party groups of the Ministry of Internal Affairs and the Ministry of Public Security in November 1961³⁵ and the "Provisional Regulations of the State Council on Determining the Organizational and Political Boundaries between Striking against Speculation and Profiteering and the Banning of Long-Distance Trafficking of Private Commerce."³⁶ (4) Documents of guiding character issued by central political-legal organs, such as the "Summary of the Experiences of Handling Cases of Sexual Assault of Underage Girls and Opinion on Sentencing Crimes of Sexually Assaulting Underage Girls" decided on by the Supreme People's Court in November 1954.³⁷ Another example is the "Summary of Criminal and Civil Case Trial Procedures by People's Courts at all Levels" issued by the Supreme People's Court in October 1956.³⁸ (5) Policies, statutes, and documents of normative or guiding character issued by Party and government organs or judicial institutions at the local level. Among all these legal sources, the one that should actually be of utmost importance, namely, state legislation, has to be described as comparatively weak. Fundamental laws both in terms of substance and procedure in criminal and civil case adjudication were not finalized in the Maoist period. The most important impact on the judiciary was presented by a small number of particular and often unrelated laws and statutes, as well as the large number of documents drafted and issued in the name of Party, government, or judicial institutions.

This composition of legal sources basically continued into the period of the Cultural Revolution. With the exception of a very small number of statutes that were criticized as public security organs, procuratorates, and courts came under attack, the vast majority of pre-existing legal sources were not abolished. The 1954 Constitution, the 1950 Marriage Law, and the 1954 "Regulations on Detention and Arrest," among others, remained effective throughout. The wording of several articles of the Constitution even became widely known within society during this period because these were quoted in central documents.[39] Some statutes, such as the "Regulations for the Punishment of Counterrevolutionaries" and the "Regulations for the Punishment of Corruption," continued to serve as the basis of case decisions during the early phase of the Cultural Revolution. While they were no longer directly referred to later on, they continued to influence case handling. Due to the changes in the political climate, some statutes, as well as documents of normative or guiding character, naturally lost their validity. Especially in the case of the latter two types of documents, rather often during the Cultural Revolution some regulations or guiding opinions aimed at specific periods or incidents lost their validity.

In addition to these formerly existing legal sources, a few new laws and regulations came into effect. The National People's Congress passed a Constitution, the State Council enacted a few administrative regulations, and there existed many political documents and leaders' speeches with legal validity. These new legal sources were largely in line with the earlier legal sources in terms of guiding thought, drafting principles, and composition. The emergence of some policies that clearly failed to meet the principles of the regular legal system was not a characteristic of this period alone. As early as the 1950s, behavior that should have been declared illegal according to existing PRC laws frequently went unpunished, especially during political movements.

In official propaganda materials, and in a few scholarly works, one finds the claim that changes with regard to legal sources during the Cultural Revolution mirrored the destruction of the legal system. This viewpoint is usually illustrated with reference to the "Six Articles on Public Security." Some officially compiled chronicles and books even depart from conspiracy theories, claiming that this or that clique enacted the "Six Articles" in order to "usurp the highest power within the state and the Party" and dissolve the standards for criminal conviction set by the "Regulations for the Punishment of Counterrevolutionaries" in order to be able to persecute cadres and the masses at will.[40] This claim lacks even the most basic factual proof. The CCP Center and the State Council jointly issued the "Six Articles." They established the fundamental policies on crime during the Cultural Revolution period, most importantly by way of strengthening the "dictatorship over the enemy," by protecting the "revolutionary masses," and by using the law to punish counterrevolutionary acts. The document contains regulations on punishing counterrevolution that are similar to the 1951 "Regulations on the Punishment of Counterrevolutionaries." However, because the former is only a policy document, unlike the "Regulations," it does not contain specific standards to determine the length or severity of the respective penalties. As for the crime of "malicious slandering" (*edu gongji*),[41] which resulted in the imprisonment of many people and has often been brought up as an example of the destruction of the socialist legal system, it is not in conflict with the "Regulations" or other CCP policies in this realm. Among the examples of counterrevolutionary acts listed by the "Regulations" are speech crimes like "carrying out counterrevolutionary propaganda and agitation, or fabricating and disseminating rumors."[42] The crime of "malicious slandering" within the "Six Articles" does not exceed the range of activities laid down in the "Regulations" with regard to counterrevolutionary crime. From a professional point of view, it can even be argued that, according to the stipulations of the "Six Articles," only attacks against Mao Zedong or Lin Biao constituted a crime. This effectively limited the range of determining this type of crime. After the end of the Cultural Revolution, in the process of negating the previous movement, the authorities did not do away with this type of legal regulation, which was perceived as a product of the Cultural Revolution. Instead, they emphasized that utterances containing defamatory attacks against Party and state leaders should be handled according to criminal standards.[43] It thus becomes evident that the crime of "malicious slandering" did not only exist during the Cultural Revolution and that regulations regarding this type of crime should not, in simplifying fashion, be taken as proof of the destruction of the previously existing legal system.

Continuities within the Judicial System

For a long time after the establishment of the People's Republic of China, there were few regulations within national legislation regarding the judicial system. Given that neither a criminal nor a civil procedure law had been passed, these passages derived from the Constitution, the organic laws of the people's courts and procuratorates, and several other statutes. Apart from these, many other components of the judicial system were established by the issuing of documents with normative or guiding character by institutions like the CCP Center, the Central People's Government, the Supreme People's Court, the Supreme People's Procuratorate, and local Party committees or local courts. Because these documents derived from different organs, systematic correspondence between the documents and national legislation, as well as between the documents, was lacking. Instead, due to the influence of political forces, frequent changes took place in the system. The general situation concerning the judicial system thus has to be characterized as extremely complicated.

Judicial functions were mainly taken on by specialized institutions such as public security organs, procuratorates, and courts prior to the Cultural Revolution. The public security organs were predominately responsible for placing cases on file, pre-trial investigations, and the detention and arrest of a suspected criminal. Among these, all tasks with the exception of arrests were decided on and carried out by the public security organs themselves. Moreover, they could propose the arrest of a suspect. However, the arrest was only to be carried out after obtaining authorization through procuratorates and leadership organs.[44] The procuratorates were tasked with preparing the indictment and conducting part of the investigations. Furthermore, they were to supervise the courts in matters of sentencing and implementation of verdicts. The courts were in charge of trial work in civil and criminal cases. Besides setting up criminal and civil adjudication tribunals, depending on the respective nature of the case, they also installed adjudication committees (*shenpan weiyuanhui*). These were staffed by the chief justice and his deputy, members of the court's Party group, as well as the heads of the tribunals. The function of the committee was to discuss and decide on difficult cases in the respective jurisdiction. In hearing cases, the courts practiced the systems of judicial hierarchies and appeals. Both civil and criminal law procedure followed a two-stage appeal process. If the implicated parties were dissatisfied with the first verdict, they had the right to appeal their sentence once. Yet, in the early years of the PRC, counterrevolutionaries who had received a death penalty or a prison sentence were barred from appealing their verdicts.[45] The courts were also supposed to implement public trials, the rule of avoidance, the collegiate system, people's assessors, the adversary system, the circuit system, specified decision mechanisms, and the system of adjudicative supervision. However, some of the systems and mechanisms had characteristics that set them apart from comparable systems in other countries—for example, case sentencing. Besides the fact that ordinary cases were heard and tried by courts while difficult cases were first heard by the court and then discussed and decided upon through adjudication committees, as stipulated through national legislation, criminal cases still had to await approval by political leadership organs. Before a criminal case verdict was officially proclaimed, the court in charge had to report to leading bodies at the same or higher political levels. Only after obtaining approval would the court verdict become effective.[46] Occasionally, after a major criminal case had been decided upon, public sentencing rallies would be convened with many people participating, during which the verdict was proclaimed. According to the principles established in the early 1950s, public security organs, procuratorates, and courts should have practiced a system of divided work responsibilities and mutual constraint. In terms of implementation, however, this division of responsibilities was not always carried out. During the Great Leap Forward, for example, the phenomenon of having all three units jointly adjudicate cases was noteworthy.[47]

In addition to the specialized institutions, i.e. the public security organs, procuratorates, and courts, there were a number of other bodies and organizations that directly or indirectly took part in judicial work. Among these were three institutions, namely leadership organs, as well as peripheral and temporal organizations. It was no novelty that leadership organs played a crucial role. For a long time, China has been characterized by a system in which the CCP has taken the lead with regard to every aspect of politics and society in unified and concentrated fashion. This system has two characteristics. On the one hand, it has been marked by a fusion of power (*quanli jizhong*). Local power is concentrated in the Party's leadership organs, while national power is concentrated in the CCP Center. On the other hand, however, the system has simultaneously been characterized by a confusion of powers (*quanli hunhe*). After the founding of the PRC, all types of powers were merged in the leadership organs, since they had the authority to lead and take part in all kinds of affairs. While they combined different powers and exercised them in unified fashion, below these organs, other bodies were set up according to the principle of work division. With regard to the judicial system, the CCP Center and Party committees at lower levels not only exercised their authority by drawing up guidelines and policies, as well as deciding on work duties, but they also immediately took part in the handling of cases, as described above. Thus a system, in which Party committees approved arrests and decided on case verdicts, emerged prior to the Cultural Revolution.

Peripheral organizations included security departments (*baowei bumen*) established in industrial and administrative work units and rural people's communes, as well as urban and rural militia organizations. These two types of organizations had the function of helping the public security organs in regulating criminal activities, investigating cases, arresting suspects, and supervising those individuals within a unit or people's commune serving administrative or criminal sentences. Among the temporary organizations, finally, were the "people's tribunals"[48] established during the land reform campaign with the specific task of handling campaign-related cases. Other institutions that emerged at various times included "work groups" (*gongzuozu*) and "case examination groups" (*zhuan'anzu*). The status of the people's tribunals was still reasonably clear-cut. They were a specific type of court that handled relevant cases according to special procedures. As to the question of what type of institutions the other two ultimately belonged to, an easy definition is not possible. They can, more or less, be viewed as temporary working bodies established to serve certain functions within a system characterized by a confusion of powers. Some workgroups and case examination groups commanded definite quasi-legal powers. They were authorized to put a case on file and to engage in investigations. Just like public security organs or procuratorates, they could take compulsory measures toward investigation targets. Therefore, the organization of the pre-Cultural Revolution judicial framework was comparatively distinct. Some extra-legal organizations could take part in the execution of legal authority. This sets the system apart from its Western counterparts, in which courts form the core of the judiciary.

This judicial system underwent major changes during the Cultural Revolution that may be divided into three distinct phases. The first period covers the latter half of 1966. Although the mass movement had already begun and local Party and government organizations occasionally rendered defunct, the political-legal system as such was not yet paralyzed. Therefore, the public security organs, procuratorates, and courts continued to handle civil and criminal cases within the accustomed system. The second period covers the years between 1967 and 1971. Due to the criticism of legal organs, the system fell into a state of paralysis. Some of the previously existing systems, rules, and mechanisms ceased to function. Most scholarly works, therefore, refer to this period when discussing the destruction of the legal system. Taking the more complex contemporary realities into account, the judicial framework truly experienced severe shocks during these years, but these did not result in changing its basic nature. The basic organizational structure of the judicial system did not change. It still consisted of professional organs, leadership organs, peripheral organizations, and temporary organs. Only the concrete institutions underwent changes. The professional organs, such as the courts, were replaced by military control committees or security departments of the respective revolutionary committees.[49] The local Party committees, as leadership organs, were replaced either through Party committees within the military or through local revolutionary committees. Among the peripheral and temporary organizations, the militia system prominently continued its existence. Furthermore, the number of case examination groups increased significantly. Among the aforementioned institutions, the change within the professional organs was most pronounced, yet the previously existing system was not completely turned on its head. The pre-Cultural Revolutionary judicial framework had already been characterized by a concentration of political power and a fragmentation of administrative authority. Judicial powers remained firmly in the hands of the leadership organs, while professional institutions, like the courts, served their respective functions and carried out concrete casework.

The paralysis of the judicial institutions during the Cultural Revolution did not fundamentally change this basic framework. There were numerous continuities between the former judicial institutions and their successors, and not only with regard to their basic functions. It is interesting to note that, even in the new institutions, certain internal organs such as "public security groups" or "procuratorate and court groups" were set up, partly staffed by members of the former judicial organs, and assumed concrete case handling. This practice, to some extent, had the flavor of reintroducing parts of the downsized former organs within the new structures.

Furthermore, there were also certain continuities related to specific judicial mechanisms and systems during the second period. Cultural Revolutionary sources refer to at least the following five types: (1) in some provinces, the two-stage trial and appeal system was still in place. Defendants who did not accept the first verdict continued to appeal their sentences.[50] (2) Some provinces and regions continued to rely on the approval of arrests by leadership organs. In the case of ordinary suspects, prefecture-level revolutionary committees or Party committees in army units above division level were to approve their arrests. The arrests of suspects at the county level or above, as well as special cases, were approved by either the provincial revolutionary committee or Party committees within the military at the provincial level.[51] (3) The indictment system was upheld either through the military control committees in charge of the previous judicial organs or through security departments within the revolutionary committees.[52] (4) Public sentencing rallies also continued and were carried out in most localities. Especially in serious criminal cases, this was the preferred mode of passing judgment. (5) With regard to criminal sentencing, particularly for cases in which convicts were to be immediately executed, provincial-level revolutionary committees or their respective military counterparts had to verify the verdict and pass it on to the CCP Center for approval. In all other cases, provincial, prefectural, and county-level revolutionary committees or the Party committees in corresponding military institutions were to approve the sentences.[53] During the One Strike, Three Antis campaign in 1970, the power to decide on death penalty cases was lowered to provincial-level leadership organs.[54] Yet, generally speaking, even during this most chaotic period of the Cultural Revolution, the continuity of the basic features of the legal system was not completely interrupted.

The third phase began in 1972, when public security organs and courts were gradually reestablished following the change of attitude toward them among the Cultural Revolutionary leadership circles. The procuratorates, abolished in 1968 as part of the administrative downsizing, remained defunct. At the same time that institutions reemerged, most of the judicial mechanisms and systems were implemented anew. Courts at the provincial level circulated all types of documents in order to recreate the previous system and decided to carry out a few technical modifications of the rebuilt structures. This situation continued until the end of the Cultural Revolution.

The Continuity of the Legal Order

The notion of the "legal order" (*falü zhixu*) is often used to describe the social order created, regulated, and protected by the respective laws. A true legal order can only exist in countries practicing rule of law. For a long time after 1949, China did not adhere to the principle of rule of law. Therefore, a legal order of relative importance existed only within certain limits. The Chinese legal order encompassed both a political order and a regular social order. The political order was predominantly created and regulated through the CCP's political measures. Laws only fulfilled a protective function within confined spaces. The regular social order was created, regulated, and protected through laws, yet during political campaigns it would also be influenced by politics.

Scholarly descriptions of how the legal order was destroyed during the Cultural Revolution are often imprecise. There were mainly three types of phenomena that signified severe disruptions, or even a destruction of the legal order. The first consisted of the fact that the numerous illegal actions taken by mass organizations, especially during the early period of the movement (1966–1968), were not punished according to legal procedures. These actions included the beating, arresting, or killing of people, battles between opposing factions, the destruction of private and public property, and the demolition of cultural artifacts.[55] The second phenomenon relates to acts committed by power organs outside the established legal procedures. These include arrests, imprisonment, and even massacres of common people or of those who were "movement targets" (*yundong duixiang*). The killing of the "Four Types of Elements" in Daxing County near Beijing carried out by low-level power organs in August 1966 is a case in point.[56] Further examples include the military suppression of rebel factions in the first half of 1967 in Qinghai and other places,[57] and the massacres carried out by armed forces and people's militias in Guangxi in 1968.[58] The third phenomenon relates to the reliance on torture and illegal persecution through political-legal organs and all types of case examination groups. If compared to the destructive activities of mass organizations, the illegal and brutal actions of state and Party institutions were much more pronounced and represent the worst breach of the legal order during the Cultural Revolution. Thus, it has to be confirmed that the legal order suffered severe devastation during the Cultural Revolution and that chaotic phenomena seldom witnessed in peaceful times appeared.

Yet, the level of destruction did not reach a state of "lawlessness." Despite the social turmoil, the underlying political order was protected by the national legal system and continued to exist. This political order encompassed two parts. The first part refers to the order comprised of Party rule, state power, and the social system. The leadership of the CCP, the socialist system, and the dictatorship of the proletariat were not easily opposed or attacked. Violators continued to receive harsh punishment. The second part refers to the order of political identities (zhengzhi shenfen), determined through class background and political performance.[59] Political identities decided the social rank and rights of an individual. The rights of those deemed to belong to an enemy class were curtailed, and those who violated these restrictions were punished. These two basic parts of the political order were not destroyed during the Cultural Revolution period. All thoughts or acts that were deemed to oppose the Party, socialism, or the dictatorship of the proletariat were strictly forbidden and persecuted. "Counterrevolution" continued to be harshly suppressed. At the same time, the order of political identities was gradually strengthened in accordance with the course of the movement. Freedom of residence and movement of alleged "enemy elements" and their families was strictly limited.[60] Even during the Cultural Revolution, there were very few examples of those attempting to overthrow the basic political order. Although the search for counterrevolutionaries was carried out incessantly during these ten years, the number of counterrevolutionary cases, on average, was lower than during the decade prior to the Cultural Revolution. According to official statistics, between 1966 and 1976, political-legal organs handled 280,000 counterrevolutionary cases nationwide.[61] Between 1956 and 1965, in Beijing, Shanghai, Sichuan, Gansu, and Shaanxi alone, about 420,000 counterrevolutionary cases were dealt with at first instance.[62] Furthermore, most of the alleged counterrevolutionary cases fall into the category of "unjust, false, and mistaken cases" that were reversed after the Cultural Revolution. Real attempts at destabilizing Party rule rarely occurred.[63]

It would also be inappropriate to characterize the social order during the Cultural Revolution as being in a state where no laws were upheld. Although authorities used the method of breaking existing conventions to launch the movement, they were far from discarding all control over the underlying social order. While in some places and during specific periods of time illegal activities were condoned to suit the aims of the Cultural Revolution, the policy toward ordinary crime remained consistent otherwise. During the ten-year period, many documents were passed to optimize the current order and to target criminal activities. Ordinary crime was mostly dealt with according to the established regulations. Furthermore, some concentrated efforts were organized, such as those targeting crimes against sent-down youth,[64] or when the five northwestern provinces jointly organized an attack against criminals on the run.[65] The 1970 nationwide One Strike, Three Antis campaign also included a concentrated effort at combatting selected types of ordinary crime; others were tracked down in the process of targeting counterrevolution in particular. With regard to penalties, Cultural Revolutionary verdicts usually took a comparatively harsh stand on ordinary crime. Among the case files that this author was able to access, there are numerous examples, such as the case of a man who was sentenced to death for having engaged in illicit relations with six women and for having had extra-marital sexual intercourse.[66] In another case, someone had to serve a ten-year prison sentence for having illicitly obtained money with an accumulated worth of less than 1000 yuan.[67] While ordinary crime increased during the Cultural Revolution, the increase was moderate. If one compares the crime rate for ordinary crime in the ten years before the Cultural Revolution with that during the movement itself, according to currently available materials, the increase in the national crime rate stayed below fifty percent.[68] In some provinces, the number of ordinary crimes recorded during the Cultural Revolution was even lower than before the movement.[69] If one takes the ordinary crime rate as a yardstick and further accounts for the population growth during this ten-year period, which was around twenty-eight percent, the increase might even be lower. This also tallies with memories of many people who lived through that period. With the exception of illegal persecutions carried out by authorities and mass organizations against individuals, personal rights were not randomly infringed upon. Thus it would be an overstatement to claim that the Cultural Revolution completely destroyed the existing social order.

Summary

As the brief analysis above makes clear, the destruction of the legal system during the Cultural Revolution was not as serious as commonly believed and did not result in a state of lawlessness. Although destruction of a certain degree cannot be negated in some areas, other parts of the pre-existing legal system continued or were even strengthened during the Cultural Revolution. The destruction of the legal system should not, in all instances, be considered as the sole cause for Cultural Revolutionary legal calamities. In some cases, these instead arose from strengthening malpractices of the pre-existing legal system. By only focusing on the aspects of destruction of the legal system, the complexities of the contemporary legal situation cannot be satisfyingly explained. The background of the "ten years of turmoil" makes it easy to overlook the continuously harsh control of authorities over society and the continued existence of a national legal system. It may also lead to wrong judgments of post-1949 history. By overemphasizing the differences between the Cultural Revolution and the periods before and after it, its disasters appear unrelated to the foundations of the political system. We should, therefore, adjust our ways of thinking about law during the Cultural Revolution. Complementing the dominant, "evaluative" mode of research, which emphasizes destruction, should be a second type of approach. This new approach should focus on the continuation and strengthening of the prior legal system in order to achieve a more complete, fact-based view of the role of law during the Cultural Revolution.

Notes

1. For an English translation see Anita Chan, Stanley Rosen, and Jonathan Unger, eds., *On Socialist Democracy and the Chinese Legal System: The Li Yizhe Debates* (Armonk: M.E. Sharpe, 1985).
2. See for example Wang Nianyi, *Da dongluan de niandai* [A Decade of Great Upheaval] (Kaifeng: Henan renmin chubanshe, 1988) and Yan Jiaqi and Gao Gao, *Turbulent Decade: A History of the Cultural Revolution*, trans. and ed. D. W. Y. Kwok (Honolulu: University of Hawai'i Press, 1996).
3. Yang Yifan and Chen Hanfeng, eds., *Zhonghua renmin gongheguo fazhi shi* [A History of the Legal System of the People's Republic of China] (Harbin: Heilongjiang renmin chubanshe, 1997); Han Yanlong, ed., *Zhonghua renmin gongheguo fazhi tongshi* [A Comprehensive History of the Legal System of the People's Republic of China], 2 vols. (Beijing: Zhonggong zhongyang dangxiao chubanshe, 1998); Cai Dingjian, *Lishi yu bianҏe: Xin Zhongguo fazhi jianshe de licheng* [History and Transformation: The Course of Establishing New China's Legal System] (Beijing: Zhongguo zhengfa daxue chubanshe, 1999) and Guo Chengwei, ed., *Xin Zhongguo fazhi jianshe 50 nian* [Fifty Years of Establishing New China's Legal System] (Nanjing: Jiangsu renmin chubanshe, 1999).
4. See Feng Mengcheng, "Dui 'wenhua da geming' zhong 'wufa wutian' xianxiang de pouxi" [Analysis of the Phenomenon of "Lawlessness" during the "Cultural Revolution"], *Dangshi yanjiu ziliao*, no. 6 (2001): 31–36 and Cao Shouliang, "'Wenhua da geming' shiqi de fazhi gongzuo gouchen" [A Review of Legal Work during the Period of the "Cultural Revolution"], *Langfang shifan xueyuan bao*, no. 12 (2015): 57–62.
5. See Li Xihai, "Wo guo 'wenhua da geming' shiqi de fanzui yanjiu" [Research on Crime during our Country's "Cultural Revolution" Period], *Henan sheng zhengfa guanli ganbu*

xueyuan xuebao, no. 3 (2008): 49–54; Dan Zhengping, "Wenhua da geming: Shenquan zhengzhi xia de guojia zuicuo" [The Cultural Revolution: State Crimes in a Theocracy], *Modern China Studies*, no. 3 (2003), http://www.modernchinastudies.org/us/issues/past-issues/82-mcs-2003-issue-3/1299-2012-01-06-09-16-39.html; and Yang Xiangxi, "Shenpan 'wenge sharen'an' meiyou shixian" [The Adjudication of "Cultural Revolutionary Murder Cases" Is not Subject to Time Limitations], February 21, 2013, accessed January 18, 2018, http://star.news.sohu.com/20130221/n366610084.shtml.

6   See Han, *Fazhi tongshi* 2, 581.
7   See Wang Renbo and Cheng Liaoyuan, *Fazhi lun* [On the Rule of Law] (Jinan: Shandong renmin chubanshe, 1989), 349. Most official writings on the period, including the verdict against the alleged Gang of Four, use this type of characterization.
8   Yang and Chen, *Fazhi shi*, 28–29; Li Buyun, "Fazhi he renzhi de genben duili" [The Basic Opposition between Rule of Law and Rule of Man], *Xiandai faxue*, no. 2 (1981): 36–39; Li Anzeng, "'Wenhua da geming' chengyin de fazhi yinsu tanxi" [A Discussion of Legal Factors as a Cause for the "Cultural Revolution"], *Zhonggong dangshi yanjiu*, no. 6 (2004): 31–36.
9   On the development of the legal system in the base areas, see Trygve Lötveit, *Chinese Communism 1931–1934: Experience in Civil Government* (London and Malmö: Curzon Press, 1979), 106–144. See also Zhang Xipo and Han Yanlong, eds., *Zhongguo geming fazhi shi* [A History of the Chinese Revolutionary Legal System] (Beijing: Zhongguo shehui kexue chubanshe, 2007).
10 At the meeting of the Fourth National People's Congress in January 1975, CCP Politburo Standing Committee member Zhang Chunqiao in his "Report on the Revision of the Constitution," stated the following: "The practice of the past twenty years has proven that [the 1954 Constitution] is correct. Its basic principles can still be applied today." Quoted in You Lin, Zheng Xinli, and Wang Ruipu, eds., *Zhonghua renmin gongheguo guoshi tongjian* [Comprehensive Mirror of the History of the People's Republic of China], vol. 3 (Beijing: Hongqi chubanshe, 1993), 438.
11 Deng Xiaoping, "Uphold the Four Cardinal Principles," March 30, 1979, in *Selected Works of Deng Xiaoping (1975–1982)* (Beijing: Foreign Languages Press, 1984), 166–191.
12 Marx referred to this concept in his "Critique of Hegel's Philosophy of Right." It received further explanation in his "The Civil War in France" and Lenin's *State and Revolution*. For the CCP, this concept became the basic theory used to discuss the relationship between state and law.
13 Mao Zedong, "Some Questions Concerning Methods of Leadership," in *Selected Works of Mao Tse-Tung*, vol. 3 (Beijing: Foreign Languages Press, 1965), 117–122.
14 For the official version of the speech, see Mao Zedong, "On the Correct Handling of Contradictions among the People," in *Selected Works of Mao Tse-Tung*, vol. 5 (Beijing: Foreign Languages Press, 1977), 384–421.
15 See Han, *Fazhi tongshi* 1, 443–44 and Di si jie quanguo sifa gongzuo huiyi mishuchu, ed., *Di si jie quanguo sifa gongzuo huiyi wenjian* [Documents of the Fourth National Meeting on Judicial Work] (Beijing: Falü chubanshe, 1958), 44. Additionally see Chen Shouyi, "Xin Zhongguo faxue sanshi nian yi huigu" [A Look Back at Thirty Years of Chinese Jurisprudence], *Faxue yanjiu*, no. 1 (1980): 1–10.
16 See Mao Rongguang, "Yong jieji fenxi de guandian lai chuli anjian: Zai Shanghai faxuehui zuotanhui shang de fayan jilu" [Using the Viewpoint of Class Analysis to Solve Cases: Records of Speeches Held at the Shanghai Law Conference], *Faxue*, no. 7 (1958): 8–11;

Yang Daqun and Shen Guansheng, "Zai xingshi anjian zhong ruhe qufen liang lei maodun de yijian" [Opinion on How to Distinguish the Two Types of Contradictions in Criminal Cases], *Renmin sifa*, no. 9 (1959): 4–7 and Zhu Jiliang, "Guanyu fanzui de maodun xingzhi wenti: Xuexi Mao zhuxi 'Liang lei maodun' xueshuo de yidian tihui" [On the Problem of the Nature of Criminal Contradictions: Some Insights from Studying Chairman Mao's Theory of "Two Types of Contradictions"], *Zhengzhi yu jingji*, no. 1 (1960): 6–10.

17 Article 11 of *The Constitution of the People's Republic of China* (Beijing: Foreign Languages Press, 1975), 19.

18 This theory was developed by Mao Zedong in the 1960s. Its basic premise was the continuation of classes and class struggle during the entire socialist period. According to Mao, it was possible that the proletarian power would be overthrown and capitalism would be restored. He thus deemed it necessary to continue solving problems by revolutionary means. The "targets of revolution" still consisted of the former "oppressive classes," along with members of a "newly emerging" exploiting class. The latter was perceived to consist of representatives of capitalism emerging from all levels of the Party-state itself, as well as so-called "people in power taking the capitalist road." This theory was the basic justification for Mao Zedong's unfolding of the Cultural Revolution.

19 The "smashing of the public security organs, procuratorates, and courts" was a major slogan and practice during the Cultural Revolution. It referred to attacks against organs of all three sectors and criticism of its representatives. The attacks gained force in early 1967 as the leadership claimed that the organs had executed the "revisionist" line of Liu Shaoqi in the seventeen years since the founding of the PRC. Attacks were accordingly stepped up and most of the associated personnel were sent to factories or to the countryside, leading to a state of (semi)paralysis. This situation continued until 1971, when the leadership revised its standpoint and ended this practice.

20 Jiang Qing, Xie Fuzhi, and other leaders of the Cultural Revolution claimed that public security organs, procuratorates, and courts had been "carried over from capitalist countries" and that they represented "things of the capitalist class and feudalism." These statements were based on their understanding of Marxist doctrines regarding the class nature of law. See Han, *Fazhi tongshi* 2, 609.

21 This theory forms part of Mao Zedong's concept of "continuing revolution under the dictatorship of the proletariat." According to classic Marxist definitions, the notion of "dictatorship of the proletariat" mainly refers to suppressing acts of resistance by enemy classes. Although in CCP history the scope of dictatorship was expanded to include the realms of thought and culture early on, this practice was not elevated to the level of theory. Mao gradually expanded its reach and it had a major impact during the Cultural Revolution. It was finally written into the 1975 Constitution. See Article 12 of *Constitution of the People's Republic of China*, 20.

22 The "Six Articles" were proclaimed in a document authored by the CCP Center and the State Council in January 1967 under the title of "Guanyu zai wuchan jieji wenhua da geming zhong jiaqiang gongan gongzuo de guiding" [Regulations on Strengthening Public Security Work during the Great Proletarian Cultural Revolution], in Guofang daxue dangshi dangjian zhenggong jiaoyanshi, ed., *'Wenhua da geming' yanjiu ziliao* [Research Materials on the "Cultural Revolution"], vol. 1 (Beijing: Zhongguo renmin jiefangjun, Guofang daxue dangshi dangjian zhenggong jiaoyanshi, 1988), 247. For a translation see Flora Sapio, https://florasapio.blogspot.de/2011/06/notorious-six-articles-on-public.html, accessed August 30, 2017.

23 See Article 5 of the version of the CCP Constitution adopted by the Ninth Party Congress, as well as Article 7 of the version passed by the Tenth Party Congress, reprinted in You, *Guoshi tongjian* 3, 421 and 431.
24 See Article 16 of *Constitution of the People's Republic of China*, 25–26.
25 This charge existed for several decades and basically referred to activities aimed at the destruction of the socialist economy. The charge was officially abolished with the revision of the Criminal Law in 1997.
26 "Zhonggong guanyu fandui tanwu daoqie, touji daoba de zhishi" [CCP Instruction on Opposing Graft and Theft, as well as Speculation and Profiteering], see You, *Guoshi tongjian* 3, 1442.
27 The author took part in these types of discussions at his work unit during the Cultural Revolution. The famous case of Yu Luoke in Beijing also included so-called "mass discussions." Yu Luoke was charged as a counterrevolutionary and sentenced to death for his famous treatise *On Family Background* (*Chushen lun*). On January 9, 1970, the military control committee in charge of Beijing's public security and courts distributed materials on twenty convicts, including Yu Luoke, to many work units, and called upon them to "organize the revolutionary masses for ardent discussions, to come up with opinions on how to handle the cases and to advise the military control committee accordingly" (quoted from author's personal copy of the document). Yu Luoke was executed on March 5, 1970. The Beijing City High People's Court proclaimed him innocent in 1979.
28 *Fazhi wenxian xuanbian* [Selection of Documents on the Legal System], vol. 1 (Beijing: Zhongguo shehui kexue chubanshe, 1981), 87.
29 Mao Zedong, "*Zai Beidaihe zhengzhiju kuoda huiyi shang de jianghua*" [Speech at the Enlarged Meeting of the Politburo at Beidaihe], August 21, 1958, in *Mao Zedong sixiang wansui* [Long Live Mao Zedong Thought] (Wuhan: Gang ersi Wuhan daxue zongbu, 1968), 109.
30 Ibid.
31 Zhonggong zhongyang wenxian yanjiushi, ed., *Jianguo yilai zhongyao wenxian xuanbian* [Selection of Important Documents since the Founding of the PRC], vol. 3 (Beijing: Zhongyang wenxian chubanshe, 1992), 14–15.
32 See Mao Zedong, "Fan tewu douzheng bixu jianchi yi ge bu sha dabu bu zhuo fangzhen" [In the Struggle against Spies We Need to Uphold the Guideline of Killing None and Capturing Only a Few], accessed August 30, 2017, http://www.people.com.cn/GB/shizheng/8198/30446/30452/2207454.html. See also "On the Ten Major Relationships," in *Selected Works of Mao,* vol. 5, 284–307.
33 The last document may be found in Jiangxi sifating, ed., *Sifa gongzuo shouce* [Handbook on Judicial Work] (n.p.: Internal publication, 1958), 101.
34 Sichuan sheng gaoji renmin fayuan, ed., *Sifa gongzuo shouce* [Handbook on Judicial Work] (n.p.: Internal publication, 1975), 27–69.
35 See Wang Fang, ed., *Dangdai Zhongguo de gongan gongzuo* [Public Security Work in Contemporary China] (Beijing: Dangdai Zhongguo chubanshe, 1992), 236. The Ministry of Internal Affairs was a state organ working closely in tandem with the Ministry of Public Security. It was set up in November 1949 and mainly dealt with civil affairs, before being abolished as part of the "simplification of structures" during the Cultural Revolution in December 1968. In March 1978, it re-emerged under the name of Ministry of Civil Affairs.
36 Henan sheng renmin jianchayuan, ed., *Sifa gongzuo shouce* [Handbook on Judicial Work], vol. 1 (n.p.: Internal publication, 1978), 282–286.

37 Jiangxi sheng sifating, ed., *Sifa gongzuo shouce* [Handbook on Judicial Work] (n.p.: Internal publication, 1955), 125–129.
38 See He Lanjie and Lu Mingjian, eds., *Dangdai Zhongguo de shenpan gongzuo* [Adjudication in Contemporary China], vol. 1 (Beijing: Dangdai Zhongguo chubanshe, 1993), 73–74 and 606.
39 The most frequently employed quotation was Article 87 of the Constitution: "Citizens of the People's Republic of China enjoy freedom of speech, freedom of press, freedom of assembly, freedom of association, freedom of procession and freedom of demonstration." In the early Cultural Revolution, many big-character posters and signboards used this article as justification for their "rebellion." Some central documents also referred to it, such as the "Ten Regulations by the CCP Center on Grasping Revolution and Promoting Production (Draft)," issued in December 1966, which was meant to stimulate workers to establish organizations and take part in the movement: "According to the regulations of the Constitution of the People's Republic of China, the working masses have the right to establish revolutionary organizations during the Cultural Revolution." See You, *Guoshi tongjian*, 376–77. The author was a middle-school student during the Cultural Revolution and first encountered this information about the Constitution through these types of publications.
40 Shaanxi sheng difang zhi bianzuan weiyuanhui, ed., *Shaanxi shengzhi: Shenpan zhi* [Chronicle of Shaanxi Province: Volume on Adjudication] (Xi'an: Shaanxi renmin chubanshe, 1994), 363.
41 The crime of "malicious slandering" was one type of counterrevolutionary crime stipulated in Article 2 of the "Six Articles." The number of people sentenced as counterrevolutionaries according to this article was fairly high. A famous example is the Ma Yingxing case from Shaanxi province. Ma was designated a rightist in 1957 and afterward sent to the infamous Jiabiangou camp in Jiuquan for "reeducation through labor," where many people died of hunger during the great famine of 1959/60. Due to some critical remarks he had made about Lin Biao, Kang Sheng, and Chen Boda, as well as the course of the movement at the beginning of the Cultural Revolution, Ma was branded a counterrevolutionary and put to death on the charges of "spreading reactionary sayings" and "attacking the proletarian headquarters." He was posthumously rehabilitated and recognized as a revolutionary martyr in August 1979. Gansu sheng difang shizhi bianzuan weiyuanhui, ed., *Gansu shengzhi: Shenpan zhi* [Gansu Provincial Chronicle: Volume on Adjudication] (Lanzhou: Gansu wenhua chubanshe, 1995), 410–11.
42 See Article 10, Item 3. Reprinted in Zuigao renmin fayuan Xibei fenyuan, ed., *Sifa gongzuo shouce* [Handbook on Judicial Work] (n.p.: Internal publication, 1954), 165.
43 On December 17, 1981, the Central Political-Legal Commission, with the verification and approval of the top Party leadership, stipulated that "maliciously slandering or defaming state and Party leaders should be dealt with as a criminal act according to Article 10 of the Criminal Law and other relevant articles" and that "sentencing should distinguish between the crimes of counterrevolutionary propaganda and incitement and the crime of defamation according to the regulations of the relevant provisions of the Criminal Law," in "Guanyu dui edu gongji, feibang Zhongyang lingdao tongzhi shifou goucheng fanzui wenti de yijian" [Opinion Regarding the Question of whether Maliciously Slandering or Defaming Central Leading Comrades Constitutes a Crime or Not], in *Sifa shouce* [Handbook on Judicial Work], vol. 2, ed. Zuigao renmin fayuan yanjiushi (n.p.: Internal publication, 1983), 321–24.

44   On the rule that arrests first require approval by the procuratorate, see Article 12 of the "Organic Law of the People's Procuratorates" and Article 3 of the "Regulations of the People's Republic of China on Arrests and Detentions" from 1954. "Zhonghua renmin gongheguo daibu juliu tiaoli," in *Sifa gongzuo shouce*, ed. Jiangxi sheng sifating, 78 and 397. References to approval through leadership organs mainly appear in documents, for example in two regulations issued in the name of the Political-Legal Party Group of the Gansu Provincial Government, circulated with the approval of the provincial Party leadership: "Guanyu Gansu sheng dangnei pizhun daibu renfan de zanxing guiding" [Provisional Regulations Regarding Inner-Party Approval for Arrests of Criminals in Gansu Province, June 1955] and "Guanyu daibu shenpan gongzuo zhong zhixing dangnei pizhun zhidu de zanxing guiding" [Provisional Regulations on Implementing a System of Inner-Party Approval for Arrests and Adjudication, September 1956]. Based on these two documents, the Gansu Provincial High People's Court ruled that arrests through courts had to be sent to prefecture-level Party committees for approval. In the case of active counterrevolutionary crimes, the approval could also be obtained after the arrest. In March 1958, the Gansu Provincial Party Committee decided that arrests requested by the courts should be commented on by the court Party committee or its leading member and sent for approval to the Party committee at the same administrative level. After obtaining the approval, the arrest should be carried out "according to the law." *Gansu sheng: Shenpan zhi*, 441.

45   The "Notice of the Government Administration Council and the Supreme People's Court on Suppressing Counterrevolutionary Activities," issued in July 1950, stipulated that all counterrevolutionaries sentenced to death had no right to appeal their sentences. "Zhengwuyuan, zui gao renmin fayuan guanyu zhenya fangeming huodong de zhishi," in *Sifa gongzuo cankao ziliao* [Reference Materials for Judicial Work], ed. Hunan sheng renmin fayuan sifa ganbu lunxunban (n.p.: Internal publication, 1950), 154. In September 1951, the Central People's Government's Supreme People's Court, Supreme People's Procuratorate, and the Ministry of Justice declared that counterrevolutionaries sentenced to prison or death had similarly no right to appeal their verdicts. Zuigao renmin fayuan Dongbei fenyuan, ed., *Sifa gongzuo shouce* [Handbook on Judicial Work], vol. 1 (n.p.: Internal publication, 1953), 210. This system remained in practice until December 1955, when the State Council, the Supreme People's Court, the Supreme People's Procuratorate, and the Ministry of Justice stipulated that counterrevolutionaries sentenced to prison or death also had the right to appeal their sentences. Heilongjiang sifating, ed., *Sifa gongzuo shouce* [Handbook on Judicial Work] (n.p.: Internal publication, 1956), 207–8.

46   In March 1958, the Gansu Provincial Party Committee issued a regulation dictating that death sentences had to be approved by the CCP Center; sentences ranging from fifteen years to life imprisonment had to be approved by prefecture or city-level Party committees; sentences below fifteen years were to be approved by county-level Party committees. Criminal cases that had been examined and approved by the provincial high people's court, with the exception of death penalty cases, were to be approved by the Party group of the high people's court. The sentencing of criminal cases, at first instance accepted by middle people's courts at the prefecture or municipal level, should without exception, be approved by Party committees at the same level. In cases of a higher-level court revising a lower-level court's decision, a Party committee at the same level should approve the change. *Gansu shengzhi: Shenpan zhi*, 447.

47 Between 1958 and 1960, a so-called "judicial great leap" took place. In order to speed up case handling, some regions changed the previously established procedures and had public security organs, procuratorates, and courts jointly handle cases. Sometimes the three institutions were even fused into one as a new type of judiciary, thus breaking the previous principles of mutual constraint, see Yang and Chen, *Fazhi shi*, 782.
48 See "Renmin fating zuzhi tongze" [General Rules for Organizing People's Tribunals], in *Jianguo yilai* 1, 351–54.
49 Given the attacks on the former "organs of dictatorship," the Cultural Revolutionary authorities had the military exercise control over public security organs and courts in order to maintain social stability. Military control committees thus took over the handling of criminal cases. Most verdicts handed out in this period were issued in their name. Additionally, the "defense departments" (*baowei bumen*) of many revolutionary committees took on judicial functions. In some provinces and cities, these departments even came to handle criminal cases directly.
50 See for example Daniel Leese, "Revising Political Verdicts in Post-Mao China. The Case of Beijing's Fengtai District," in *Maoism at the Grassroots: Everyday Life in China's Era of High Socialism*, ed. Jeremy Brown and Matthew D. Johnson (Cambridge, MA: Harvard University Press, 2015), 110.
51 *Gansu sheng: Shenpan zhi*, 441–42.
52 According to an interview with a former member of a sentencing group within the Gansu Provincial Revolutionary Committee's Defense Department, the handling of criminal cases at the time also included taking care of indictment procedures.
53 *Gansu sheng: Shenpan zhi*, 463–64.
54 In January 1970, the CCP Center issued a "Notification on Striking against Counterrevolutionary Destructive Activities." The document stipulated that "the killing of people has to be approved by revolutionary committees at the levels of province, city, or autonomous region. The Center has to be notified in order to register the case. In important cases that require immediate action, a telegram to the Center asking for approval is deemed sufficient." "Guanyu daji fangeming pohuai huodong de zhishi," *Zhongfa* [1970] no.3 (January 31, 1970), reprinted in *Chinese Cultural Revolution Database*, ed. Song Yongyi (Hong Kong: Universities Service Centre, 2006).
55 This type of phenomenon was rather common during the Cultural Revolution. That the beating and even killing of people by members of mass organizations should not be dealt with through legal means was approved by members of the Cultural Revolutionary leadership several times. In July 1966, deputy head of the Cultural Revolution Small Group Jiang Qing stated: "We should not advocate beating people, but beating people is not a big deal! [...] If people are beaten in the tempest of a revolution, this is not a bad thing. If good people beat bad people, it serves them right," see You, *Guoshi tongjian* 3, 489. In August 1966, Politburo member and Minister of Public Security, Xie Fuzhi, at an enlarged conference of the Beijing Public Security Bureau stated: "Things stipulated in the past, irrespective of whether they derive from the state or public security organs, should not be done away with. [...] If the masses beat people to death, this is something I am personally opposed to. But if the masses detest bad people, we cannot dissuade them from doing so and should not force [them]." In the same month, during a meeting with leading public security officials from Gansu, Shaanxi, Hubei, and Beijing, Xie stated: "Should Red Guards who killed people, be sent to prison? In my opinion, if someone has been killed that is that. We should not care at all. [...] This cannot be handled according to common

practice and must not be treated as a criminal case. [...] If you detain and arrest the people who beat others, you will make a mistake." See Wang, *Da dongluan*, 73. According to the recollections of Wu De of the Beijing Municipal Committee, both he and Xie Fuzhi believed that it was a grave matter when killings first happened in Beijing in mid-1966 (Wu wrongly cites the year as 1967). They contemplated issuing documents in order to reign in these murderous activities but they ultimately met with resistance from Mao Zedong. This indicates that the policy was decided at the highest level. Zhu Yuanshi, ed., *Wu De koushu. Shi nian fengyu jishi: Wo zai Beijing gongzuo de yixie jingli* [Recollections of Wu De. Chronicle of Ten Years of Storms: Some of My Experiences while Working in Beijing] (Beijing: Dangdai Zhongguo chubanshe, 2004), 28–29.

56 Wang, *Da dongluan*, 69–70.
57 See Roderick MacFarquhar and Michael Schoenhals, *Mao's Last Revolution* (Cambridge, MA: Belknap Press of Harvard University Press, 2006), 179–80.
58 Among the official accounts for Guangxi, see for example "Zhonggong Guangxi Zhuangzu zizhiqu dangwei guanyu 'wenhua da geming' yilai Guangxi ruogan lishi wenti de yijian, taolun tigang" [Opinions of the CCP Guangxi Autonomous Region Party Committee on Several Historical Problems in Guangxi since the "Cultural Revolution," Discussion Draft] (January 1983), in *Chinese Cultural Revolution Database*.
59 See for example the fairly important "Zhengwuyuan guanyu huafen nongcun jieji chengfen de jueding" [Decision by the Government Administration Council on the Division of Rural Class Statuses] from August 1950 and several additional regulations reprinted in Sichuan sheng gaoji renmin fayuan, ed., *Sifa gongzuo shouce* [Handbook on Judicial Work] (n.p.: Internal publication, 1975), 27–121.
60 See Article 4 of the "Six Articles on Public Security Work," which banned class enemies, "targets of dictatorship" and their relatives from travelling, as well from joining or setting up organizations.
61 *Dangdai Zhongguo de shenpan gongzuo* 1, 138.
62 According to the relevant local chronicles, Beijing recorded 13,832 such cases, Shanghai 43,237 cases, Sichuan 267,277 cases, Gansu 57,664 cases, and Shaanxi 39,026 cases. See Beijing shi difangzhi bianzuan weiyuanhui, ed., *Beijing zhi: Zhengfa juan: Shenpan zhi* [Chronicle of Beijing: Political-Legal Series: Volume on Adjudication] (Beijing: Beijing chubanshe, 2008), 91–92; Shanghai tongzhi bianzuan weiyuanhui, ed., *Shanghai tongzhi: Gongan sifa juan* [Comprehensive Chronicle of Shanghai: Volume on Public Security and the Judiciary] (Shanghai: Shanghai renmin chubanshe, 2005), accessed August 30, 2017, http://www.shtong.gov.cn/Newsite/node2/node2247/node4570/node79195/node79213/userobject1ai103492.html; Sichuan sheng difangzhi bianzuan weiyuanhui, ed., *Sichuan shengzhi: Jiancha, shenpan zhi* [Chronicle of Sichuan Province: Volume on Procuratorates and Adjudication] (Chengdu: Sichuan renmin chubanshe, 1996), 350–51; *Gansu shengzhi: Shenpan zhi*, 277; Shaanxi sheng difangzhi biancuan weiyuanhui, ed., *Shaanxi shengzhi: Shenpan zhi* [Chronicle of Shaanxi Province: Volume on Adjudication] (Xi'an: Shaanxi renmin chubanshe, 1994), 301–2.
63 In 86.52 percent of the 11,984 counterrevolutionary cases handled in Gansu Province during the Cultural Revolution (involving over 13,000 people), the original verdict was revised. 5,270 people were proclaimed innocent. *Gansu shengzhi: Shenpan zhi*, 283. Among the cases in which the original verdict was upheld, and which continued to be classified as "counterrevolutionary," was a case from Qin'an County dated May 1972, in which a follower of the Unity Sect (*Yiguan dao*) had styled himself as emperor, claimed

his upcoming enthronization in Beijing, and predicted the coming of the Third World War. Forty-five people were implicated in this case. Gansu sheng difangzhi bianzuan weiyuanhui, ed., *Gansu shengzhi: Gongan zhi* [Provincial Chronicle of Gansu: Volume on Public Security] (Lanzhou: Gansu wenhua chubanshe, 1995), 175.

64 See for example *Dangdai Zhongguo de shenpan gongzuo* 2, 625; You, *Guoshi tongjian* 3, 200–1 and 1443; Liu Xiaomeng and Shi Weimin et al, eds., *Zhongguo zhiqing shidian* [Encyclopedia of Chinese Educated Youth] (Chengdu: Sichuan renmin chubanshe, 1995), 512–517; He Lan and Shi Weimin, eds., *Monan qing: Nei Menggu shengchan jianshe bingtuan xie zhen* [The Situation South of the Gobi: The True Story of the Inner Mongolian Production and Construction Corps] (Beijing: Falü chubanshe, 1994), 299–331.

65 *Gansu shengzhi: Gongan zhi*, 296.

66 Author's recollection of a case from Gansu Province charged on the crime of "counterrevolutionary adultery."

67 See *Gansu sheng: Shenpan zhi*, 343.

68 Statistics on ordinary crime during this period are scarce and the officially propagated numbers are incomplete. Furthermore, the standards for filing a case varied over time. The author's estimate is based on a combination of various sources that indicate a number of just under 2.6 million criminal cases filed between 1956 and 1965. As far as the incomplete statistics on the Cultural Revolution are concerned, the highest estimates indicate approximately 3.8 million criminal cases, rendering an increase of around 47 percent. Compare Kang Shuhua, "Xin Zhongguo chengli yilai de fanzui fazhan bianhua ji qi lixing sikao" [Thoughts on the Changes and Development of Crime and its Rationality since the Founding of New China], in *Fanzuixue luncong* [Anthology of Crime Studies], vol. 1 (Beijing: Zhongguo jiancha chubanshe, 2003), 409–436 and Wu Pengsen, "Zhongguo xingshi fanzui 60 nian: Fanzui yu shehui de hudong" [Sixty Years of Criminal Deeds in China: Interactions between Crime and Society], in *Anhui shifan daxue xuebao*, no. 3, (2012): 292–305.

69 In Gansu Province, for example, in the decade between 1955 and 1965, a total of 87,173 criminal cases were recorded, while between 1966 and 1976 some 65,742 criminal cases were officially recorded. This would indicate a decrease by 24.6 percent. *Gansu shengzhi: Gongan zhi*, 262–63. It should also be noted that the national crime rate rapidly increased by over 60 percent in the decade after the Cultural Revolution.

Michael Schoenhals
2 The Intelligence Sleeper Who Never Was
Han Fuying and Case 5004

A terminological complication that bedevils the study of law and politics in the PRC concerns the word "case" (*anzi, anjian,* or simply *an* in Chinese). In the courts and by the police it was used with relative specificity and came with considered sub-definitions of what counted as counterrevolutionary, historical, major, etc. cases. At the same time, when the need arose to quantify cases for the sake of scoring political points, overscrupulous attempts at terminological precision for the sake of keeping an accurate tally were not always seen as helpful by the men and women who served as Communist Party perception managers.[1] What was the point, they appear to have wondered, of fidgeting with semantic minutiae when intelligence and facts in any case were to be fixed around policies already decided by Chairman Mao and the CCP Center?

For historians, one way of resolving methodological problems arising from terminological complications like this one is to introduce one's own definition. In response to a rhetorical question posed as "What is a case?," one could declare—drawing inspiration from a well-known line (1.12) in Ludwig Wittgenstein's *Tractatus logico-philosophicus*—that the totality of facts determines what is a case, and also whatever is not a case. However, such a definition has a way of complicating assertions, arguments, and calculations that rely on pre-existing Chinese data. After all, it is usually the specific referent of that data that historians must grapple with, and not what we ourselves may prefer to speak of as "cases."

The strategy adopted in this chapter is neither that of crafting a novel definition, nor one of pretending that legal/political keywords can be left forever undefined or that conceptual precision in any case has become an overrated quality in twenty-first century post-truth discourse on Chinese communism. In what follows, the focus is on an example of a specific subset of the totality of cases, a subset with a definition developed after 1949 in documents emanating not with the PRC judiciary but with the Central Ministry of Public Security (CMPS). Labelled *zhuan'an* in Chinese, such cases arose only in response to events or circumstances serious enough to warrant a predicated investigation.[2] In this respect, not only were they distinct from lesser case categories such as the routine investigation or probe of alleged criminal conduct discussed by Jeremy Brown in his chapter; the

---

For valuable comments on earlier drafts of this chapter, I want to thank Thomas Kaiser, David Chambers, and Jeremy Brown.

https://doi.org/10.1515/9783110533651-003

CMPS definition also dispensed with references to the PRC judiciary. A *zhuan'an* was exclusively a public security matter and the totality of facts surrounding it triggered, authorized, and made budgetary allowances for the use of dedicated operational resources and investigative methods, including physical surveillance, the non-consensual monitoring of private correspondence, and targeted development and tasking of special so-called "case agents" (*zhuan'an teqing*).[3]

The chapter rests on the surviving archival record of one *zhuan'an* and seeks to illuminate certain generic procedural aspects of its investigation.[4] A key implication of the story told—of how a recent graduate from Guangxi Medical University in 1956 came to be suspected of being a sleeper agent recruited and planted in the PRC by GMD intelligence—is that even something as serious as a predicated investigation could now and then prove totally devoid of elements impacting balefully on the lives of its human target(s). Perhaps this should not come as a surprise. Chinese public security officers did, after all, have and make use of the option of closing down their investigations without filing any charges when those investigations found no evidence of wrongdoing.

Context of Case 5004: CCP Security Risk Assessment

The context of Case 5004 (5004 *hao zhuan'an*, as it was designated by the Guangxi Provincial Public Security Bureau [PSB] in April 1956) was a nationwide personnel security risk assessment in China's government, military, and CCP organs and in state-run economic, cultural, and educational entities. Arising from the by no means unfounded fear of employees exploiting legitimate access to their organization's assets for unauthorized purposes, the assessment was spoken of in the militant language of the times as the "internal elimination of counterrevolution" (*neibu sufan*).[5] At its most intense, in the second half of 1955, but lasting until the end of the decade, it proactively sought information on links between known individuals and suspected counterrevolutionary threats.[6] A staggered top-down affair, it aimed at identifying so-called Remnant or Hidden Counterrevolutionaries (RHCs) and at adopting robust countermeasures to mitigate any risks they might pose. In September 1958, an ad hoc CCP Central Group of Ten (on which the CMPS was represented by the Minister of Public Security Luo Ruiqing and two of his deputies) leading and monitoring its progress, estimated that over a period of three years, the *neibu sufan* assessed an estimated 18,512,082 CCP and non-CCP personnel. Of this total, a full 98.65 percent were given a clean bill of health.[7]

One procedural aspect of the security risk assessment was the definition of its goals in terms of target numbers against which actual performance was measured. Quantitative estimates that took past trends as well as current and emerging threats into account became a critical metric for determining its rate of success. This is unlikely to have been a complete secret at the time. However, details—such as what a target number might be for a specific city or province (the aggregate level from which regular monthly reports on actual performance reached the CMPS) or how the number of RHCs identified, or instances of counterrevolution disrupted, might have deviated from goals—were only known to a select number of senior public security officers, who were under intense pressure to meet those same targets. In a top-secret ministerial notification dated March 16, 1957, provincial public security bureaus were told that, while they were under obligation to respond truthfully to inquiries from members of people's congresses and political consultative congresses concerning how many people had actually been arrested in the course of the *neibu sufan*, they were strictly forbidden from talking about target numbers.[8]

A second procedural aspect of the assessment involved a temporary lowering of minimum standards for the launch of predicated case investigations. Prior to the *neibu sufan*, fairly stringent criteria had applied to the formal conversion of a routine RHC probe into a predicated investigation—a conversion that the performance metrics counted as an "upgrade" (*tisheng*). As explained in the official 1954 CMPS Case Work Manual, a predicated investigation of a security threat was only to be launched under one of three circumstances, namely when (1) the presence of an active *tewu* or counterrevolutionary activity has been confirmed; (2) the target is in contact with an enemy intelligence organization; or (3) an examination of the known facts positively identifies the target as a counterrevolutionary suspect.[9] Early on in the course of the *neibu sufan*, however, a revised Central Group of Ten rulebook authorized the launch of investigations under no fewer than seven, less stringent circumstances. For example, as revised, the original second criterion now allowed for predicated investigation when a target was suspected of "maintaining contact with *tewu* organs or *tewu* personnel and [therefore] strongly suspected of being a dispatched or stay-behind *tewu* suspect element."[10] This reformulation not only affected the workload of operational departments nationwide, but also the security risk assessment of countless individuals. Previously, a person would have had to be in contact with an enemy intelligence organization in order for a red flag warning to be raised; but now, all it took was staying in touch with, for example, an overseas relative with links to (i.e. current or former personnel serving) such an organization.[11]

Citizen Han Fuying

The individual at the center of Case 5004 was a young Hakka woman by the name of Han Fuying, born in XX County, Fujian Province, in 1932.[12] After migrating with her parents to the city of Liuzhou in what was then Guangxi Province as a teenager, and attending middle school there, she passed the entrance exams for the Guangxi Medical University in September 1950.[13] At the time, the university campus was in the city of Guilin, but in summer 1954 it moved to the provincial capital of Nanning. Upon graduation in July 1955, her work assignment remained temporarily on hold and she remained on campus pending the outcome of the *neibu sufan*. In the words of her university president—who chaired the powerful ad hoc troika that reviewed and approved all security risk assessments—she had an unresolved problem that made her a prime target.[14] After close to half a year in limbo, she was finally given a temporary position as an instructor in the clinical medicine section of the local School of Nursing. It was during her tenure there that the Cultural Protection Division of the Guangxi PSB launched its predicated investigation.[15]

Han Fuying came from a well-to-do family. Her father had graduated from Sun Yat-sen University in Guangzhou in 1930 and, after a teaching career, served as a county magistrate and local tax official in Fujian. In 1947, he had come to Liuzhou at the invitation of an old friend from school to assume the directorship of the recently established Jianhua Cigarette Factory (his wife and children followed him in 1948 and 1950), a major private business venture in Guangxi's rapidly expanding tobacco industry.[16] For a few years after the founding of the PRC, he served as a delegate for one of China's small democratic parties on the Liuzhou Municipal People's Congress. He came under attack for corruption and financial irregularities, however, in the so-called Five Antis campaign that targeted tax evasion, bribery, cheating on government contracts, theft of economic intelligence, and misappropriation of state assets. As a result, when the Jianhua Cigarette Factory was nationalized in 1954, he found himself demoted to a deputy managerial post. A file on him kept by the Liuzhou Municipal CCP United Front Department stated that he had "stolen state intelligence, offered bribes, and evaded taxation."[17] In late 1955, the Liuzhou Municipal PSB had him down as rather "full of himself, in a bourgeois way," but added on a substantial note that he was *not* known to have corresponded with Hong Kong and, "for now," appeared "unproblematic" overall.[18] In addition to a brother who had a job in the Liuzhou Railway Planning Division, Han Fuying also had a sister who attended one of Liuzhou's most prestigious middle schools when the *neibu sufan* began.[19]

At first glance, there was little in Han Fuying's behaviour that should have made her a person of interest to the public security organs. In 1950, already prior to entering university, she had joined the Communist Party's New Democratic Youth League.[20] When the university authorities asked her to update and amend her CV, she was forthcoming with information about herself, her family, relatives, and "substantive personal relationships" (*guanxi*). At the height of the *neibu sufan*, she was often awake at night doing nobody knows what—so fellow students in her dormitory claimed. But perhaps she merely worried about the fact, as recorded in her university file, that she was going deaf in one ear. She had a lot of friends with whom she enjoyed dancing and going to the movies, and quite a few of those friends were "ideologically backward." But there was really nothing in what she herself said or did that was suspicious.[21] Han Fuying's only problem had to do with her relatives and, specifically, one of her overseas relatives. On its own, this had sufficed to complicate and prolong her security risk assessment. When as a sixteen-year-old she arrived in Guangxi from Fujian, she had travelled with her mother by boat via Hong Kong where she had stayed for forty-eight hours with an uncle of hers by the name of Han Feng. And that uncle was an old GMD *tewu*!

Becoming a Security Risk

According to what her brother had told Han Fuying, her uncle Han Feng had been "progressive" as a young man and at one point possibly even active in the CCP underground.[22] He had attended university, but after being arrested and incarcerated for two years by the GMD, he had "betrayed the revolution." During the War of Resistance against Japan, he had travelled to India, Burma, and Maritime Southeast Asia on behalf of GMD intelligence.[23] At war's end, he had remained in service with the Second Bureau of the Ministry of National Defense of the Republic of China (ROC) as an intelligence officer, active mainly in Hong Kong and Southeast Asia. At some point after the outbreak of civil war in China in 1946, he had told his relatives that he had abandoned what he called the "perfidious trade" of espionage and become a businessman, a claim that Han Fuying's father believed to be truthful.[24]

The Guangxi Medical University *neibu sufan* troika was unsure about how to deal with the relationship (to the extent that one deserving of the name existed) between Han Fuying and her *tewu* uncle. As far as matters relating to security were concerned, the troika reported directly to the Cultural Protection Division of the Guangxi PSB and, in a long submission in autumn 1955, it elaborated on what it knew. Numerous extended conversations with Han Fuying did suggest that her link to Han Feng entailed nothing more than the ordinary relationship between a niece and her distant uncle. But, on the other hand, there was the fact that he was—or at the very least, given that up-to-date information on his current status or whereabouts was unavailable, for a long period had been—a GMD *tewu* whom she had met in person on the eve of her arrival in Guangxi in 1948. Clearly, this was important, given what in the *neibu sufan* counted as a legitimate reason for launching a predicated investigation. The university knew, because she had told them as much, that Han Fuying and her mother had briefly stayed with Han Feng in Hong Kong and that she herself had subsequently corresponded with her uncle. According to what she herself had said, her father had told her about Han Feng's past in late 1951 and insisted she cut her ties with him so as not to "get into trouble." The university president believed her assurances to be true, namely that she had not corresponded with Han Feng after that. It was under these circumstances that he proposed to the provincial Cultural Protection Division that she be assigned a job at the local School of Nursing, a school he described as a "low risk" employer.[25]

In November 1955, however, new and potentially damaging information suddenly came to light. The *neibu sufan* troika discovered that when the campus had still been in Guilin, a university security cadre had been told by the Guilin municipal PSB that an address on Connaught Street, Hong Kong, from which Han Fuying had received a letter written by Han Feng in 1951 belonged to "an organ of British Southeast Asia intelligence"![26] This discovery prompted a letter from the university president to the Cultural Protection Division with request for clarification. If the information proved accurate, the decision to deal with Han Fuying as proposed might warrant reconsideration. Fortunately for everyone involved, it turned out that the address from which Han Feng had sent his letter was not, as the Guilin security cadre had remembered, "4/F 23 Connaught Road" but "24 Connaught Road Central." As for whether No. 23 really was British intelligence, this needed to be checked with Guilin but was clearly irrelevant to assessing Han Fuying's security risk.[27] In mid-December 1955, the head of the Cultural Protection Division told his colleagues he supported the Medical University president's wish to give Han Fuying a qualified bill of health and allow her to take up a teaching position at the School of Nursing. But at the same time, he also ordered Han to be secretly subjected to control and "in particular, be put under technical control [*jishu kongzhi*]," which meant that her private mail was now to be systematically opened and read.[28] In other words, without knowing it, she was about to become the target of a major investigation predicated on the totality of the circumstances surrounding the relationship between her and her *tewu* uncle, including the presence of fragmentary but particularized derogatory information, descriptive and specific to events and activities such as their meeting in 1948 and their subsequent correspondence.

A GMD Sleeper Agent?

To some of the officers in the Guangxi PSB Cultural Protection Division, the information about Han Fuying's case bore the disturbing hallmarks of a sleeper agent intelligence operation mounted by the GMD.²⁹ What seriously intrigued one particular officer—Tan Yanhua, a young woman who belonged to the same age cohort as Han Fuying and who was singled out specifically by the division head to arrange for Han's correspondence to be monitored and read—was the possibility, no matter how remote, that Han Fuying's contact with her uncle in Hong Kong had an intelligence nexus. After having managed to invalidate the Guilin claim concerning a link to British intelligence, Tan continued to collect all the information she could find on Han and her uncle (her father and brother as well), to see if there might be something else that prompted suspicion. One of the first things she discovered was that whereas Han Fuying had said that she had last corresponded with Han Feng in 1951, and after that neither written to nor received any letter from him, the Guilin PSB had in the course of the *neibu sufan* passed on information to the Cultural Protection Division stating that in actuality, Han Fuying had remained in touch with her uncle c/o Yuqiao Enterprises at 24 Connaught Road Central until, at the very least, November 1953. And not only that: the address in question turned out to belong to a senior GMD intelligence officer who used it as a cover for the "bandit" Chinese People's Anti-Communist National Salvation Army General Headquarters!³⁰ Furthermore, there was an intermediary, living in Guilin, through whom Han Fuying had supposedly stayed in touch with her uncle. He was a tobacco merchant (known as "an extreme reactionary") whose small business had been on the radar of the municipal PSB for some time after having occasionally forwarded mail and funds from overseas to GMD intelligence assets inside the PRC.³¹

As far as Han Feng's exact status was concerned, Tan was able to find a description of him as a GMD *tewu* operating illegally in Hong Kong. His name appeared in a document compiled in 1954 by the Social Affairs Department of the CCP Center's South China Sub-Bureau outlining the organization, personnel structure, etc. of the Protection of Secrets Bureau of the ROC Ministry of National Defense.³² Under these circumstances, although the Cultural Protection Division did not have any intelligence proving that this was indeed the case, Tan and some of her colleagues reasoned that, at the very least, "the enemy might want to exploit" Han Fuying.³³ In the winter of 1955–56, their opinion of just what kind of intelligence nexus they faced evolved gradually and, by late March 1956, some of them had concluded that Han Feng's "loving care" for Han Fuying, "seems to be tending toward [*si you ... de qushi*] profiling for an agent in place and developing an organization. And there are signs it is in anticipation of becoming at some point able to collect intelligence on us."³⁴

The details of the give and take between the head of the Cultural Protection Division and his junior colleagues, and the decision to burrow deeper into Han Fuying's circumstances, are scantily documented. One of the performance goals set for PSB operational divisions was to mount and manage a minimum number of predicated investigations, and it seems possible that an aspiration on the part of the Cultural Protection Division to oversee *n* investigations may have influenced their deliberations. On record, however, is only a very simple justification agreed upon, namely that a case be made of Han Fuying and a predicated investigation launched "to attack the enemy with greater precision."

A Case is Built

To launch its predicated investigation of Han Fuying, the Cultural Protection Division had to receive permission from the provincial PSB. The Guangxi PSB, in turn, had to inform the CMPS Cultural Protection (Sixth) Bureau in Beijing and briefly summarize (in the form of a *li'an baogao* or "case launch report") what motivated it and how it was to be conducted.[35] The drafts of the cover note and report sent to Beijing reveal how, from the very outset, the officers involved disagreed about how confidently and explicitly they should claim to be "on to something" and just what that might be. In a first draft of the cover note to the CMPS Sixth Bureau, for example, they claimed to have a "highly important lead ... on a suspect we have strong reason to believe is a sleeper agent dispatched by the enemy." The division head, however, appears in the end to have seen no reason to make such an extravagant claim, because he crossed out the sentence in question and replaced it with nothing more than a terse claim that there was a "*tewu* suspect lead" that merited investigation. It was with his wording unchanged that his superior in turn signed off on the cover note in the name of the Guangxi PSB.[36]

The carefully worded case launch report, after having seen numerous revisions, was sent off to Beijing in one original and four carbon copies.[37] It followed a strict, pre-set pattern and arguably the most important of its constituent parts was the one entitled "basis for launch of case." It read in full:

> In summer 1948, Han Fuying followed her mother to Hong Kong where, for two nights and one day, the two of them stayed in the home of Han Feng. When they left Hong Kong for Liuzhou, Han Feng saw them off, urging Fuying to study diligently, to get better at maths, physics, and chemistry, one day become an engineer, and not waste her life on trivial things. After Han Fuying had settled in Liuzhou, Han Feng sent copies of the *Sing Tao Daily* and coffee by post, arranged to have people [travelling to Liuzhou] carry with them things like a watch for her mother and sister and corresponded regularly with them. While exercising technical control, the Guilin Municipal Bureau [of Public Security] discovered in 1953 that Han Fuying corresponded with Han Feng at Yuqiao Enterprises, 24 Connaught Road Central, via Sima Kang in the XX Tobacco Co., located on Sun Yat-sen Road Central, Guilin. However, according to a notification issued by our superior levels in 1953, the [Hong Kong] address is the communications address of the bandit operative Xu Kekang. In its *Enemy Situation*

> *Documentation* (*Diqing ziliao*) dated June 1955, the [CCP] South China Social Affairs Department states: "Han Feng is a desk officer in the Hong Kong Intelligence Station (where he manages intelligence tasks) of the Protection of Secrets Bureau." Subsequently, an investigation into Sima Kang in Guilin, who had forwarded their correspondence, prompted suspicions of him being counterrevolutionary. He had in the past forwarded letters and money on behalf of so-and-so in Guilin, at a residential address identical to one used by enemy operatives for letters and funds.
>
> Based on the above circumstances, we maintain that Han Feng's "loving care" for Han Fuying, in combination with the fact that Sima Kang was asked to forward their correspondence, throws serious suspicion on Han Fuying as being a dispatched [operative]. In order to achieve clarity with respect to her [true] status and background, we now launch this predicated investigation of her case (*li wei zhuan'an zhencha*).[38]

The Cultural Protection Division explained that the investigation had been assigned the code designation Case 5004.[39] Given that the registration number of the case launch report to Beijing was [1956] 5 zhuan bao zi No. 1, it would appear to have been the first predicated investigation launched by the division in 1956.[40] Its code designation had not been picked at random: the number five indicated that it would be managed by the Fifth (Cultural Protection) Division, and the number four—if praxis in Guangxi corresponded to that in other provinces—stood for the month of April, in which it was being launched, rather than a serial number.

The Cultural Protection Division was in no hurry to crack Case 5004 and, in line with CMPS policy at the time, was taking a long-term view.[41] Han Fuying did not, after all, pose an immediate threat in the way that a suspected saboteur or assassin might have done.[42] The case launch report explained that the division expected to employ the usual range of operational instruments for the sake of clarifying whether Han Fuying's true "status and background" did have an intelligence nexus. Ultimately, officers argued that she might even prove to be someone who could be controlled for purposes of "understanding threats posed by the enemy" given that relationships like that between her and her uncle, in Tan Yanhua's words, "are what the enemy develops and exploits."[43]

The rank of officers formally assigned to lead predicated investigations and their corresponding task forces was always a good indicator of just how important a case was judged to be. The Guangxi PSB's Case 5004 was not high priority and was run by one Liu Runhua, a mere deputy section head, and two of his junior colleagues Zeng Xiangrong and Wang Chunsheng.[44] On the task force were an additional handful of junior officers, including Tan Yanhua, whose names were not mentioned in the *li'an baogao* to the CMPS and who may well have been enlisted simply in order to keep it at minimum strength when some members, in due course, found themselves overwhelmed by other, more pressing tasks.

Deploying Operational Resources

Given how much Case 5004 depended on the presumed exchange of letters between Han Fuying and the "enemy," as represented by her *tewu* uncle, the task force's most important operational resource was, not surprisingly, technical control. Aside from intensifying the monitoring of her correspondence with Han Feng, the report to Beijing explained that the Nanning officers would also ask their colleagues in Guilin to inspect any correspondence forwarded via Sima Kang. As they believed to have failed to do so in the past, the authors of the report also promised to henceforth make every effort not to miss any letters.[45] By August 1956, they had submitted a formal inter-provincial request for help (for a period of six months, subject to renewal) to the Fifteenth Division of the Guangzhou Municipal PSB, which employed some of the PRC's most experienced postal inspectors at the choke point through which mail from and to the British colony of Hong Kong was routed. The task force requested that they monitor the contents of any suspicious mail from or to Han Fuying's aunt who happened to live in Guangzhou.[46] After six months, the Fifteenth Division wrote back saying that nothing of interest had been discovered, whereupon further monitoring was suspended.[47]

A second operational resource to be deployed by the task force was that of a case agent, which in the present context meant a covert informer. In its report to Beijing, the Cultural Protection Division announced that it would attempt to recruit an informer to "report on [Han Fuying's] daily life and movements." Confidently, the report explained "given that Han is quite active socially, it should prove possible to find an agent with a similar personality who can get close to her, intentionally establish emotional ties, and thereby win her confidence."[48] Progress on this score was swift and after Han had taken up her new teaching position at the School of Nursing (where she became instantly popular with the students), the task force was able to report on July 30, 1956, how "She shared her thoughts with our agent XX, saying 'In the past, I always worried about how my problem would be resolved, but now I am relieved,' and 'both the school leadership and the Party organization show concern for me, and have even arranged for me to get a hearing aid. This all shows that the organization is really looking after me!'"[49]

That her new employer should "show concern for" and be "looking after" Han Fuying may of course have been simply because she was a promising and popular teacher. But it seems likely that it was motivated by more than that. In its case launch report, the Cultural Protection Division noted that Han had become "somewhat alarmed" by the fact that her relationship with her uncle had made her a prime target in the *neibu sufan* and, as a result, delayed her job assignment. Now, if she really was on a GMD intelligence mission, the division speculated, this may well have forced her to conclude that the public security organs were closing in on her. Clearly, this was not good, since it would put her on her guard. "For this reason," the report argued, "we must first of all research this matter together with her unit's leadership and do a good job of allaying her fears, so as to stand an even better chance of discovering problems."⁵⁰ In other words, it may well have been that the goodwill she was shown by her new employer was initially intended to make her lower her guard, assuming that her experience in the *neibu sufan* had, so to speak, rattled the suspected "enemy."

In the end, it was neither technical control nor a case agent that would provide the task force with the information it needed to claim progress in its predicated investigation. Instead, it proved to be what the case launch report had described as the "mutual exchange of intelligence, for the purpose of promoting the unfolding of the case [*yi tuidong anqing fazhan*]," between the officers in Nanning, the Liuzhou Railway Public Security Division, and the Guilin, Liuzhou, and Guangzhou PSBs.⁵¹

Correspondence Misdated? External Investigation I

On three separate occasions in the spring, autumn, and late winter of 1956, the Cultural Protection Division sent Case 5004 task force members on so-called external investigation (*waidiao*) missions. Such missions had become increasingly common across China in the course of the *neibu sufan*. They did not always involve very clear tasking of the officer(s) concerned, to a point where even the CMPS magazine *People's Public Security*, in September 1956, felt compelled to expose what it described as barely disguised tourism and excursions, the real purpose of which was not to examine records or debrief sources but "sightseeing and shopping."⁵² It is worth noting, in this context, that the Nanning officers had all been properly tasked and returned from their missions with information that proved critical to the unfolding of Han Fuying's case, albeit not always as anticipated.

The first member of the task force to conduct an external investigation was Wang Chunsheng, who visited first Guilin (some twelve hours from Nanning by train) and then the regional communication node of Liuzhou (half-way between Guilin and Nanning) for a week in early May 1956. Before setting out, he drafted a long outline of what he intended to investigate, but it failed to enthuse his superior officer who in its stead wrote down a simple list of key points on which the rationale behind Case 5004 hinged and that therefore needed verification/clarification.⁵³ While in Guilin, the most important point Wang needed to verify was whether the date ascribed to the "1953 technical material" (i.e. the intercepted correspondence between Han Fuying and her *tewu* uncle) was that of their correspondence per se, or merely that of the public security document that mentioned it. Furthermore, was the failure to discover any additional correspondence after 1953 due to an absence of "technical control" or was it because control had continued but no actual correspondence had taken place?[54] At a meeting with his Guilin counterparts on May 5, 1956, Wang was given the unsettling news that not only had no records whatsoever been kept of postal intercepts made prior to 1954; as of 1954, subsequent to internal restructuring, the municipal officers' assumption was that any "technical control" called for would be exercised by their superiors in the provincial capital of Nanning. A quick check of the relevant files found no secondary record from 1954 or later hinting at the existence of "technical control" mentioning Sima Kang or Han Feng. And not just that: the careful perusal of the existing archival records showed that the last confirmed date on which Han Fuying and Han Feng had corresponded was October 8, 1951. After that, nothing![55]

From Guilin, Wang Chunsheng travelled to Liuzhou where he investigated files on Han Fuying's father and brother. The files showed that, in the early stages of the *neibu sufan*, Han Fuying's sister had informed on their father and volunteered trivial but particularized (seventeen items in total) derogatory information on him to the CCP branch in her school. When she had been about to enter middle school in 1951, for example, her father had told her to keep quiet about their landlord family background. In 1952, her father had told his children that he really did not want them to join any organizations, including the Communist Party's Youth League, but rather just wanted them to stay out of trouble. In recent years, he had in private spoken critically of the Soviet Union on numerous occasions while, at the same time, singing the praises of the United States.[56] In February 1956, her middle school CCP branch had shared its assessment of Han Fuying's sister with the Liuzhou PSB. It described her as "a comrade and member of the Youth League with a clear history, who in the course of the present *sufan* movement, has performed admirably as an activist."[57]

At a meeting on May 9, 1956, in the offices of the division of the Liuzhou PSB tasked with counterintelligence and the ferreting out of RHCs, Wang Chunsheng's local hosts floated the idea of recruiting Han Fuying's sister as an informer. But Wang was apparently not convinced that she was agent material and, according to his own minutes of the meeting, he said as much:

> The question of whether she may be exploited: my own view is that since she has [already to some extent] informed on her father, we should henceforth, if we pay careful attention to how we go about it, be able to get some relevant information from her on her father and brother. But we must not rashly employ her to monitor her father [because]: (1) Their relationship is that of father and daughter; (2) She is too young; (3) Even though her relationship with her father may recently have deteriorated ... she will not necessarily have any more important information to share.[58]

Later in summer 1956, at a meeting between senior Nanning PSB officers and the task force to discuss how Case 5004 was progressing, Wang Chunsheng reaffirmed his opposition to the recruitment of Han Fuying's sister as an agent to inform on her own father (and brother). Wang's immediate superior concurred, but went on to argue that more might be done to improve the conditions under which the already active informer XX at the School of Nursing operated. Would it perhaps not be possible, he asked, to physically bring Han Fuying and XX closer together by "changing the way in which dorm rooms are assigned"? In addition, perhaps the informer's application to join the CCP could be quietly put on hold, since once she had become a Party member, he argued, her operational utility would "diminish."[59]

Focusing on Father Instead? External Investigation II

The first external investigation found that the original assumption that Han Fuying, despite her own claims to the contrary, had continued to correspond with her *tewu* uncle had almost certainly been in error. Did Han Fuying really deserve to be classified as a suspected GMD sleeper agent? Given that she had already been assigned a job where there was no chance of her coming into contact with classified matters or discovering anything of intelligence value, did it even make sense to regard her as a security risk? As time progressed, members of the task force in Nanning started asking themselves whether the primary focus of their predicated investigation really ought to be on Han Fuying: would shifting attention to her father and brother not perhaps be more appropriate? As the record reveals, that is what their colleagues in Liuzhou believed.[60]

By early October 1956, the time was ripe for a member of the Case 5004 task force to make a second visit to Liuzhou. This time around, Zeng Xiangrong went to visit the Liuzhou PSB and Liuzhou Railway Public Security Division. Through the bureau, he arranged to meet the officer in charge of security in the nationalized Jianhua Cigarette Factory. Zeng brought with him a long list of a questions, most of which concerned only Han Fuying's father and brother.[61] Aside from providing him with background on substantial personal relationships maintained by her father, and a transcript of an interview with Han Fuying's sister conducted by a Liuzhou officer, Zeng's visit yielded little he did not already know. "In the course of my investigations," he complained upon his return to Nanning, "I did not unearth anything new." The only significant outcome of the visit had been to independently confirm facts already known.[62] Han Fuying's own story about her correspondence with her *tewu* uncle, for example, tallied perfectly with what her sister had been telling the Liuzhou PSB.

Where is Uncle? External Investigation III

One important question that vexed the officers running Case 5004 concerned the current whereabouts of Han Feng. Where was he and what exactly was he doing? In November, Tan Yanhua argued that "At this point, if we can confidently state that he is actually tasked with turning [intelligence] assets [in the PRC], then we can also achieve clarity in [all of] the other questions."[63] However, the information the task force had managed to collect on Han Feng was contradictory and, more importantly, out of date. Was he still in Hong Kong? Was he still working for GMD intelligence, and if so, doing what, exactly? In search of answers, on November 9, 1956, they sent a letter to the CMPS asking the ministry to "please investigate (or forward to the South China Social Affairs Department and ask them to find out) whether the *tewu* Han Feng remains in Hong Kong and if so what his cover is, what his activities are, and whether or not his tasks include the recruitment of assets inside China."[64] A reply from the CMPS First (Political Protection) Bureau arrived after eight weeks, informing them that no information in the matter was to be had in Beijing. Given that the South China Social Affairs Department no longer existed, the best thing to do, the CMPS First Bureau suggested, would be to turn to its successor, the Guangdong Provincial PSB, for help.[65]

When the inconclusive answer from the CMPS First Bureau arrived, Wang Pinzhong, a junior member of the Case 5004 task force, was already in Guangzhou making inquiries. Her colleagues waited until they heard back from her before deciding what to do next.[66] In early January, she sent them a long letter reporting on the status of her inquiries and telling them that, unless there was anything else, she would soon be returning to Nanning. Unfortunately, in definitely resolving the crucial issue of Han Feng's current whereabouts, she explained, her efforts had all been in vain:

> The final question of whether he is in Hong Kong at present and involved in any *tewu* activity: After checking with the Political and Legal Department of the Guangdong Provincial CCP Committee (where some of the comrades from the original South China Social Affairs Department now work), the Guangdong Provincial Public Security Bureau, and the Guangzhou Municipal Public Security Bureau, I was in each instance unable to find information confirming that he is active in Hong Kong. Furthermore, when interrogated, a hard-core Guomindang dispatched operative from the same organization as Han Feng currently locked up in Guangzhou Municipal Prison said that he did not know Han Feng and was unable to share any information about him. I have really racked my brains and

considered every option, but I am unable to provide any answers and cannot think of what more to do. In my view, it is very hard to come up with clear answers to questions concerning the ongoing activities of *tewu* overseas. It is only those who are inside China who can be effectively controlled and monitored, allowing one to discover things, etc.[67]

Once back in Nanning, Wang Pinzhong shared the few additional snippets of information (of questionable reliability) that she had picked up with her colleagues. Seen as possibly worth taking seriously was a factoid provided by a student in the Department of Physics at Sun Yat-sen University, whose father had been a friend of Han Feng's. The student remembered hearing in 1954 that Han Feng had been charged with conducting *tewu* activity and forcibly expelled from Hong Kong to Taiwan by the British colonial authorities.[68] Not given much credence, on the other hand, was what a different source had told Wang, that Han Feng had managed to stay on as a *tewu* in Hong Kong until the so-called Kowloon Riots of October 1956 (in which GMD operatives were held by the Hong Kong governor to have been "responsible for some of the most significant outbreaks of violence").[69] What happened to him after that was a total mystery.

A Case Unravels

The progress of Case 5004 was duly monitored in Beijing. When the CMPS Sixth Bureau had not received an update from the Guangxi PSB in early 1957, it mailed off a brief reminder that read in full: "What is the current work status of Case 5004? Please report."[70] Guangxi had probably failed to update Beijing because the case had, in effect, collapsed. On June 29, 1957, in a proposal addressed to the CMPS Sixth Bureau, the Guangxi PSB sought to explain why the case should be closed down:

> Originally, at the time when the case was launched, the reason we suspected she might be a sleeper agent was only because (1) a higher-level circular had declared Han Feng to be a *tewu* element, (2) Han Fuying had met with the *tewu* Han Feng in 1948, and (3) the two of them had been in contact by mail in 1953. We opened the case rashly without checking whether there was any reason to doubt that the two had remained in contact. Now we can see that our grounds were actually insufficient.
>
> The issue of communication between Han Fuying and Han Feng: Our original claim that the two were still in contact in 1953 was based on slipshod work on our part. The [mail intercept] document that the Guilin Municipal Bureau sent us in 1953 had neither a year nor a day written on it, and the only thing we had to go by was the date (November 14, 1953) on which it had been registered by the Guilin Municipal Bureau Investigation and Research Section.

As a result, we mistakenly concluded that [Han Fuying and Han Feng] were still in contact in 1953. We have since checked and with the exception of one letter from Han Feng to Han Fuying in October 1951 (in the course of the *sufan* campaign, Han Fuying said that she and Han Feng had corresponded on two occasions) in which he encourages her to study hard, we have found no proof of the two of them having remained in contact.

Even though Han Fuying had gone to Hong Kong in 1948 and met with Han Feng, she does not know much about Han Feng's circumstances. So, for example, the information she provided in the course of the *sufan* campaign was all based on what she had been able to find out through her father, whom she had specifically asked in order to have something to share with the [Party] organization. At the time (in 1948), Han Fuying was still (at the age of sixteen) a child and Han Feng is therefore unlikely to have tasked her. In addition, over these past years Han Fuying is not known to have been in contact with the *tewu* [Han] Feng in Hong Kong or engaged in any suspicious destructive activity. She has been active in her work as an outstanding teacher. Consequently, there are insufficient grounds to treat her as a dispatched *tewu* suspect (*paiqian tewu xianyi*). In view of all of this, we are of the opinion that the above case should be closed and that [Han Fuying] should merely be put under long-term observation and monitoring.[71]

On July 9, 1957, the CMPS Sixth Bureau replied in writing to the Guangxi PSB, agreeing to its proposal to close Case 5004, to suspend further operational work (*chexiao zhuan'an zhencha*), and to henceforth limit itself to long-term observation and monitoring.[72]

Procedure under Pressure

For historians to draw general conclusions from a single predicated investigation is, of course, impossible. The unspectacular launch, unfolding, and quiet closure of Case 5004 may have represented something like the public security norm at the time, but this cannot be confidently asserted without access to additional data. That data, furthermore, would have to meet certain minimum standards of independence from the politically motivated massaging of facts so defining of public perception management in the Mao era. A predicated investigation by the Harbin PSB launched on the eve of the founding of the PRC on grounds similar to those of Guangxi's Case 5004 did, for example, lead to the filing of charges against a GMD *tewu* suspect and was quickly turned into a major film, *The Case of Xu Qiuying*.[73] But while the plot unfolding on the silver screen in theaters across China made the operational work of Harbin's public security task force appear reassuringly professional and solid, behind the scenes it turned out to have been far less so in real life. In summer 1956, the Heilongjiang Higher People's Court decried it as having in real life engendered a major "mistaken case."[74]

There is one important procedural aspect of Case 5004 that was unquestionably emblematic of a wider trend, documented in a classified study carried out by the Changchun Municipal PSB in the third quarter of 1956. The study, which looked at substantive data sets concerning *zhuan'an* from the first six months of the year, identified a direct link between the *neibu sufan* and spikes in the overall number of predicated investigations mounted and aborted. Drawing on the study's findings, in December 1956, the CMPS issued a stark warning to senior public security officers nationwide, cautioning them against letting security risk assessment performance goals expressed in quantitative terms trigger predicated investigations of historical matters without first ensuring that those same matters still entailed a clear and immediate security risk.[75]

A condensed version of the Changchun study reached the Guangxi PSB in the final days of 1956, and if/when the senior officers in the Cultural Protection Division read it, they would quickly have seen the unsettling similarities between their own Case 5004 and the *zhuan'an* it criticized. In Nanning like in Changchun, political pressures had admittedly led to a lack of proper oversight. Senior officers had permitted what never should have been a predicated investigation in the first place to be mounted, in the hope of meeting performance goals. In Changchun, it was said, mere hunches had in some cases been turned into leads, while in others unconvincing leads had been upgraded from routine probes to *zhuan'an*. Some officers had only collected and put their trust in information that appeared to strengthen their cases and, as a result, their work had become faith rather than fact based.

The Changchun study did not hesitate to single out the CCP Central Group of Ten's revised rulebook (that had lowered the threshold for the launch of predicated investigations) as a particularly problematic aspect of the *neibu sufan*. It was partially blamed for the high rate of mounted and later aborted/nullified cases during an intense phase when highly dubious predicated investigations had been allowed to consume operational resources and, in the process, draw attention away from the "cases that really are important."[76]

One particular self-critical passage in the Changchun study could equally well have been penned by the Nanning officers who had looked in vain for an intelligence nexus connecting Han Fuying to the "enemy." The Changchun officers had stressed that the aim of predicated investigations and proper motive behind the deployment of operational resources could only be to "discover the enemy and attack the enemy." Hence, they admitted, if under these circumstances,

> we mount no small number of *zhuan'an* that really amount to cases not based on firm factual suspicions, and if [in the end] the rate of cases that need to be nullified is very large, not only will the number of enemies that we dig up be very small, but we will also have wasted manpower and resources. Even if one is able to launch countless cases of this kind,

it still does not count as an achievement. Consequently, in the future we need to maintain quality when launching cases ... . When examining reports spelling out why a case has to be launched, leading cadres must not be too accommodating: cases that are not sufficiently well motivated and that do not fulfill the launch criteria spelled out in the *Case Work Manual* must be firmly rejected.[77]

In addition to undergirding this general finding, what Case 5004 illustrates historically is how cases that never reached the PRC judiciary might have come about in the politically charged atmosphere of a security risk assessment and hunt for RHCs. The full case file lends itself well to a "thicker" extended description and analysis of the people, processes, procedures, and public security routines involved—in particular of key aspects of operational work. As for the fate of Han Fuying, as the coda below bears out, it was in the end never that much affected.

After the Event

In spring 1957, after the Guangxi PSB had aborted Case 5004, Han Fuying was given a permanent position as a doctor in what is today the No. 1 Hospital attached to Guangxi Medical University.[78] At the same time, the closed file on Case 5004, as regulations stipulated, was transferred from the Cultural Protection Division to the archive of the Guangxi PSB. It remained in the archive until 1961, when Han Fuying received a job transfer to the Hospital attached to XX University and moved permanently with her husband from Nanning to Harbin, the capital of Heilongjiang Province, some 3,953 kilometers to the north by train.[79] That same year in July, the case file was mailed to the Harbin Municipal PSB accompanied by a simple, in part pre-printed form that explained: "We are now forwarding to you one bag/bags of archival records pertaining to 1 person/persons by the name of Han Fuying who has received a work transfer to your municipality."[80]

In Harbin, the public security organs took only a fleeting interest in Han Fuying and Guangxi's Case 5004. An officer did take a brief look at the file and concluded that at issue had been a "*tewu* problem involving overseas connections" and that, as a result, one might want to monitor eventual contacts between Han and persons overseas. Possibly only to be on the safe side, an inquiry was put to the local PSB inspectors of international posts and telecommunications, but by February 1962 nothing untoward had been discovered.[81] Thereafter, nobody ever took an interest in Case 5004 again.

At some point, probably after 1979 when national policy vis-à-vis senior members of the medical profession shifted decisively away from stressing "redness" to rewarding "expertise," Han Fuying received a promotion and moved with her husband to Beijing, where she first worked at the research institute of the Chinese Academy of Sciences, the Chinese Academy of Medical Sciences, and a ministry hospital. After formally retiring, she became affiliated, as a senior advisor, with one of the most prestigious public hospitals in China. Repeatedly assessed by her employers as an "advanced worker," she was awarded the honorific designation 8 March Banner Bearer by the PRC Ministry of Health.

Notes

1. For an explanation of the term "perception management," see https://en.wikipedia.org/wiki/Perception_management, last modified October 22, 2017.
2. The term "predicated investigation" is one used and carefully defined by the United States Federal Bureau of Investigation in *The Attorney General's Guidelines for Domestic FBI Operations* (Washington DC, August 2009), 20–23.
3. On case agents, see Michael Schoenhals, *Spying for the People: Mao's Secret Agents, 1949–1967* (Cambridge: Cambridge University Press, 2013), 68–76.
4. I purchased the original closed file (a single volume, altogether over 200 pages, referred to below as *5004 zhuan'an anjuan* [File on Case 5004]) at a flea market in Beijing in the winter of 2012. I was given to understand by the man who sold it to me that it was to have been destroyed after having been weeded out from a municipal PSB archive at the start of the post-Mao era of "reform and opening up." Instead of pulping or burning it as they were meant to, the persons or person who took custody of the file decided to preserve it on the assumption that future historians might well one day take an interest in it.
5. "Internal" here merely refers to the fact that the assessment was a closed affair, conducted within the units concerned. In this respect, it differed from the earlier Suppression of Counterrevolutionaries campaign that had very much taken place in public.
6. See Wang Xiaoping, "Wushi niandai sufan yundong de lailong qumai tanjiu" [Probing the Twists and Turns of the 1950s Campaign to Eliminate Counterrevolutionaries], *Xibu xuekan* [West Journal], no. 4 (2014): 14–21.
7. *Quanguo sufan yundong tongjibiao* [Nationwide Statistics from the Campaign to Eliminate Counterrevolutionaries] (Beijing: Zhongyang shiren xiaozu bangongshi, September 1, 1958), table 1.
8. Zhongyang gonganbu, "Guanyu zhunbei quanmian jiancha sufan gongzuo de tongzhi" [Notification on Preparing for a Comprehensive Examination of the Elimination of Counterrevolutionaries], telegram dated March 16, 1957.
9. Zhang Minghe, "Zai di san ci [Hebei] quansheng gongan huiyi shang de zongjie baogao" [Summing Up Report at the Third Hebei Provincial Public Security Conference], *Gongan jianshe* [Public Security Construction], no. 99, (September 30, 1954), 38; Mu Fengyun, ed., *Zhuan'an zhencha* [Predicated Investigations] (Beijing: Zhongguo renmin gongan daxue chubanshe, 1987), 35. As employed by public security officers at the time, the term *tewu* referred to operatives or assets of hostile intelligence services. Among ordinary Chinese it was often simply a term of abuse thrown indiscriminately at persons suspected of links to external enemies of the PRC state. In this chapter, because of its inherently "fuzzy" meaning, *tewu* has been mostly left untranslated.

10 Zhongyang shiren xiaozu, "Guanyu zhuan'an xiaozu jige wenti de guiding" [Stipulations to Govern Some Case Group Matters] (March 6, 1956), in Zhongguo renmin jiefangjun zong zhengzhibu baoweibu, ed., *Sufan yundong wenjian xuanbian* [Selected Documents from the Campaign to Eliminate Counterrevolutionaries] (Beijing: n.p., 1959), 36.
11 All the same, predicated investigations triggered by the *neibu sufan* remained comparatively rare. If the total number of simple, straightforward personnel security risk assessments was in the tens, or even hundreds, of thousands in a given province, the number of *zhuan'an* in that same province rarely exceeded a few dozen.
12 I have anonymized her and her family and other targets of investigation. Public security officers and other officials are referred to by their true names.
13 Wei Bike, "XXX cailiao" [Documentation Concerning XXX], in *5004 zhuan'an anjuan*, 170. In 1957, Guangxi Province was renamed Guangxi Zhuang Autonomous Region.
14 Ibid., 172; Wei Bike, "Zhi sheng gonganting wu chu han" [Letter to Fifth Division of the Provincial PSB] (November 26, 1955), in *5004 zhuan'an anjuan*, 169.
15 Public security entities charged with "cultural protection" (*wenbao*) were responsible for security, including counterintelligence, in China's cultural, educational, media, public health, etc. sectors.
16 "Yanjiu 5004 zhuan'an" [Researching Case 5004] (November 26, 1956), in *5004 zhuan'an anjuan*, 53. The name of the factory has been altered.
17 Excerpts from "Zhonggong Liuzhou shi tongzhanbu dang'an" [CCP Liuzhou Municipal United Front Department Archive], in *5004 zhuan'an anjuan*, 92–93.
18 Liuzhou shi gonganju, "Zhi Guangxi sheng gonganting han" [Letter to Guangxi Provincial PSB] (December 16, 1955), in *5004 zhuan'an anjuan*, 63.
19 Liuzhou tielu guanliju gonganchu, "XXX cailiao zhengli" [Consolidated Documentation Concerning XXX] (March 10, 1956), in *5004 zhuan'an anjuan*, 146. On the Liu River Middle School, see http://baike.baidu.com/view/451805.htm, accessed January 18, 2018.
20 "Cailiao dengjibiao" [Records Registration Form], in *5004 zhuan'an anjuan*, 180.
21 Guangxi sheng gonganting wenbaochu, "XXX xiansuo li'an baogao" [Lead on XXX Case Launch Report] (April 19, 1956), in *5004 zhuan'an anjuan*, 14; Wei Bike, "XXX cailiao," in *5004 zhuan'an anjuan*, 172.
22 "Gei XXX de xin" [Letter to XXX] (June 22, 1955), in *5004 zhuan'an anjuan*, 175.
23 Ibid.; "XXX de cailiao zhengli" [Consolidated Documentation Concerning XXX] (March 26, 1956), in *5004 zhuan'an anjuan*, 24.
24 Ibid.; "Gei XXX de xin" [Letter to XXX] (July 5, 1955), in *5004 zhuan'an anjuan*, 176.
25 Wei Bike, "XXX cailiao," in *5004 zhuan'an anjuan*, 170–172.
26 The precise circumstances surrounding this discovery are murky and not recorded in detail in the *5004 zhuan'an anjuan*.
27 Tan Yanhua, "Gei Kang chuzhang biantiao" [Note to Division Chief Kang] (November 28, 1956), in *5004 zhuan'an anjuan*, 173.
28 "Guangxi sheng gonganting wu chu piyu" [Remark by Guangxi Provincial PSB Fifth Division] (December 18 [?], 1955), in *5004 zhuan'an anjuan*, 169.
29 See Guangxi gonganting shizhi bangongshi, "Guangxi tewu huodong qingkuang he jiefang chuqi de fante douzheng" [The Activities and Struggle Against *Tewu* in Guangxi Shortly After Liberation] *Gonganshi ziliao* [Public Security History Materials], vol. 32 (1994), 18–33.
30 Tan Yanhua, "Gei Kang chuzhang biantiao" [Note to Division Chief Kang] (November 24, 1956), in *5004 zhuan'an anjuan*, 168; Tan Yanhua, "Gei Kang chuzhang biantiao" (November 28, 1956), in ibid., 173.

31 Wang Chunsheng, "Zhai zi XXX dang'an" [Excerpts from Archive on XXX] (May 5, 1956), in *5004 zhuan'an anjuan*, 182; Guangxi sheng gonganting wu chu, "Guanyu XXX de qingkuang" [Circumstances Surrounding XXX] (April 11, 1956), in *5004 zhuan'an anjuan*, 36.
32 Guangxi sheng gonganting, "Zhi Liuzhou tielu gonganchu han" [Letter to Liuzhou Railway Public Security Division] (September 23, 1955), in *5004 zhuan'an anjuan*, 60–61. In principle, regional and provincial CCP Social Affairs Departments, the predecessors of the PRC's regional and provincial government PSBs, were all to have been abolished in the winter of 1949–1950. Some, however, continued to exist as Party entities under their original names for a number of years, including the Social Affairs Department of the CCP Center's South China Sub-Bureau, located in Guangzhou.
33 Tan Yanhua, "Gei Kang chuzhang biantiao" (November 28, 1956), in *5004 zhuan'an anjuan*, 173; "Guanyu XXX xiansuo li'an de yijian" [Opinion Concerning Lead on XXX Case Launch] (March 30, 1956), in ibid., 34.
34 Ibid, 33; Guangxi sheng gonganting wu chu yi ke, "XXX xiansuo li'an baogao gao" [Draft of Lead on XXX Case Launch Report] (March 30, 1956), in *5004 zhuan'an anjuan*, 18.
35 For an overview of predicated investigation work in the PRC prior to the 1990s, see Mu Fengyun, ed., *Zhuan'an zhencha*.
36 Guangxi sheng gonganting, "XXX xiansuo li'an baogao gao" [Draft of Lead on XXX Case Launch Report] (April 16, 1956), in *5004 zhuan'an anjuan*, 11.
37 Ibid.
38 Guangxi sheng gonganting wenbaochu, "XXX xiansuo li'an baogao" (April 19, 1956), in *5004 zhuan'an anjuan*, 14.
39 Ibid., 15.
40 Guangxi sheng gonganting, "XXX xiansuo li'an baogao gao" (April 16, 1956), in *5004 zhuan'an anjuan*, 11.
41 Guangxi sheng gonganting wenbaochu, "XXX xiansuo li'an baogao" (April 19, 1956), in *5004 zhuan'an anjuan*, 14.
42 See *Zhongguo renmin gongan shigao* [Draft History of the Chinese People's Public Security] (Beijing: Jingguan jiaoyu chubanshe, 1997), 251–52.
43 Tan Yanhua, "Gei Kang chuzhang biantiao" (28 November 1956), in *5004 zhuan'an anjuan*, 173.
44 Guangxi sheng gonganting wenbaochu, "XXX xiansuo li'an baogao" (April 19, 1956), in *5004 zhuan'an anjuan*, 15.
45 Ibid.
46 Guangxi sheng gonganting, "Qing Guangzhou shi gonganju dui XXX de tongxun guanxi jinxing jishu kongzhi" [Requesting Guangzhou Municipal PSB Subject Correspondence Linked to XXX to Technical Control] (August 28, 1956), in *5004 zhuan'an anjuan*, 64–65.
47 Guangzhou shi gonganju, "Zhi Guangxi sheng gonganting han" [Letter to Guangxi Provincial PSB] (February 21, 1957), in *5004 zhuan'an anjuan*, 75.
48 Guangxi sheng gonganting wenbaochu, "XXX xiansuo li'an baogao" (April 19, 1956), in *5004 zhuan'an anjuan*, 15. See also "Guanyu XXX xiansuo li'an de yijian" (March 30, 1956), in *5004 zhuan'an anjuan*, 34.
49 "Dui XXX zhuan'an gongzuo de qingkuang baogao" [Report on the Progress of Work on XXX Case] (July 30, 1956), in *5004 zhuan'an anjuan*, 40.
50 Guangxi sheng gonganting wenbaochu, "XXX xiansuo li'an baogao" (April 19, 1956), in *5004 zhuan'an anjuan*, 15.

51 Ibid.
52 Ding Guanyin, "Cong sufan diaocha gongzuo zhong de wenti tanqi" [Some Observations Prompted by Issues Arising from Investigations in the Campaign to Eliminate Counterrevolutionaries], *Renmin gongan* [People's Public Security], no. 11 (September 30, 1956), 23–24.
53 Wang Chunsheng, "XXX zhuan'an waidiao gongzuo jihua" [Plan for External Investigations into the Case of XXX] (April 20, 1956), in *5004 zhuan'an anjuan*, 100–101.
54 Six-point handwritten note entitled "Guilin ju: Wang" [Guilin Bureau: Wang] (n.d.), in *5004 zhuan'an anjuan*, 101; and almost identical five-point note on Guangxi Provincial PSB stationery entitled merely "Gui" [Guilin] (n.d.), in *5004 zhuan'an anjuan*, 161.
55 "Zai Guilin shi gonganju dui XXX youguan wenti diaocha qingkuang" [Status of Investigation into Matters Concerning XXX at the Guilin Municipal PSB] (May 5, 1956), in *5004 zhuan'an anjuan*, 99.
56 "Zhai jianju XXX cailiao" [Derogatory Information Provided by XXX] (n.d.), in *5004 zhuan'an anjuan*, 93–94.
57 Liujiang xian zhongxue hanjia sufan dangzhibu, "Piyu" [Remark] (February 8, 1956), in *5004 zhuan'an anjuan*, 94. On *biaoxian*, see Andrew G. Walder, *Communist Neo-Traditionalism: Work and Authority in Chinese Industry* (Berkeley: University of California Press, 1988), 132–35.
58 Wang Chunsheng, "Zai Liuzhou shi gonganju yike yanjiu XXX an youguan gongzuo wenti" [Researching Matters Relating to the XXX Case in the First Division of the Liuzhou Municipal PSB] (May 9, 1956), in *5004 zhuan'an anjuan*, 98.
59 "Yanjiu 5004 zhuan'an," in *5004 zhuan'an anjuan*, 48. The unstated assumption at the time appears to have been that a non-CCP target (e.g. Han Fuying) would hesitate to open up to and confide in a Party member the way he or she might do to an "ordinary" friend or colleague. For more on this topic and what public security officers believed made a good informer, see Schoenhals, *Spying for the People*, 110–21.
60 "Dui XXX an de fenxi yijian ji zuofa" [Analyzing and Approaching the Case of XXX] (August 30, 1956), in *5004 zhuan'an anjuan*, 50.
61 "Dui 5004 zhuan'an qu Liuzhou ying nongqing yixia wenti" [These Matters Relating to Case 5004 Should be Clarified While in Liuzhou] (n.d.), in *5004 zhuan'an anjuan*, 103.
62 "Yanjiu 5004 zhuan'an," in *5004 zhuan'an anjuan*, 53.
63 Ibid., 54.
64 Guangxi sheng gonganting, "Zhi Zhonghua renmin gongheguo gonganbu han" [Letter to PRC Ministry of Public Security] (November 9, 1956), in *5004 zhuan'an anjuan*, 66–67.
65 Gonganbu di yi ju, "Zhi Guangxi sheng gonganting han" [Letter to Guangxi Provincial PSB] (December 28, 1956), in *5004 zhuan'an anjuan*, 68.
66 Yang XX, "Dui Gonganbu [56] gong 1 wu zi 816 hao laiwen de pishi" [Instruction on How to Handle Letter 1-V-816 [56] from Ministry of Public Security] (January 4, 1957), in *5004 zhuan'an anjuan*, 69.
67 Wang Pinzhong, "XXX an zai Guangzhou de diaocha qingkuang jianbao" [Update on Investigation of XXX as Conducted in Guangzhou] (January 7, 1957), in *5004 zhuan'an anjuan*, 128–29.
68 Guangxi sheng gonganting, "Zhi Zhonggong Fujian sheng jiaoyuting dangzhibu han" [Letter to CCP Branch of the Fujian Provincial Bureau of Education] (August 31, 1957), in *5004 zhuan'an anjuan*, 87.
69 Ibid.; Hong Kong Governor Alexander Grantham quoted in Richard J. Aldrich, Gary D. Rawnsley, and Ming-Yeh T. Rawnsley, eds., *The Clandestine Cold War in Asia, 1945–65: Western Intelligence, Propaganda and Special Operations* (London: Frank Cass, 2000), 73.

70　Gonganbu di liu ju, "Cuibao 5004 an gongzuo qingkuang" [Request for Update on Progress of Case 5004] (February 11, 1957), in *5004 zhuan'an anjuan*, 10.

71　Guangxi sheng gonganting, "Guanyu chexiao 5004 an de baogao" [Report Suspending Case 5004] (June 29, 1957), in *5004 zhuan'an anjuan*, 3–9. It was by no means unusual for former targets of aborted or inconclusive predicated investigations to be put under "long-term observation and monitoring" for a period of time. On this point, the treatment of suspected counterrevolutionaries in Mao's China and that of suspected terrorists in today's United States bears striking similarities. Compare the following passage in the official March 2013 *Watchlisting Guidance*, as issued by the US National Counterterrorism Center: "An individual who is acquitted or against whom charges are dismissed for a crime related to terrorism may nevertheless meet the reasonable suspicion standard and appropriately remain on, or be nominated to, the Terrorist Watchlist. Each case should be evaluated on the facts of the underlying activities, the circumstances surrounding the acquittal or dismissal, and all known derogatory information to determine of the individual should remain on the Terrorist Watchlist." See page 38 of https://theintercept.com/document/2014/07/23/march-2013-watchlisting-guidance/, last modified July 23, 2014.

72　Gonganbu di liu ju, "Guanyu chexiao 5004 an baogao de piyu" [Permission to Suspend Case 5004] (July 9, 1957), in *5004 zhuan'an anjuan*, 2.

73　See https://baike.baidu.com/item/%E5%BE%90%E7%A7%8B%E5%BD%B1%E6%A1%88%E4%BB%B6/3607483, accessed January 18, 2018. The film title in Chinese is "sanitized" and speaks only of an *anjian* rather than a *zhuan'an*. At the time, the latter term was, like numerous other examples of "operative" terminology (e.g. "case agent," "technical control"), not meant to be shared with the general public.

74　See the exposé "Xu Qiuying an zhenxiang: 'zhengzhi mousha' 40 nian hou bei pingfan" [The Truth about the Xu Qiuying Case: Verdict of "Political Murder" Overturned after Forty Years], last modified May 23, 2009, http://history.news.163.com/09/0523/20/5A1C8LKJ00011247.html

75　Changchun shi ganganju, "Guanyu zhuan'an gongzuo cunzai de wenti he gaijin yijian de baogao" [Report on Problems in Case Work and How to Resolve Them] (October 1956), *Gongan jianshe*, no. 182 (December 25, 1956): 10–12.

76　Ibid., 11.

77　Ibid., 11–12.

78　"XXX de zonghe cailiao (zhai zi benren dang'an)" [Consolidated Record Concerning XXX: Excerpts from Her File] (June 6, 1962), in *5004 zhuan'an anjuan*, 186.

79　Ibid.

80　Guangxi Zhuangzu zizhiqu gonganting, "Gong 2 zhi zhuan zi di 209 hao" [Public Security Transfer Note 2/209] (July 7, 1961), in *5004 zhuan'an anjuan*, 1.

81　Ibid.

Wang Haiguang
3 A Different Category of Life
The Counterrevolutionary Case of a Rural Schoolteacher

On February 4, 1970, two days before the Chinese New Year, Li Fugui, a thirty-five-year-old primary schoolteacher and father of four, was taken by public security organs in Hailong County, Jilin Province, on the suspicion of being an "active counterrevolutionary."[1] Seen through the lens of class, the errors that this son of a landlord was accused of having committed were sufficient grounds not only to detain him, but also to extort denunciations and confessions from his entire family. The case against him was fabricated, but it can still reveal something about the criminal process in the Chinese countryside during the Cultural Revolution. It not only demonstrates that the legal system was impaired during the movement, but also shows how the investigation of political crime was conducted at a time when formal procedures of legal work were rejected. Moreover, the case sheds light on how the Cultural Revolution came to upset the close relations between people in rural communities. As such, it improves our understanding of how political movements affected but also adapted to local society.

Li's class background made him a member of the "Four Types of Elements" (*si lei fenzi*), consisting of landlords, rich peasants, counterrevolutionaries, and bad elements as well as their families. He was one of the hundreds of thousands of these Four Types who suffered political persecution—some even became victims of mass killings—during the Cultural Revolution.[2] Although the persecution faced by these people is crucial to our understanding of violence during the Cultural Revolution, it has frequently been overlooked in previous historical scholarship with its main focus on cities and the fate of cadres and intellectuals.

To be sure, the Cultural Revolution began as an assault on the cadre bureaucracy, with devastating consequences for many cadres and their families, but the persecution they suffered was structurally different from that of the Four Types. The attacks on cadres were especially vicious in 1966 and 1967, but with the restoration of Party leadership, overthrown cadres were the first to benefit from reconciliatory policies and many were "liberated" in the early 1970s, meaning that at least some of them could return to their former positions.[3] The Four Types also suffered at the hands of Red Guards and rebels during the tumultuous beginning of the Cultural Revolution. Then, following the establishment of revolutionary committees and military control committees, they became targets of a new wave

---

Translated and edited by Amanda Shuman

https://doi.org/10.1515/9783110533651-004

of violence. To consolidate the power of the revolutionary committees, both legal and illegal persecution was employed against the Four Types and other "reactionary elements" in the name of the people's democratic dictatorship.

Li Fugui came under investigation during the Cleansing of the Class Ranks campaign and was accused of active counterrevolution during the subsequent One Strike, Three Antis campaign. Both movements employed military force and police terror in the name of restoring order and suppressing political crime. Li's case improves our understanding of what these campaigns meant for politically stigmatized and vulnerable people in the countryside.

This chapter is based on Li's original case file from the Hailong County Public Security Bureau in Jilin. The file is complete. It contains 500 pages systematically detailing the entire process, from criminal evidence and initial hearing to review and rehabilitation decision. It includes investigation materials, interrogation records, comprehensive reports, witness testimonies, verification materials, suggestions for handling the case, confessions, and the Public Security Bureau's rehabilitation decision; in total, 150 documents. The narrative accounts are extremely detailed, but what makes this file exceptional is the rare inclusion of the original criminal evidence, including a damaged Mao Zedong portrait.

Using these original sources, this chapter analyzes Li's active counterrevolutionary case file from the angle of rural society micro-politics to understand two interconnected themes: the political and social environment for those at the bottom of society during the Cultural Revolution, and furthermore the occurrence and handling of political cases dealing with "malicious slandering" (*edu gongji*). It makes every effort to use this case to demonstrate the effect of the Cultural Revolution on the overall political environment within a rural community, and in particular on the situation of human rights for those with "reactionary" family backgrounds. Furthermore, it describes the politicized process of investigation and trial, and the factors that went into reaching a verdict.

The Ambiguity and Impact of Class Status: Li's "Landlord" Family

Li Fugui was born in 1935 in Hailong County to a family later classified as landlord.[4] In 1956 he married Wang Zhi, whose own family background was that of a lower-middle peasant. They subsequently had four children. Li Fugui's father lived with his son's family. From 1956 until the Cultural Revolution, Li Fugui worked as a teacher at six different primary schools.[5]

Party officials initially assigned families in the countryside with a class status to determine the local redistribution of land. Early experiments with land reform were made in the Jiangxi Soviet and later in Communist-controlled areas during the Civil War, before it was implemented nationwide after the founding of the PRC. The Li clan included several well-known wealthy families, and in Li's grandfather's generation, the family was still very well-off. When the family land was divided up among sons in the following generation, his father, Li Changgeng (born in 1914 and hereafter "Old Li"), had still received some land. However, Old Li liked to gamble when he was younger,[6] and had sold and pawned off the land he had inherited until there was little left. Six years prior to land reform, which in this area began in 1947, just twenty-one *mu* of land remained.[7] By the time of land reform, the family's situation had declined to that of an ordinary peasant family. As a child, Li Fugui needed to help his family; he did not enter school until the age of twelve, at a time when the Communist forces were already in control of the Northeast.

Hailong County was one of the first areas in Northeast China to be captured by the CCP, which is why land reform began as early as 1947. At that time, the county's land reform policies and regulations let only those classified as poor peasants join farmers' cooperatives. Later, middle peasants with good conduct (*biaoxian*) were allowed to join, while landlords and rich peasants remained barred from participation.[8] At the time of land reform, Old Li was assessed and given the status of a middle peasant. As a child, Old Li had studied six years. According to the case file, he had some basic education and was fairly eloquent. During land reform, he had shown a lot of enthusiasm and not only joined the peasant association, but also become a cadre.

Upon becoming a cadre, the case file describes Old Li as arrogant and self-important. He himself later explained that at the time he had "enthusiastically climbed the bureaucratic ladder with the intent of joining the Party."[9] Instead, he was categorized as a "corrupt element" in the Three Antis and Five Antis campaigns. The expressed goal of these intertwined campaigns, which were set in motion nationwide in 1951–52, was to eliminate corruption, bureaucracy, and economic crime among Party and state cadres as well as the industrial and commercial elite. In Jilin Province alone, denunciations and confessions led to the identification of as many as 34,361 so-called "corrupt elements."[10]

It is worth noting that the decision to classify Old Li as a landlord was not taken until 1953, after land reform had been completed. Because his new class status marked him as a reactionary, he was expelled from the cadre ranks and sent back to his village to labor under supervision of the masses. From a purely economic standpoint, Old Li should have been considered a "bankrupt landlord" (*pochan dizhu*) at the time of land reform. According to the stipulations of the Government Administration Council's "Decision on the Division of Rural Class Statuses": "After a landlord goes bankrupt and relies on [his] own labor as the main source of livelihood for one year, [he] should be granted a change of status."[11] However, class status was not a simple expression of economic circumstances. Old Li privately told his son that the real reason for his landlord class status was that, as a cadre, he had had poor relations with his colleagues and had offended some people; this was their revenge. Or, in the words of a 1969 confession, he had behaved "like a bureaucrat of the old society by oppressing the people" and done things that were "harmful to the people."[12] Thus, Old Li's landlord label was less the result of having exploited the peasants' land, than it was based on his own misconduct and poor social relations.

In February 1960, Hailong County carried out an evaluation of its Four Types. Each production brigade submitted a report to the Party committee of their respective commune, containing suggestions on what position each individual was to have within the commune. In addition to formal commune members (*zhengshi sheyuan*), people's communes also included three other ranks of people: informal commune members (*fei zhengshi sheyuan*), who were prohibited from voting and collective decisions, those laboring under mass supervision (*jiandu shengchan*), and those who had been sentenced to *guanzhi*—a punishment involving surveillance and limited freedom of movement without imprisonment. The CCP had employed measures comparable to *guanzhi* already during the Civil War, when it was used against class enemies and counterrevolutionaries, and it was codified as a punishment for corruption in one of the earliest criminal statutes of the PRC.[13] Old Li had originally been classified as an informal commune member, but now the production brigade suggested that he should be put under *guanzhi*. What was suggested, then, was a legal measure. However, the suggestion was sent for approval to two Party organs: the commune's Political and Legal Affairs Department as well as its Party committee. They opted for an administrative solution that was similar in practice but considered less severe. They decided that Old Li should be "criticized and struggled against" and then put under mass supervision.[14] That year, Hailong County examined a total of 2,708 people and determined that 924 of them were to be counted as formal commune members, 597 as informal commune members, 538 were to work under mass supervision, and 59 were to be put under *guanzhi*. The status of the remaining 590 people was left unsettled for the time being.[15]

Old Li and his entire family suffered as a result of his landlord label. As class was inherited patrilineally, the label cast a shadow over his children's social and political future. In 1962, the whole family moved from Tongxin to Heping Village for Li Fugui's job. From his case file it is possible to infer that Li was a hard worker, who was seen in a favorable light by his colleagues.[16] Yet, because Li was tainted by his father's landlord class status, he was never able to get ahead. He resented this, thinking that if he resolved the issue of his family background then he could become a school administrator.[17]

In 1964, during the rural Socialist Education movement, the county's Socialist Education work team went to Heping to "squat on spot" (*dundian*).[18] It was responding to a nationwide call to clearly define class statuses, which began in the countryside and later expanded into the cities, a point expanded upon in Puck Engman's chapter. The team convened a general assembly and read aloud documents related to class. At the meeting, Old Li carefully listened to the work team's explanation of the State Council's 1950 decision on class status, which gave him some hope for changing his landlord status. One passage in particular seemed to have a direct bearing on his case, namely, "The temporal standard for fulfilling landlord status is calculated backward from the moment of local liberation; those who spent three consecutive years living as a landlord fulfill landlord status."[19] Because Old Li's situation did not appear to meet these criteria, he thought that he might have found a way to revert his status. He then returned home and told his son that, according to this document, the family's status did not meet the requirements of landlord. The family had eighty-one *mu* of land prior to the division of family land in 1939. However, later, sixty *mu* was mortgaged and the rights to that land had already been lost. Li Fugui then asked his father how the family had received a landlord label. Old Li told him that it was only in 1953 during the movement to Suppress Counterrevolutionaries that the family had received it. At the time, Old Li said, he did not know the national regulations and the family had been incapable of doing anything about it. They discussed the matter of whether or not they could have the class status changed back.

Li eagerly wished to get rid of this family burden. After hearing what his father said, he went to consult with the head of the school where he worked. Li was told that without sufficient land one could not be evaluated as landlord; it was a question of exploitation not personal relations—Li's situation could be changed. However, when Li took the matter to the head of the Socialist Education work team, he got a cursory answer: "Have faith in the masses and faith in the Party."[20] Appeals to the head of the production brigade and a Party member were similarly rebuffed. The matter was complicated by the fact that Li's family had moved from Tongxin Village; any decision to revise the father's class status needed to be taken there. Moreover, many older villagers knew that Li's family had had land in the past and that Old Li had gambled and fallen into debt. The consensus was that a landlord reduced to poverty was still a landlord. Even if the attempt had succeeded, it is unclear if it would have had much effect. Had Old Li's status been changed to that of a "bad element," he would have remained one of the Four Types. Not only did Old Li's status remain the same, the attempt to "reverse the verdict of his landlord father" became one of Li Fugui's crimes during the Cultural Revolution.

The Deterioration of the Rural Political Environment

The launch of the Cultural Revolution brought disaster to the Four Types. In the summer of 1966, Red Guards in the cities subjected countless people categorized as Four Types elements to criticisms and beatings and ransacked their homes. Moreover, tens of thousands were banished from the cities and sent to the countryside. In the countryside, persecution of the Four Types grew even more severe as they became targets for class struggle; they were subjected to public struggle sessions, beaten, and even killed. In Heping Village, Old Li became one of the targets of public denunciation. In 1967, he was criticized for a range of purported crimes, such as having been a "capitalist roader" by keeping a small private plot of land for cultivation; in this he was not alone as many farmers had done the same to survive the Great Famine in 1959–1961. The class struggle motive of the Cultural Revolution necessitated that people struggled against Old Li and other members of the Four Types, but a consequence of these struggles was the overall deterioration of community relations of the countryside.

At the same time that his father was publicly denounced, Li Fugui faced increasing hardship due to his class background, especially in his work as a teacher. At the beginning of the Cultural Revolution, teachers were the first to come under attack by Red Guards.[21] Unsurprisingly, teachers with "bad" family backgrounds became particularly vulnerable. Students frequently viewed such teachers through the distorted lens of class struggle, nitpicking and closely watching the movements of these "class enemies" and taking any pretext to attack them. Li's case illustrates how quickly the situation could escalate.

On June 13, 1966, the CCP Center and State Council had called for a temporary suspension of classes at universities and schools, but on October 14, 1967, the Party ordered schools to "resume classes to make revolution"[22] (*fuke nao geming*). Shortly thereafter, the school to which Li had been assigned, the Tongxin Primary School, reopened its doors. Even though classes had resumed, Li found it difficult to get students in the frame of mind to study. During one incident recorded in Li's file, unruly students stood on the desks and caused disorder. Li provocatively asked them: "So you want to rebel?" When students complained about this response, the school ignored them. In rural primary schools, teachers would often adopt stern methods to maintain order in the class and parents generally understood and supported this strict attitude. However, during the Cultural Revolution, such methods were considered from a class perspective. Teachers with a "good" class background could get away with it, but for teachers with a "bad" class background, strict discipline could easily be considered as "an act of class revenge" and an "abuse of poor and lower-middle peasant children."

One day in December 1967, Li went to turn on the stove in the cold classroom for his students, but he did not have any kindling for the fire. He saw on the classroom floor a few stained notes that the former teacher had written down from *Quotations from Chairman Mao*. He added them to the fire. Some students asked him how he could burn the Chairman's quotations. He responded that the pages were dirty and could not be used. This class had several students transferred from another school who knew that Li was a landlord's son, and they used this incident as an excuse to find fault with him. After class, they posted a big-character poster saying that Li did not respect Chairman Mao. But when the school investigated the situation, it decided that the students were just causing trouble, and Li was simply transferred to yet another class.[23] Li reluctantly continued working for another month at Tongxin Primary School, but felt that the situation was becoming unbearable and thus transferred to Jianshe Primary School.

On November 14, 1968, the *People's Daily* published an article by Hou Zhenmin and Wang Qingyu, two primary school teachers from Maji Commune in Shandong's Jiaxiang County.[24] Hou and Wang suggested that state-run primary schools nationwide be put under the direction of local production brigades. Primary school teachers were to return to their brigades, which would give them work points rather than having the state pay their salaries. The *People's Daily* also organized a forum on this transfer of state-run primary schools, at which no opposing views could be aired.[25] Shortly thereafter, the management of rural primary schools was transferred to the production brigades. In December 1968, Jianshe Primary School was transferred. Li returned to the brigade where, after being obliged to attend a seven-day study class, he was sent into the fields to do farm work. In a very short period of time, he had gone from being a schoolteacher receiving a state salary to an agricultural laborer compensated in work points. At the time, this demotion was referred to as "accepting re-education from poor and lower-middle peasants."

The Deterioration of Li's Neighborhood Relations

Rural society, where family and community relations had remained important, became distorted through the discourse of class struggle. The friction that occurred daily in rural neighborhoods, such as disputes over trivial matters, and small household affairs—all rose to the level of class struggle. Social life became ruled by political principle, and ordinary people often could not avoid it in their daily lives. Seemingly innocent issues could have serious consequences; a fallout between neighbors might continually escalate into a major conflict. Li's relations with his neighbors deteriorated in precisely this way.

The Li family's neighbors were the Wen, Yu, and Lin families, all of whom had a poor peasant class status. Nevertheless, prior to the Cultural Revolution, Li's relations with these neighbors seem to have been peaceful, and they all had frequent contact with one another. For example, Li's wife and Yu's wife were about the same age, and everyday they would visit each other's homes with their children, do household chores together, and chat. While the Li family became increasingly isolated, given that their political class status had effectively turned them into untouchables, the other families had little to fear—with poor peasant class statuses, they enjoyed strong political backing. They benefited from the policies of the Cultural Revolution thanks to a member of the Wen family becoming a member of the Heping Brigade Revolutionary Committee.

A series of incidents provoked or escalated personal animosity between Li Fugui and his neighbors. It began when a member of the Yu family—who despite his poor peasant background had been convicted as a counterrevolutionary for his days as a bandit—was publicly criticized and denounced. One of the accusations against him was that he had taken liberties with Li's ten-year-old daughter. Li became livid and gave him a good beating. In another incident, the eldest daughter of the Wen family climbed onto a roof. Li was scared that she would fall, so he shouted to her to get down. Afterward, Wen told Li that he had frightened his daughter and coerced him to pay four yuan in compensation. Another confrontation began with a rally for a group visiting from a nearby middle school. To mark the occasion, the loudspeakers broadcasted a set on "Wishing Chairman Mao eternal life without end." The father in the Yu family, Yu Yunpeng, complained that the loudspeaker was noisy and cursed the broadcast, saying, "what a crock of shit, [they] still say eternal life without end [*wanshou wujiang*], [but it should] be 'eternal death without end' [*wansi wuliang*]." Li reported this to the military propaganda team, but when they questioned Yu he denied it and instead accused Li of having cursed the broadcast. Because the military propaganda team did not handle neighbor quarrels at that time, they were both dismissed. Yu then teamed up with his neighbor to talk to Li; a confrontation that ended in yet another quarrel. Following these politically augmented confrontations, relations between the Li and Yu families were thoroughly strained.

The incident that would have the most severe consequences involved a set of Chairman Mao portraits hanging in Li's home. In spring 1968, Li bought and hung up three portraits of the chairman. One day at the end of April, the wife of Yu Yunpeng brought the family's four-year-old to the Li house for a visit. While playing on the *kang*, the child tore off the lower part of a portrait of Mao Zedong and Lin Biao displayed on the wall. One of Li's daughters saw what had happened and shouted that the child had torn up the portrait. When Li returned home and discovered this, he had his wife try and paste the portrait back together. When this failed, the portrait was taken down. A few days later, the Yu family's eldest child had a fight with Li's eldest daughter, during which she yelled that the Li family had dug out the eyes of Chairman Mao in the portrait. Li later claimed that he had not thought too much of it at the time; after all, it was Yu's own child who had torn the portrait.[26]

That same year in June, however, Li was at Jianshe Primary School when the schools started the Cleansing of the Class Ranks campaign, which was meant to eliminate "enemies" of the revolution but extended to anyone thought to be an opponent of the newly inaugurated revolutionary committees. When Li heard that some teachers had been exposed for having dug out the eyes of Chairman Mao in portraits, he became worried and told his wife. The next day, she burned the damaged portraits of Mao and Lin and used newspapers to cover the wall where their portraits had been.

In Li's neighborhood, the Cleansing the Class Ranks campaign was organized by a Mao Zedong Thought Propaganda Team consisting of PLA soldiers and commune members with a poor or lower-middle peasant status. Li's neighbor, Yu Yunpeng, and several others went to the propaganda team and accused the Li family of having destroyed a Mao portrait. This was considered a serious political incident and the propaganda team responded immediately by sending people to Li's house to investigate. On the night of March 2, 1969, Li was attending a meeting when one of his neighbors led the propaganda team to the house for inspection. They took the newspapers off the walls to try and find the torn portraits of Mao and Lin Biao, but found nothing. Since the propaganda team could not find any "incriminating evidence," they abandoned the matter. During the New Year festivities, Li's family bought five new Mao portraits and hung them in their home.

In May 1969, Old Li clashed with neighbor Yu. While working together in the fields one day, Yu cursed the production brigade and team leaders. Relations between the Li and Yu families were tense, and Old Li took the opportunity to report Yu to the production brigade leader. Upon hearing about this, Yu first attempted to pick a fight with Li Fugui, but when that failed he sought backup from the Lin brothers, Lin Ke and Lin Qingxue. Together with them, Old Li and Yu were called to the office of the brigade revolutionary committee where Lin Qingxue complained that he was unable to maintain "supervision" over the unruly Old Li. The latter retorted: "In what way can't you supervise me?! Wherever there are poor and lower-middle peasants, I can be supervised," and added: "It just depends on behalf of whom you are wielding power!" Lin was taken aback by this response. When Lin purported to lodge a complaint on behalf of the progressive peasantry, Old Li reversed the situation by suggesting that the complaint demonstrated that

Lin was not representing the peasantry at all. Lin then asked angrily, "For whom are you saying I wield power?" Old Li evasively answered that he did not know. Lin Ke asked: "Old Li, what power are you asking for?" Old Li responded, "I have not asked for power." Lin Ke fired at him: "How so? You still want power!" When Lin Ke saw that Old Li was not backing down, he hit him.[27]

When Li Fugui heard that his father had been struck, he went to see Lin Ke. Li complained that this kind of behavior was not in line with the nonviolent struggle that Chairman Mao had called for. Lin justified his actions by saying that he had just put the proletarian dictatorship into practice.[28] When Li tried to appeal to the head of the brigade instead, he was not only rebuffed, but also warned not to attempt to reverse his father's verdict. Li again invoked the authority of Mao Zedong's instructions, stating that: "Chairman Mao called for a struggle with words [wendou], [we] must not struggle with violence [wudou]."[29] Li threatened to take the issue a level higher, to the commune military propaganda team, but the cadre objected to the idea, noting that the "unruly lodging of complaints" was not allowed.[30]

Malicious Slandering in the Classroom

Li went to the village to "receive re-education" and, together with the commune members, began to work in the fields. Because he had been engaged in teaching for so long, he found working in the fields extremely difficult and was unable to earn many work points. Many of the other teachers previously sent to the countryside had already returned to their teaching posts, and Li was restless to do the same. In private, he asked his father: "With a family background like ours, can I still return to teaching?" He did not have to wait long for an answer. On August 18, 1969, Gao Xianheng, a former colleague, who was in charge of the Heping Primary School of Heishantou Commune Heping Brigade, received a notice from his superiors that Li was to be transferred to the commune for a short period of time. Heping Primary School had few teachers, so when Gao asked Li to temporarily fill in and teach the fifth-grade, Li agreed.

Li Fugui highly valued this opportunity to return to teaching. The fifth-grade class at Heping Primary School had twelve students, all fifteen to sixteen years old, with a low education level and a poor track record in classroom discipline. Gao had given his Chinese and math books to Li in order to prepare—one duty in particular was to give students a vocabulary review and dictation. During three days of review, Li discovered that some students would change the character "叛" as in the word 叛徒 (pantu, "traitor/renegade") to "判" as in the word 批判 (pipan, "criticize/criticism"). They would also change the characters of "恩" and "查" in the name of the Albanian Labor Party leader, Enver Hoxha (恩维尔·霍查, Enweier Huocha), to "思" and "香" respectively. Li marked these and other words in his book for the dictation test to be held on the fourth day.

The dictation test, held on August 25th, did not go as planned. Li read each word aloud three times in the order they appeared in the book, and then asked the students to write it down. The first word he read aloud was "Enver Hoxha." After reading it aloud three times and asking the students to finish writing, he went on to read the second word: the two characters of *pantu* – "traitor." After he read it aloud two or three times, a student interrupted the test, asking: "Teacher Li, is Enver Hoxha not the leader of the Albanian people? How can we put his name together with 'traitor'?"

Li tried to explain that this was the order in which the words appeared in the book and that they were separated by punctuation. But the student continued with his questions: "Is the one who's writing this wrong supposed to be the teacher or the student? I'm not writing [it]!" Li did not dare to further engage with this student, so he conceded with the following words instead: "I accept your objection," and then had the students cross out the word. He continued the vocabulary test with two additional words and then had them write the word 'traitor' again.[31]

The day after this incident, Gao returned to the school. After hearing about what had happened, he immediately looked for students of the fifth-grade and carried out an investigation to acquire detailed knowledge of what had taken place, and helped Li with several days of work. Li also wanted to engage the students in criticizing rampant anarchism in the school system so as to restore order in class. In this, he had some support from central-level policies. On August 28, the CCP Center had circulated an order calling for an end to violent struggle, restoration of discipline, and stabilization of social order.[32] However, the students resisted Li's attempt and continued to criticize him for his error.[33] Gao and Li discussed the matter. Li said that, since this event had taken place, he was afraid that other people would say his choice of word order had been deliberate. He further added that he would be unable to teach a class with these students, and was thus transferred to teach the second grade instead, where he only lasted a week. When Gao went to Hailong County to attend a meeting, Li was driven out of the school and went back to the production team to work in the fields.[34]

Building the Case against Li

Yet the classroom incident was not over. Heping Brigade Revolutionary Committee leaders took steps to turn the incident into a serious political case, ordering Li to immediately conduct thorough self-criticism and write a confession of his crimes. They also wanted Old Li to write a confession. Between September 13 and 27, Li provided the brigade revolutionary committee with three confessions. Because the first two were rejected on the basis of not being detailed enough, his third confession contained several points that expressed his political error in the language of the Party: (1) he had not distanced himself from his landlord family background; (2) he had violated Party policies (by keeping a small plot of land); (3) he had not held high the red banner of Mao Zedong Thought (referring to the incident at the school); and (4) he had practiced liberalism (referring both to comments he had made about the brigade cadre not meeting the requirements of a Party member and to his inability to work properly). The confession also mentioned the incident involving the neighbor's child who had torn the portrait in Li's house. Quoting Mao from the Yan'an rectification campaign, Li assured that he would "learn from past mistakes in order to avoid future ones" and urged the Party to "cure the sickness to save the patient."

At the same time, the brigade revolutionary committee started a broad investigation among teachers and students, with the goal of collecting evidence against Li. The committee secretary had several of the fifth-year students from Heping Primary School write testimonies about the "poisonous" things that Li had done in the classroom. The committee also sought out students at Jianshe Primary School and had them testify to Li's burning of the Mao quotes and his disciplining of lower and middle peasants' children. It also sought out Lin Ke to testify that Li, provoked by the beating of his father, had taken a stand against the lower and middle peasants. Heping Primary School director Gao provided the committee with a testimony concerning the incident in Li's classroom and gave an account of what had happened.

The Heping Brigade Revolutionary Committee issued its "Opinion on Handling the Li Fugui Matter" on October 16, 1969. Li was charged on six points: (1) maintaining the reactionary attitude of a landlord and using his position in the classroom to insult and beat the children of poor and lower-middle peasants; (2) submitting to the "evil wind of reversing verdicts" by seeking to revise his father's class status; (3) engaging in the malicious slandering of Chairman Mao; (4) attacking Enver Hoxha, Mao's "close comrade-in-arms;" (5) rejecting re-education from poor and lower-middle peasants; (6) sabotaging rectification and construction of the Party by claiming that the brigade secretary had insufficient qualifications. Based on Li's overall behavior, the brigade Party branch and brigade revolutionary committee agreed that Li should be removed from his teaching responsibilities and put under *guanzhi* as an active counter-revolutionary.[35] To strengthen the case even further, they boosted the political status of one of the key witnesses (who went from being a member of the Youth League and the commune to a Party member and coalmine worker) and included additional testimonies. Finally, Li handed over a seven-page written self-criticism, the longest one yet. With the suggestions and seal of the Heping Brigade Revolutionary Committee, the file was sent to the commune's revolutionary committee for examination and evaluation.

On October 25, 1969, the Heishantou People's Commune Revolutionary Committee issued its opinion, finding that Li was "indeed maintaining the reactionary position of a landlord's child, and was not suitable for work in the education sector." Thus, it approved the suggestion to remove Li from his teaching position. The committee also ordered that he be "sent down" to participate in agricultural labor, where he would have to "accept poor and lower-middle peasant supervision of his reform process." By suggesting that Li was an active counterrevolutionary, the brigade revolutionary committee had turned the matter into a criminal case, which meant that it had to be evaluated by the Hailong County People's Protection Department. The department, however, concluded that the facts of the case were still unclear. As a result, the commune rejected the charge of active counterrevolution.[36]

Pursuing the Matter of the Vandalized Mao Zedong Portraits

This could have been the end of the matter, but in early 1970, Hailong County began the One Strike, Three Antis campaign and the Heping Brigade Revolutionary Committee once again set out to "mobilize the masses." The county, commune, and brigade all established case examination groups. The primary objective of the One Strike, Three Antis campaign was to strike down active counterrevolutionaries, which created a rationale for bringing up Li's case once again. By using new "revelations" from the neighbors' two small children, the brigade revolutionary committee once again accused Li of the "counterrevolutionary act" of having slashed the Chairman Mao portraits in his home.

The Hailong County Revolutionary Committee People's Protection Department, a body that had taken over the responsibilities of public security, procuratorate, and courts in early 1968, had a direct hand in the investigation and trial of the case. The department had a wide range of responsibilities, which not only included investigation and adjudication of ordinary as well as political crimes, but also war preparations. An army representative led each of its various offices, with a local cadre as second-in-command.[37] On January 3, 1970, the department sent a soldier named Zhang to the Heping Brigade to investigate Li's active counterrevolution case. That same day, following a struggle session against Li, Zhang carried out a preliminary interrogation of Li about his intention and motivation for attempting to revise his father's class status.

With the assistance of the brigade revolutionary committee, the local public security bureau established a case examination group consisting of seven people. The case examination group conducted intense interrogations of Li, focusing in particular on the destroyed portrait of Chairman Mao. On the first day, they began interrogations at half past five in the morning; on the second day, they first interrogated him in the morning and then for three hours in the middle of the night.[38] Using this "conveyor belt" tactic, meaning that the interrogators took turns questioning Li during drawn-out sessions in order to tire him out, the case examination group held seven interrogations over six days. The group also collected witness testimonies from more than ten people, including the teacher Gao and students present during the purported attack on Enver Hoxha. They also interviewed the people involved in the attempt to revise Old Li's class status, as well as the neighbors and children who had reported on the destroyed Mao Zedong portraits.

The investigation brought forth a new accusation, namely, that Li had also pierced Mao portraits in his home. This was brought to light by the son of his neighbor Wen and the son of neighbor Yu, who at the time were also under scrutiny for petty theft.[39] These two reported to the brigade secretary that Li had pierced the eyes of Chairman Mao portraits. On February 1, the case examination group organized members of the militia to carry out a detailed search of Li's home. They wrote a report on the spot in which they stated that the eyes and mouth in the Chairman Mao portraits had marks from pins and knives. Among these were portraits of Mao Zedong sitting in a bamboo chair and on a sofa, and a portrait from a 1968 New Year's Day newspaper editorial, all of which, the report concluded, had been intentionally damaged. It further hypothesized that the adults were responsible for the damage.[40]

Heping Brigade planned to hold a struggle session against Li the next day. Li rushed home and told his wife that Old Li would have to take the blame for having pierced the eyes and mouth on the portrait of Mao sitting on the bamboo chair. He reasoned that if he himself were arrested, no one would be left to care for the family.[41] Reluctantly, Old Li agreed to take the blame.[42] This act later led to accusations that Li had colluded with his family to make their testimonies tally and had attempted to shift responsibility for the crime onto the "old landlord." But when Li returned home on February 5, he decided there was no point in further dragging his father into the matter. His father later saw him being led away by armed militiamen, who were taking Li to the county seat for his case to be heard. Old Li tried to console the rest of the family by reminding them that it is "Party policy to show leniency to offenders and, upon a good confession, he will be dealt with leniently."[43]

Investigating the Case of Active Counterrevolution

Li was brought to the Hailong County Revolutionary Committee People's Protection Department, where he was detained at the local labor reform unit, known as the Red Guard Company Study Class. In this way, the process of formally investigating his active counterrevolution case began. The process was divided into two parts. While the Hailong County People's Protection Department questioned Li, the brigade questioned his father and his wife. The goal of this parallel questioning was to corroborate Li's testimony.

Because it concerned a potential counterrevolutionary crime, the interrogation of Li fell upon the county's Political Protection Group, which questioned him five times over a period of four days. The group also requested Li to write four further confessions, in which he fully admitted to all the charges.[44] At the brigade, Li's wife testified that her husband had pierced the portraits of Mao Zedong and that the two of them had colluded on three separate occasions to make their stories consistent.[45] With this, the brigade was satisfied and on February 23, it sent its opinion to the People's Protection Department to consult when reaching their verdict. In addition to its own opinion on how to judge the case, the brigade revolutionary committee attached comments from all the units that Li had come into contact with: the production teams, the leading group for education, and the case examination group. The units differed on the correct punishment for Li; the most lenient advocated *guanzhi* and the most severe proposed that he be sentenced harshly as a counterrevolutionary. The overall message was that the revolutionary masses would accept nothing less than a conviction. It is worth noting that, in addition to the seal of the Heping Brigade Revolutionary Committee, the opinion bore the private seal of the head of the committee, a sign of the extent to which he had become personally involved in the matter.

The case entered its final phase in March/April 1970, as the One Strike, Three Antis campaign reached its high point. Taking over the entire process, the People's Protection Department continued its interrogation of Li and also questioned his father and wife. The Political Protection Group subjected Li to intense interrogation in order to extort a confession and, to pressure him further, organized a public struggle session.

As this new round of interrogation began, Li repudiated what he had told the case examination group a year earlier when under duress, but the interrogators rejected this turnabout, considering it to be a mere tactical move. The political security group collected new testimonies from local neighbors, who provided the group with an important piece of information: Li and his neighbor Yu had become bitter enemies as a result of a whole series of issues between their two families.[46]

After having collected all possible material and criminal evidence, the investigators compiled a complete set of material on Li's counterrevolutionary case that listed four major types of crime, largely corresponding to those that the case examination group had identified in its investigation.⁴⁷ They determined that Li had maliciously slandered Chairman Mao and Enver Hoxha; submitted to the "evil wind of reversing verdicts;" deceived the people, engaged in bourgeois factionalism, attacked the revolutionary committee, and sabotaged socialist construction; and sabotaged education and beaten the children of poor and lower-middle peasants.

Based on the People's Protection Department's investigation, the Heishantou People's Commune Revolutionary Committee revised its conclusion from six months earlier. It now described Li as a "counterrevolutionary element that has earned the bitter hatred of the people," guilty of "major crimes and utmost evildoing." The committee requested the public security organs to arrest Li and pursue the matter legally.⁴⁸

Following the revolutionary committee's conclusion, the Political Security Group of the Hailong County People's Protection Department compiled its final report on the case, which opened up for adjudication of Li's case. It read:

> Criminal Li Fugui was born into a reactionary landlord family, has been hostile to the Party's policies, [and] claimed his reactionary landlord father has been treated unjustly. From 1968 onwards, [he] has used his own hands and needles to defile portraits of Chairman Mao. When leading his school class during a test, [he] openly made students write "Enver Hoxha traitor," as a means of attacking the proletarian headquarters. After the incident, [he] made deceptive use of the criticism of anarchism, [while] actually suppressing the revolutionary actions of the students.

The report affirmed that Li was guilty of active counterrevolution and stated that it would be impossible to assuage the people's anger without severe punishment. The report concluded by noting that the Political Protection Group was unanimous in its opinion that Li had to be arrested and severely punished.⁴⁹

Case Review and Reversal

From the point of view of basic legal principles, there are many flaws in this report. It was full of political stock phrases and offered little in the way of concrete facts. Furthermore, the evidence pertaining to the motivation behind the crime, which was key to determining if it had indeed been counterrevolutionary in nature, originally came from Li's confession during the case examination group's investigation in late 1969. However, when the Political Protection Group had questioned him about this, he had repudiated his earlier testimony. As such, it should not have been accepted as evidence.

The report was submitted to the Hailong County People's Protection Department for approval. However, the group reviewing the case quickly discovered flaws in the cited evidence. To clear up the matter, the department decided to send out yet another group to re-examine the case, this time selecting cadres with greater experience. Awaiting the result of the re-examination, the department released Li Fugui from detention in late May 1970. At that point, Li had been held in custody for a total of 105 days.

The actual re-examination of the case did not begin until six months later, in late November 1970. The case reviewers first sought out Li Fugui in his workplace to discuss the matter with him.[50] They also questioned his wife, who told them that she actually did not know who had pierced the Chairman Mao portraits. She now claimed that her previous assertion that her husband was the culprit, had been made under duress.[51] The case reviewers additionally sought out other people involved in order to further understand the situation, including Old Li, who said he did not know who had pierced the portraits.[52] Also questioned were the neighboring families, who had been the first to report the piercing of the portraits, to have them retell what had happened. Finally, the case reviewers organized a discussion with the production team in which Li had worked to inquire about his conduct since returning to the fields to work.[53]

Now working under the hypothesis that the case had been fabricated, the case reviewers went through the evidence again. Although the facts regarding the classroom incident involving the Albanian Party leader had already been made clear, they were still unable to make sense of the matter of the damaged Chairman Mao portraits. Each person said something different. As in the earlier investigations, this issue became the focus. The case reviewers turned to three groups of witnesses to gain clarity. First, they sought out Li's neighbors who had participated in the search of his house. They then heard from the people in the Poor and Lower-Middle Peasant Propaganda Team who, when carrying out the search of Li's house during the Cleansing of the Class Ranks, had been unable to find any evidence.[54] This was a strong indication that there was no foundation for the case. Finally, they heard from a member of the original case examination group who had investigated the case in the winter of 1969–70.[55] From these new testimonies, it seemed that the origin of the case had been a conflict between Li and his accusers, and that it had been built on evidence extorted through forced confessions. The brigade secretary also seemed to have played a significant role in investigating the case.

Supplementary inquiries about Li's character, general conduct, and conflict with other people in the village helped the case reviewers in their consideration of the testimonies.[56] Li Fugui, his wife, and his daughter, all denied having anything to do with the destruction or piercing of the Mao portraits.[57] Among the accusers, on the other hand, some were no longer willing to testify against Li.[58] Finally, the case reviewers sought out the children who had first reported the incident to the authorities. Questioned by the case reviewers, the children gave contradictory stories and, when pressed on the issue, admitted that they had fabricated the accusations.[59]

After all this, the accusations of active counterrevolution were finally put to rest. On August 7, 1971, the Hailong County Protection Department issued a notice addressed to the Heishantou Commune concerning Li Fugui's case, which said: "In the case of Li Fugui, [we] have decided after discussion that the issue during the dictation test was an unintentional political error. The piercing of Chairman Mao portraits at the Li family has been verified. As to who committed the act, there is insufficient evidence, at present it is impossible to clarify; [one] can confirm the act [but] not the person [responsible]."[60]

After the end of the Cultural Revolution, a great number of "unjust, false, and mistaken cases" (*yuan jia cuo an*) were reversed under the banner of "fixing policy" (*luoshi zhengce*). Li was among those who saw hope for his own rehabilitation. Although he had not been formally convicted for any crime, he wrote letters to the CCP Hailong County Committee and the County Education Bureau Party Group, requesting a formal recognition that he had been unjustly detained on false charges. In his petition, Li wrote: "In November 1968, I was called back to the production team to 'receive re-education.' The result of them educating me was that I was made out to be an active counterrevolutionary." The letter denounced those who had fabricated his active counterrevolution case and explained in detail his position on the Mao portraits. Li stressed the absurdity of the charge by stating that "even the most stupid counterrevolutionary would never commit a crime using the portraits of Chairman Mao in his own home."

In February 1979, the Hailong County Public Security Bureau formally reversed Li's case. The decision read:

> [Our] opinion following the review is that there is not sufficient evidence to prove that Li vandalized the Chairman Mao portraits in his home. Equally unclear is the issue arising from the classroom incident, thus the educational detention [*shourong jiaoyu*] was unsuitable. According to the principle that "counterrevolutionaries must be eliminated wherever found, mistakes must be corrected whenever discovered," the decision of the Hailong County Public Security Bureau is to revoke the original conclusion, grant rehabilitation [*pingfan*], politically clear [Li's] name, [and] to recommend that the original work unit recompensate the wages for time spent in detention. Destroy the original materials.[61]

Although this decision left several issues unsatisfactorily resolved, it did finally put an end to Li Fugui's "criminal case."

Afterword

In 1970, during the One Strike, Three Antis campaign, Hailong County reported that it had uncovered fifty-eight political cases. Among these, it counted fifty-three reactionary written slogans (*biaoyu*), two reactionary utterances (*kouhao*), one instance where the portraits of political leaders (i.e. Mao Zedong and Lin Biao) had been vandalized, one anonymous letter, and one counterrevolutionary killing.[62] We cannot say how Li's case was categorized. Did it count as a counterrevolutionary slogan? Was it perhaps the case of defiling Mao's likeness? What we do know is that cases such as Li's were common across the country.[63]

Compared to the bewildering spectacle of high politics in this period, the case of an ordinary person like Li Fugui may seem insignificant—the unjust fate of a rural primary school teacher. Yet, the multiple dimensions of this micropolitical event makes it perhaps no less significant a subject than top-level politics; it may even be considered more substantial. In contrast to the opaque and outwardly absurd affairs of the Party leadership at the time, such as the still puzzling circumstances of the Lin Biao incident, the present case is rooted in the manifest structures of rural society that shaped a majority of Chinese lives.[64] One single case can help us gain a more fine-grained understanding of the social history of the Cultural Revolution. Indeed, an embedded reading of Li's file can improve our understanding of a wide range of issues. Here, I can do nothing more than highlight a few aspects of his case pertinent to our current understanding of the Cultural Revolution.

First, the case highlights the difference between the city and the countryside in terms of both the structure and timing of the political campaign. In contrast to the line struggles and power seizures that dominated the early and urban development of the movement, the Cultural Revolution mimicked earlier campaigns of class struggle once it reached the countryside. Its most significant impact on rural society came after the establishment of the revolutionary committees and the primary targets were the Four Types. The chaotic reshuffling of political leadership, together with the reorganization of administration and workplaces, augmented the vulnerability of Old Li and his son, who were already likely targets of class struggle.

Second, law was distorted by the requirements of the political campaign. The second among the "Six Articles on Public Security," a set of regulations issued in early 1967 that set the tone for policing during the Cultural Revolution, explained that all instances of anonymous mailing of counterrevolutionary letters, dissemination of counterrevolutionary leaflets, and writing or shouting of reactionary slogans attacking or slandering Chairman Mao and his "close comrade-in-arms" Lin Biao constituted acts of active counterrevolution. The "Articles" thus enlarged the scope of repression outlined in the 1951 "Regulations for the Punishment of Counterrevolutionaries" and consequently entailed a contraction of the legal sphere (for a different view on this particular point see the chapter by Xu Lizhi). Whereas the language of earlier regulations was strictly about opposition to the Party or the state, the "Six Articles" explicitly made attacks on Mao Zedong into crimes of active counterrevolution. The result was a barrage of cases similar to that of Li's, where acts like the involuntarily damage of a Mao portrait, were treated as grave political crimes. With the weakening or abolishment of public security organs, procuratorates, and courts, the military became administrators of the law. Soldiers replaced the police in handling cases, thereby increasing the frequency of cases such as Li's. This was a step backwards for the legal system and judicial procedure.

Third, socio-political identity took on an even greater importance. The Four Types, as the untouchables of Maoist China, had been the targets of several political movements before the Cultural Revolution. But with the proclamation of "continuous revolution," repression against the Four Types worsened and family background was solidified as a criterion of political stigmatization. An indirect effect of the strict control and insecure living conditions of the Four Types and their families, rural society as a whole was brutalized.

Finally, the Cultural Revolution signified a general deterioration of the socio-political situation in the countryside. Class struggle tore through rural communities, as everyday conflicts became instruments for political advancement. Under the banner of class struggle, politically motivated charges brought misfortune upon people with "bad" family backgrounds. In Li's case, everyday conflicts with his neighbors were amplified by the fact that he had been born into a landlord family. Further disaster was avoided only when the county revolutionary committee found little evidence to support the allegations against him.

The study of the Cultural Revolution requires many different perspectives. We must not ignore the grassroots approach and should pay particular attention to the fate of marginal populations.[65] Indeed, we may judge the degree of civilization of society at the time by the conditions under which these people lived.

Notes

1   All personal names appearing in this chapter have been replaced with pseudonyms.
2   See, for example, Yu Luowen, "Beijing Daxing xian can an diaocha" [Investigation into the Massacre in Daxing County, Beijing], in *Wenge da tusha* [Massacres during the Cultural Revolution], ed. Song Yongyi (Hong Kong: Kaifang zazhishe, 2003), 13–36; Yang Su, *Collective Killings in Rural China during the Cultural Revolution* (Cambridge: Cambridge

University Press, 2011); Tan Hecheng, *The Killing Wind: A Chinese County's Descent Into Madness During the Cultural Revolution*, trans. Stacy Mosher and Guo Jian (Oxford: Oxford University Press, 2017).
3   Cf. Warren Sun, "Jiuzheng wenge de jizuo cuowu – Zhou Enlai yu jiefang ganbu" [Rectifying the Ultra-Left Mistakes of the Cultural Revolution – Zhou Enlai and the Liberation of Cadres], in *Zhou Enlai yu ershi shiji de Zhongguo he shijie* [Zhou Enlai in the Context of Twentieth Century China and the World], ed. Liao Xinwen and Liu Jingquan (Beijing: Zhongyang wenxian chubanshe, 2015), 740–48.
4   "Li Fugui 1969 zi xie lüli" [Li Fugui 1969 Self-Written Resume].
5   "Guanyu Li Fugui richang biaoxian zuotanhui jilu, Jianshe xiaoxue" [Records from the Discussion Concerning Li Fugui's Daily Conduct, Jianshe Primary School], December 26, 1970.
6   "Lao pinnong zuotanhui" [Meeting of Old Poor Peasants], December 27, 1970.
7   "Shenxun Li Changgeng jilu" [Interrogation Record of Li Changgeng], February 21, 1970.
8   Meihekou shi difangzhi bianzuan weiyuanhui, *Meihekou shizhi* [Meihekou Municipal Chronicle] (Changchun: Jilin renmin chubanshe, 1999), 255.
9   "Li Changgeng de jiaodaishu" [Li Changgeng's Letter of Confession], September 13, 1969.
10 Zhonggong Jilin shengwei dangshi yanjiushi and Jilin sheng dang'anguan, eds., *"San fan," "Wu fan" yundong (Jilin juan)* [The "Three Antis," "Five Antis" Campaigns (Jilin volume)], (Changchun: Jilin sheng neibu ziliao chubanwu, 2002), 26.
11 Zhengwuyuan, "Guanyu huafen nongcun jieji chengfen de jueding," August 4, 1950. Available in the Maoist Legacy Database (MLD), item no. 1416.
12 "Li Changgeng de jiaodaishu."
13 Cao Zidan, "Shilun wo guo guanzhi xing cunzai de genju" [Tentative Discussion on the Existence of *Guanzhi* as a Criminal Sentence in China], *Zhongguo faxue*, no. 1 (1990), 61.
14 "Wulei fenzi pingcha shenpibiao" [Approval Form for the Evaluation of Five Types Elements], February 19, 1960, in *Dizhu fenzi Li Changgeng dang'an* [Dossier of Landlord Element Li Changgeng], ed. Zhonggong Jilin sheng Hailong xian liuba shi xiang jiceng weiyuanhui (n.p.: n.d.).
15 *Meihekou shizhi*, 206.
16 "Guanyu Li Fugui richang biaoxian zuotanhui jilu."
17 "Li Fugui xunwen bilu" [Interrogation Transcript of Li Fugui], January 3, 1970.
18 The term *dundian* translates to something like "squat on spot" or "squat at a point." The practice itself involved sending cadres with various levels of experience down to rural areas where they then worked as technicians, guides, and in similar roles for short periods of time to mobilize and work with local villagers. Gail Hershatter, *Gender of Memory* (Berkeley: University of California Press, 2011), 72–77.
19 Zhengwuyuan, "Guanyu huafen nongcun jieji chengfen de jueding."
20 "Zhang Weixin diaocha zhengshi cailiao" [Verification Materials for the Investigation of Zhang Weixin], February 21, 1970; "Li Fugui xunwen bilu."
21 Bian Zhongyun, a deputy principal of a girls' high school attached to Beijing Normal University, who was beaten to death by her students on August 5, 1966, is frequently referred to as the "first victim" of the Cultural Revolution, see *Jiyi*, no. 47 (April 28, 2010) and no. 49 (May 23, 2010). Available at http://prchistory.org/remembrance/, accessed August 25, 2017.
22 Zhonggong zhongyang, Guowuyuan, Zhongyang junwei, Zhongyang wenge, "Guanyu da, zhong, xiao xuexiao fuke nao geming de tongzhi" [Notice Concerning the Resumption of

Classes to Make Revolution in Universities, Middle Schools, and Elementary Schools], *Zhongfa* (1967) no. 316, in MLD, item no. 2096.
23. "Li Fugui shenxun jilu" [Li Fugui Interrogation Records], January 30 and February 1, 1970; "Guanyu Li Fugui richang biaoxian zuotanhui jilu."
24. "Jianyi suoyou gongban xiaoxue xiafang dao dadui lai ban" [Suggestion to Transfer the Administration of State-Run Primary Schools to the Production Brigades], *People's Daily*, November 14, 1968, 1.
25. Cf. "Guanyu gongban xiaoxue xiafang dao dadui lai ban de taolun (qi)" [Discussion on Transferring the Administration of State-Run Primary Schools to the Production Brigades (Seven)], *People's Daily*, December 12, 1968, 1.
26. "Li Fugui shenxun jilu," February 1 and February 3, 1970.
27. "Li Changgeng de jiancha jiaodai cailiao" [Li Changgeng's Self-Criticism and Confession Materials], September 13, 1969.
28. "Lin Ke de diaocha zhengshi cailiao" [Verification Materials of the Lin Ke Investigation], October 22, 1969, in Heishantou gongshe Heping dadui zhuan'anzu, *Guanyu Li Fugui de zonghe cailiao*, February 23, 1970.
29. Mao Zedong's instructions to this effect were quoted in a *People's Daily* front-page editorial on September 5, 1966.
30. "Chang Yongqing de diaocha zhengshi cailiao" [Verification Materials of the Chang Yongqing Investigation], February 23, 1970.
31. "Gao Xianheng de diaocha zhengshi cailiao" [Verification Materials of the Gao Xianheng Investigation], September 22 and October 22, 1969; January 28, 1970.
32. Zhongguo gongchandang zhongyang weiyuanhui, "Mingling" [Order], *Zhongfa* (1969) no. 55, August 28, 1969. Available in MLD, item no. 2098.
33. "Shenxun Li Fugui bilu," January 30, 1970.
34. "Gao Xianheng: Wo xiao fasheng de zhengzhi shijian de jingguo" [Gao Xianheng: The Course of the Political Incident that Transpired at Our School], September 22, 1969.
35. Heishantou gongshe Heping dadui geming weiyuanhui, "Guanyu Li Fugui de wenti chuli yijian" [Opinion on the Handling of the Li Fugui Matter], October 16, 1969.
36. Hailong xian geming weiyuanhui renmin baoweibu zhengbaozu, "Dui Li Fugui fangeming anjian diaocha baogao" [Report on the Investigation of the Li Fugui Counterrevolutionary Case], April 21, 1970.
37. *Meihekoushi shizhi*, 179, 196, 197, 215.
38. Hailong xian geming weiyuanhui renmin baoweibu, "Xunwen Li Fugui bilu," [Transcript of Li Fugui's Interrogation] January 29 to February 3, 1970.
39. "Lao pinnong zuotanhui."
40. Heping dadui geweihui zhuan'anzu, "Xianchang jiancha baogao" [Report of an Inspection at the Scene], February 1, 1970.
41. *Ibid.* See also: "Wang Zhi xunwen jilu" [Wang Zhi Interrogation Record], December 26, 1970.
42. Xian renbaobu, "Li Changgeng xunwen bilu" [Li Changgeng Interrogation Transcript], December 1, 1970.
43. *Ibid.*, December 1 and February 21, 1970.
44. "Li Fugui jiancha cailiao" [Li Fugui Investigation Materials], February 10 and 18, 1970.
45. "Wang Zhi xunwen bilu" [Wang Zhi Interrogation Transcript], February 20 and 21, 1970.
46. "Lin Fengqi zhengshi cailiao" [Lin Fengqi Verification Materials], April 17, 1970; "Chang Qinglin zhengshi cailiao" [Chang Qinglin Verification Materials], April 17, 1970.

47 "Li Fugui zonghe cailiao" [Comprehensive Materials on Li Fugui], no date given, but most likely April 1970.
48 Heishantou renmin gongshe geming weiyuanhui, "Guanyu Liu XX fangeming anjian de chuli yijian" [Opinion on the Handling of the Li XX Counterrevolutionary Case], April 17, 1970.
49 Hailong xian geming weiyuanhui renmin baoweibu zhengbaozu, "Dui Li XX fangeming anjian diaocha baogao."
50 "Li Fugui xunwen bilu," November 30, 1970.
51 "Wang Zhi xunwen bilu," November 30, 1970.
52 "Li Changgeng xunwen bilu," December 1, 1970.
53 "Heping er dui zuotanhui" [Meeting of the Second Heping Production Team], December 1, 1970.
54 "Zhang Fengyi diaocha zhengshi cailiao" [Verification Materials of the Zhang Fengyi Investigation], December 23, 1970; "Liu Xingping diaocha zhengshi cailiao" [Verification Materials of the Liu Xingping Investigation], December 22, 1970; "Yao Chunsheng diaocha zhengshi cailiao" [Verification Materials of the Yao Chunsheng Investigation], December 25, 1970.
55 "Zhao Qingguo diaocha zhengshi cailiao" [Verification Materials of the Zhao Qingguo Investigation], December 23, 1970.
56 "Liu Zisu zhengming Li Fugui zai Tongxin xiaoxue gongzuo qingkuang" [Liu Zisu Testimony on the Circumstances of Li Fugui's Work at Tongxin Primary School], December 26, 1970; "Guanyu Li Fugui richang biaoxian zuotanhui jilu, Jianshe xiaoxue;" "Lao pinnong zuotanhui."
57 "Li Xiaomei xunwen bilu" [Li Xiaomei Interrogation Transcript], December 25, 1970; "Wang Zhi shenxun bilu," December 26, 1970.
58 "Chang Qinglin zhengshi cailiao," December 28, 1970.
59 "Lin Yuansheng xunwen bilu" [Lin Yuansheng Interrogation Transcript], December 27, 1970; "Yu Xiangqian xunwen bilu" [Yu Xiangqian Interrogation Transcript], December 27, 1970.
60 Hailong xian geming weiyuanhui renmin baoweibu, "Dui Li Fugui anzi de pifu" [Reply in the Case of Li Fugui], August 7, 1971.
61 Hailong xian gonganju, "Dui Li Fugui pingfan de jueding" [Decision to Rehabilitate Li Fugui], February 17, 1979.
62 Hailong xian gonganju, "1966 zhi 1971 ge lei zhengzhi anjian zhenpo qingkuangbiao" [Overview about the State of Solved Political Cases of Various Categories between 1966 and 1971], January 1972.
63 Cf. Wang Haiguang, "Pingfan yuan jia cuo an yu san zhong quanhui qianhou de lishi zhuanzhe" [The Reversal of Unjust, False, and Mistaken Cases and the Historical Shift Around the Time of the Third Plenum], *Lilun xuexi*, 1 (1999), 16–18.
64 Cf. Wang Haiguang, "Guanyu Lin Biao shijian yanjiu de ji ge wenti" [On a Few Issues of Researching the Lin Biao Incident], *Yanhuang Chunqiu*, no. 7 (2015), 24–28.
65 Cf. Yang Kuisong, *"Bianyuan ren" jishi: Ji ge "wenti" xiao renwu de beiju gushi* [People on the Margins: The Tragic Stories of Several "Problematic" Individuals] (Guangzhou: Guangdong renmin chubanshe, 2016).

Puck Engman
4 Vetting the People's Servant
On the Principles of Revolutionary Integrity

As the Chinese Communists approached victory in the Civil War, their leaders became increasingly preoccupied with the dilemma of balancing capacity against integrity. Under the policy of the united front, they sought to retain and make use of personnel capable of administrating a modern state—including former GMD functionaries, prominent businessmen, and leaders of religious and ethnic groups.[1] At the same time, the communist leaders found it necessary to distance the "people's government" that they represented from the "criminal" regime against which the war had presumably been fought, thereby distinguishing New China from the "lawless" class society from which the Chinese people had finally been liberated.[2] To better appreciate these contradictive objectives (and their consequences) the following chapter proposes a new lens to examine purges, rectification, and personnel reform in the first thirty years of the PRC. It considers these practices as constituting a specific form of vetting. As a method of administrative disassociation, vetting consisted of evaluating the historical conduct and affiliation of Party and state personnel according to the ethical standards championed by the CCP. In the following, I turn to the personnel file of a low-level cadre in Wuhan, who was subjected to repeated investigations and probes into his past by local authorities.[3] My aim is to show how local investigators operationalized the Party's principles of integrity and standards of evaluation, and how someone who became the object of scrutiny defended himself.

To introduce the term vetting to the discussion of "purges" and "rectification" is to suggest an expansion of the universe of comparable cases, extending beyond the socialist world.[4] The comparison will remain implicit here, as the scope of this chapter is limited to an account of the development, transmission, and enforcement of the CCP's particular brand of integrity. In Party language, integrity was expressed as an amalgam of individual conduct (*biaoxian*) and class background (*jiating chushen*). Premier Zhou Enlai put it succinctly in an August 1966 criticism of his long deceased and disgraced colleague, Qu Qiubai. Zhou explained that bad class background with good conduct was at least partly good, while having a good class background with bad conduct was to "forget one's roots." Worse yet were people like Qiu Qiubai, who had both a bad class background and bad

---

For their comments and insights, I am indebted to Daniel Leese, Elisabeth Forster, Aurélia Ishitsuka, Simon Rose, Michael Schoenhals, and Amanda Shuman.

conduct. They were confined to political isolation if they wanted to avoid accusations of trying to "restore" (*fubi*) the old class society.[5] Zhou spoke at a time of radical criticism against the Party bureaucracy, but the idea of an interplay between conduct and background was far from new.

In fact, this conceptualization of integrity, which was prominent in both policy and propaganda, underlay the vetting practices of the CCP from the early 1950s to the late 1970s. Theoretically, it derived from the tension between the illegitimate past and the just future that was the socialist present, with the socialist state as the vehicle of historical progression. The past prevailed in the form of reactionary forces, both foreign and domestic, while the progressive majority—the formerly oppressed classes identified by the 1949 Common Program as the "people" (*renmin*)—embodied the future. Although every citizen (*guomin*) was obliged to follow the laws and regulations of the PRC, the right to be represented and accommodated by the people's servants was reserved for the progressive classes.[6] As Zhou Enlai's distinction between class background and political conduct suggests, the idea that anyone could reform to join the progressive majority was central to this concept of integrity, at least in theory. Proper conduct was described with words like "advanced" and "red"—in opposition to "reactionary" and "black"—to emphasize the ever-widening gap between the New China and the decadent, parasitic, and exploitative "old society."[7] In practice, however, improper conduct was easily taken as an indicator that a person's true class background might have been overlooked. Conversely, the wrong class background invited constant scrutiny of conduct, which Wang Haiguang gives further example of in his chapter. In this way, the pre-revolutionary past became the dark underbelly of the socialist present, which would repeatedly be brought to light through the "discovery" of a major reactionary or counterrevolutionary conspiracy. Beyond the headlines of the press, the CCP sought to systematize knowledge about the pre-revolutionary past of Party and state personnel through background checks.

Historical Integrity and Self-Writing

The fundamental device used to obtain working knowledge of cadres' pasts was a set of forms on which personal résumés and autobiographies (*zizhuan*) were scribbled down. Due to an urgent need of qualified personnel, the destruction or displacement of archives during the war, and general fiscal constraints, local CCP leaders had little choice but to rely on the employees' own retelling of their past.[8] However, when the Party launched initiatives to rectify the bureaucracy, these accounts were subjected to close scrutiny. For Bai Tieshang, a low-level cadre working for the Wuhan branch of the China Coal Construction Company, this meant his story was challenged through repeated interrogations into his past.⁹ As part of the process, he was made to prepare seven different versions of his autobiography between 1956 and 1977. Throughout this period, the overall story and chronology he presented his investigators with remained the same. Bai was born in Hong'an County in the 1910s. During the war against Japan, his three years of basic schooling at a rural school (*sishu*) and the introduction of a relative was enough to land him a position as a cadre in the New Fourth Army. In his very first autobiography, written in June 1956, he described his brief but tumultuous career in the army in the following way:

> In July [1941], due to my dissatisfaction with the oppression by the Japanese devils and the reactionary government, I joined the New Fourth Army [...] After an introduction by a township operative, Mao Shaodong, I became the head of an armed squad (my main responsibility was the organization of militias for self-defense, the district head was Zhang Hongzhong) [...] In April 1945, my work led me to be taken hostage by a reactionary guerilla band. *At this point, the township secretary who was with me was beaten to death and I was taken away* [emphasis in the original]. Because the puppet guerilla band was only interested in extorting money, and because people from my village vouched [for me], I was released when my mother had sold off property to raise over 30,000 yuan [in payment to the guerilla band]. In July of the same year, I was once again abducted by the puppet guerilla, and once again I was released after Bai Jinhai from my native village had vouched for me and after paying over 3,000 yuan. In October of the same year, I was again abducted by the puppet guerilla and taken to Lindian in Macheng County. That same night in Lindian, I scaled the wall and ran away. At that time, because my unit had already left, I lost [contact with] the organization; moreover, when returning to my town I could not go home, my only option was to run away to Hankou.¹⁰

Having left the army in irregular fashion, Bai thus arrived in Hankou, one of the districts in the tri-city of Wuhan, provincial capital of Hubei, where he took up the family trade of selling iron. A year after the founding of the People's Republic, Bai transitioned into coal retail. When his coal shop was incorporated into a joint public-private enterprise at the height of nationalization in 1956, he stayed on as the assistant manager. Thus, he became an insider, a functionary of the socialist state. As part of his initiation, he was required to write the autobiography excerpted above.

All of Bai's autobiographies followed a set of guidelines developed to facilitate inquiry into his past and hold him accountable for any omissions. A revised version from May 1960 appears on a printed form that summarizes the requirements of an acceptable autobiography in six points. It specifies that autobiographies must cover: (1) information on the family situation; (2) a description of the subject's surroundings at each of the described stages in life; (3) contact information of witnesses able to corroborate the account, together with a comment on their political situation; (4) a declaration, if applicable, of the reasons for joining and leaving a revolutionary organization; (5) details, if applicable, on the circumstances in which one joined or received training from a reactionary organization; (6) other relevant information.[11]

These brief instructions, which followed national standards for autobiographical writing, already give us a general idea of what discredited a cadre in the eyes of the CCP.[12] Those who drew up these instructions were clearly not motivated by a general interest in the past, but rather by concerns related to a particular understanding of the nature of "old society." The first point, for instance, gives information that can be used to determine the author's class background (*jiating chushen*). Together with individual class status (*jieji chengfen*), this marker served to separate those who had belonged to the oppressed from their former oppressors. Points four and five provide information of another kind. Here, the concern is with the author's past relation to the CCP and its political opponents. Reading Bai's file with these guidelines in mind, it is easy to understand why he became doubly suspect in the eyes of the officials. Not only was he considered a capitalist at the time of nationalization, a class status that branded him as an exploiter and potential reactionary, he was also thought to have "problems of political history" (*zhengzhi lishi wenti*), a collective term referring to any suspicions concerning an individual's historical alignment with the CCP and its allies. Thus, both Bai's political past and his class identity made him potentially unfit to serve as a cadre in the PRC.[13] An autobiography written according to the instructions above would contain details of any potential integrity issues and provide contact information to individuals who may corroborate the narrative. In this way, the ideal autobiography anticipated future investigation.

In the following, I rely on Bai's personnel file to trace the evolving, but ultimately coherent set of principles that informed the assessment of Party and state cadres' integrity throughout the Maoist era. I will follow four different examinations documented in the file. Because the CCP organs reviewed his class status as well as his political history, this file is well suited for a simultaneous study of two aspects of socialist integrity that scholars have habitually explored in separation. By tracing the repeated inquiries into the background of a single individual, I will anchor overarching principles of administrative suitability in a concrete example of vetting carried out by local Party organs and ad-hoc campaign bodies. Although the individual fate of Bai cannot be seen as representative, his file is typical to the extent that it was compiled in a standardized fashion by local officials who interpreted and evaluated integrity in keeping with national policy. The investigations of Bai Tieshang between the 1950s and the 1970s did not advance step-by-step as new data reached his superiors. Rather, they maintained a staccato rhythm that evokes Gail Hershatter's concept of "campaign time"—a politically determined temporality arranged according to Party and state initiatives.[14] Yet, as will become clear, this rhythm does not match the grand divisions of the Maoist past but corresponds instead to specific initiatives communicated via specific documents. For instance, it was not the total politicization of society during the Cultural Revolution that motivated the investigation of 1968, but rather a well-documented policy of reexamining historical problems to assure the integrity of the new revolutionary committees. The chapter ends in the immediate aftermath of Mao Zedong's death, at a moment when a new type of historical integrity was in the making. After 1978, issues related to the prerevolutionary era, already thirty years in the past, lost their importance for the evaluation of personnel suitability. In this period, integrity came instead to be understood primarily in light of affiliations and actions during the Cultural Revolution.

First Review: Cadre Examination

In September 1953, when tensions were high following Gao Gang's attempt to displace senior CCP leaders, the Second National Conference on Organization Work convened in Beijing under the auspices of Liu Shaoqi and nine other members of the Politburo. The first conference had been held two years earlier and focused on organizational consolidation and recruitment of Party members, while the second adopted key documents that became fundamental to the codification of personnel administration and screening.[15] Among these documents was the CCP Center's "Decision on the Examination of Cadres," signed on November 24, 1953.[16] The decision drew upon the experiences from Yan'an to set a standard for cadre examinations (*ganbu shencha*) that would live on well into the reform era.[17] The comprehensive screening of cadres in the PRC was a massive undertaking that took several years to complete. A historical reference work gives an idea of the extent: 17.5 percent of the cadres on the county level and above were selected for further investigation and 11.8 percent were considered to have some problems in their political history.[18] Half a century later, the CCP still maintained that the examinations had been necessary but was ambivalent about the outcome. While the scope of the examinations was criticized as too restricted in 1966, it was judged to have been excessively broad after 1978, to the point of having engendered numerous "unjust, false, and mistaken cases."[19] At the time, however, the Party presented cadre examinations as a soft alternative to violent campaigns against corruption and the hunt for counterrevolutionaries. The 1953 decision outlined a non-intrusive approach that it held to be fundamentally different from "campaign-like assaults" that "obstructed" the bureaucracy's normal operation. The drafting of the decision coincided with the First Five-Year Plan (1953–1957), which aimed to lay the foundation for Stalinist modernity through nationalization of private enterprises and collectivization of agriculture. Any concerns about integrity were secondary to the task of putting the plan into effect.

The grand finale of the First Five-Year Plan was the final stage of nationalization. This meant that private companies were incorporated into joint public-private enterprises and private personnel was assimilated into an expanding state organization. Faced with this influx of new state employees, the CCP Central Organization Department, in a final push to complete examinations by the end of 1958, ordered cadre examination offices across the country to turn their attention to the "complex" historical problems of staff in the public-private sector. To meet the deadline, the department instructed cadre examination offices to take advantage of recent campaigns to rectify the CCP and to eliminate hidden counterrevolutionaries.[20] Thus, the line between different strategies of purification became blurred, notwithstanding the normative distinction that the Party had made between good people who had committed mistakes and enemies of the people who were essentially hostile toward the socialist project.[21]

Bai's file perfectly illustrates how one campaign seamlessly led into another. A mimeographed form on the investigation of "corruption, theft, and other illegal activities" was filled out during the rectification movement of 1957. It stated that Bai had engaged in small-scale embezzlement and had been reported by one of his neighbors for having won ten yuan playing mahjong.[22] For this offense, he had received "education" from the Party committee of his work unit. A few months later, the CCP Organization Department and Cadre Examination Office of the Wuchang District approved an investigation into Bai's past, prompted by his own account of how he had been taken hostage while serving in the New Fourth Army. The investigatory outline contained a series of questions to be answered: Why had Bai's life been spared when the township secretary had been beaten to death? Had there been a deal between him and the enemy that he was covering up? Had he sold out the revolution and his comrades? Had he caused harm to the revolution?[23]

The only way to gain clarity on these questions was to collect testimonies from the people involved in the events. Because most of these witnesses were still located in or around Bai's native county, the outline was sent to the Party committee of Hong'an County. Here, the cadre examination office joined forces with the local Five Person Group, set up to carry out the Elimination of Hidden Counterrevolutionaries campaign, to proceed with the investigation.

In essence, the investigation was an assessment of Bai's historical loyalty to the communist movement. Leaving his unit without permission was an error in and of itself, but the crucial question was related to his time in captivity and the circumstances of his prompt release. A great many cadres working for the revolutionary forces had had similar experiences during the war. The 1955 August First Report, authored by the Central Organization Department, acknowledged that questions related to "turning oneself over" (*zishou*: admitting to the enemy one's affiliation with the revolutionary organization) and instances of "turning renegade" (*panbian*: surrendering information about or otherwise harming the revolutionary organization) were both extremely complex and absolutely crucial to cadre examinations. Each case was to be treated separately and investigators were instructed to take a range of exonerating and incriminating circumstances into account.[24] Integrity, then, was not directly inferred from past transgression; rather, it was the result of an overall assessment of the suitability of the cadre based on past and current behavior. Although several policy documents were circulated to define and differentiate between "turning oneself over" and "turning renegade," local Party committees were given considerable discretion in determining how to handle historical problems.[25]

The method used by the Five Person Group to reconstruct the circumstances of Bai's abduction was straightforward. It relied on the autobiography to track down the witnesses that Bai had claimed could corroborate his life story. Several of the key witnesses had died or gone missing in the war, but the Five Person Group finally managed to locate and question fourteen witnesses from Bai's past, including relatives, New Fourth Army veterans, and former members of the GMD force that had abducted him. Although the testimonies generally corroborated Bai's own version, some indicated that he had given up names to save his own life.[26] Before the questioning of witnesses had ended, Bai was asked to revise his autobiography. He now admitted to having divulged the identities of two of his immediate superiors while in captivity.[27] When the cadre in charge of Bai's case wrote up the results of the investigation, he simply summarized the relevant sections of the revised autobiography. The distinction between the suspect's own account and the conclusion of the investigation must have appeared irrelevant. The function of the revised autobiography was precisely to include historical errors "uncovered" by the investigation—discrepancy between individual recollection and the findings of the investigation was not permitted. Referring to Bai's latest text, the Party committee concluded that the account was "basically" consistent with the investigation. Despite having disclosed the names of his superiors to the enemy, Bai had not "caused damage to the revolutionary enterprise."[28] Both Bai and the Party branch committee of the coal shop signed off on the conclusion. Bai was spared punishment for what were deemed to be minor errors. Ultimately, his qualifications as a literate, experienced shopkeeper outweighed minor concerns about integrity.

The investigation of Bai relied heavily on his own confession and oral testimonies recorded by the investigators. It is not unusual for new state organizations to rely on such admissions or relax standards of proof to make up for the dearth of material evidence in the wake of violent conflict, especially when the need to restore the integrity of the administration is seen as urgent.[29] The material limits of investigation can partially explain the deeply entrenched policy of "leniency to those who confess, severity to those who resist" (*tanbai congkuan, kangju congyan*), which has become a symbol of coercive interrogations and wrongful sentences under the socialist regime. It should be noted, however, that even though the slogan originates with Mao Zedong himself, it expresses a systematic preference for and reliance on confessions that predates the CCP.[30] Without disputing that the principle has inspired abuse in the PRC, it appears to have also promoted a minimum of transparency within the local administration at a time when it lacked the resources and capacity to pursue investigation. In the context of the cadre examinations, the writing of autobiographies and confessions can be seen as a loyalty test where admission of past wrongdoing was a way to distance oneself from the old order and express adherence to the socialist project. Rather than a tool for disqualifying the politically unreliable, the autobiography created the trust necessary to keep those with bad class background or a spotty past in the administration, provided that their confessions were perceived as adequate. Compared to the simultaneous campaign to Eliminate Hidden Counterrevolutionaries, with which they were intertwined, the cadre examinations provided a reconciliatory alternative that granted second chances to those cadres who were confirmed to have given a truthful account of their past.[31]

Interlude: Great Leap

Without any written justification, Bai's social status alternated throughout the investigation of the late 1950s. With just a few scribbled characters, his class status could be changed. In the earliest records, dated June 1956, he referred to himself as a "petty merchant" but in March 1958 he entered his class status as "artisan." However, as the investigation progressed, the term "capitalist" began to appear. The first time Bai was referred to in this way is in an investigatory outline sent from Wuchang to Hong'an in June 1958. In a draft of the final decision a month later, a Party official wrote "capitalist" followed by a question mark in the field reserved for individual class status, but this was subsequently crossed out, presumably by a superior. The final decision referred to him as a "petty merchant."

The class status system turned socio-economic identity in pre-revolutionary society into a formal status that determined one's relation to the socialist state.[32] Despite the role of this taxonomy in informing both redistributive policies and the evaluation of individual trustworthiness, the criteria for inclusion in a particular category in urban areas were remarkably vague. The primary reference for the determination of class status throughout the existence of this system was the Government Administration Council's "Decision on the Division of Rural Class Statuses," adopted in August 1950. Drafted under the direction of Liu Shaoqi, the decision expanded upon directives on land reform in the Jiangxi Soviet to provide local Party officials with an authoritative guide to assign class status in the countryside.³³ As its fundamental purpose was to enable land redistribution, it is easy to understand why the "capitalist" status was not a priority. The new decision only provided the most general definitions of rural entrepreneurs, such as "artisanal capitalists," "merchant capitalists," and "peddlers." The "artisanal capitalists," for example, differed from the "artisans" in that they employed workers and had an income that derived "completely or mainly" from profits. Some additional definitions circulated over the years, but they dealt with specific issues rather than attempting to systematize the assignment of class status.³⁴ There is no evidence of a concerted effort by the central leadership to provide criteria for the assignment of class status in the cities. The absence of such documentation suggests that the assignment of class status was based on self-reporting, at the discretion of local CCP organs.

Despite lacking a clear-cut policy definition, the "capitalist" was a stock character in propaganda depictions of the pre-revolutionary order, where it usually appeared as a "parasite" or even "vampire" living off the blood of workers. Less frequently, it appeared as a patriotic ally of the revolutionary forces. This was because the national bourgeoisie had, in Mao Zedong's words, a "dual character": it was essentially an exploitative class opposed to socialism but also an important political ally in the struggle against feudalism and imperialism.³⁵ Instead of drafting laws and regulations to direct the designation of capitalists, the CCP leadership opted for conserving a certain constructive ambiguity around the capitalist figure.³⁶ Through propaganda and education, both local cadres and the masses would learn to identify capitalists in their own surroundings. In this way, identification became a social learning process through which cadres and workers developed a sense for what a capitalist looked like by incorporating the new ways of seeing present in the press, in the cinema, and on posters. As companies were supposed to have capitalists, these were found, regardless of tricky technicalities such as the degree of control over the means of production. As with categories such as gender and race, this process fostered an environment in which class became socially recognizable, rather than legally or scientifically determined. Sheila Fitzpatrick, introducing her study of class identity in the Soviet Union, writes that class was an "ambiguous" category that was "less easily identifiable to the eye" than race and gender.³⁷ However, one should be careful not to overlook the well-documented problems of modernist projects aiming to make race, gender, and ethnicity recognizable. The establishment of legitimate principles of classification and stratification has been a major objective of the modern state, but despite countless arbitrary divisions and long learning processes, categories such as these routinely fail to become readily "identifiable to the eye."³⁸ Moreover, class status in the PRC is comparable to other identities assigned by the state in that, although it was originally legitimated by science and the fantasy of visibility, it obtained, as an administrative status, an institutional force independent of the veracity of underlying scientific claims.

The ambiguities of assignment opened up for contesting official class status by way of insisting on alternative interpretations of the pre-revolutionary past. This is what Bai did in 1958 when he argued that—with eleven years of making iron, two years working in the fields, four years in the army, and five years producing coal—he could hardly be considered a capitalist.[39] However, the CCP had the means to enforce its interpretation, which it did in 1960 by confirming, without further ado, that Bai was indeed a capitalist. And yet, Bai did not see himself as a capitalist but as an artisan. The Party took this as a sign that he was resisting his class identity and was in urgent need of reform. According to the official line, the transformation of the relations of production under socialism had eliminated the material conditions on which the "exploitative mentality" of the bourgeoisie was based. Still, the bourgeois mentality did not vanish automatically; instead former capitalists had to reform themselves to become part of the people.[40] Many of those counted among the bourgeoisie possessed skills that were valued by the CCP in its efforts to modernize the economy. Several among them were able to hold important positions in the administration, at least up until the assault on the bureaucracy during the first year of the Cultural Revolution. The condition for inclusion was that they stayed on the path of personal reform.

To teach him to accept his class status, Bai was enrolled for a semester at a political school, organized by the Chinese People's Political Consultative Conference, where cadres with a bourgeois background were taught how to approach their work from a Marxist-Leninist standpoint. At the time of the Great Leap Forward, those with a class status other than worker or peasant were encouraged to approach personal reform according to the model of advancement used in production: constant competition to fulfill far-reaching targets. Capitalists from the city of Tianjin put up big-character posters promising to "open their hearts to the Party," while "rightists" made improbable pledges to "transform into leftists within one year and join the Party within two."[41]

An evaluation of Bai's progress over a semester at the school stated that he had initially clung to his participation in the revolution and self-perceived status as an artisan to reject his capitalist class status and resist education by the proletariat. Moreover, his uncommunicative, apprehensive, and passive attitude had been an obstacle to personal transformation.[42] To restore his integrity in the eyes of his superiors, Bai was forced to formally abandon his own interpretation of the past. He admitted his errors and made promises to reform. He pledged to listen to the Party, learn from the proletariat, and engage in political study in the future.[43] Furthermore, he made a detailed plan for how he could "actively participate" in the Great Leap Forward by taking part in the rustication movement, self-criticism, and working thirteen hours per day, seven days a week. To show his willingness to serve socialism, Bai set ambitious production targets and accepted the "supervision of the Party and the masses." Through such an effort, he planned to meet his goal of transforming himself into a "laborer living from [his] own labor in name as well as in reality" within two years.[44] Such lofty goals proved impossible to realize, not least because there was no policy in place to actually revise class status. Such a mechanism was introduced in the 1960s, albeit for entirely different reasons.

Second Review: Cleanup

If cadre examinations in the mid-1950s were characterized by the balanced approach to personnel reform described above, the human disaster of the Great Leap Forward came to upset that balance. Mao Zedong attributed the failure to make the leap into socialist modernity and the resulting famine to an erosion of conduct and ethics within the bureaucracy.[45] The result was the launch of a rectification campaign known as the Socialist Education movement or the Four Cleanups because it focused on four aspects of the bureaucracy. A central part of the campaign was the revival of the methods of in situ investigation, referred to as "squatting" (*dundian*), used by Mao and others during the war. Just like in Mao's own investigations, class became the primary lens through which problems were understood. Following the Chairman's 1962 exhortation to never forget class struggle, the new campaign was accompanied by the message that the failure of the Great Leap Forward was not simply the result of cadres slacking off, but rather a consequence of organized sabotage by class enemies. On May 8, 1963, for example, Mao personally selected a report from a Party meeting in Wulijie (a district at the rural outskirts of Wuhan) as reflecting exemplary political work in the countryside. One of the report's main claims was that the number of diseased cattle during the famine had been significantly higher among farmers with a reactionary class status.[46] Such dubious findings were all the more damning because Party discourse promoted a conspiracy theory according to which domestic class enemies were collaborating with hostile foreign forces to carry out capitalist restoration.[47] The campaign to answer this threat consisted of two parts: mobilizing the masses to learn about and promote class struggle and reintroducing the kind of investigatory work that was said to have led the CCP to revolutionary victory. Work teams were dispatched from the cities to the countryside in re-enactment of wartime investigations. Toward the end of the movement, the bureaus administering industrial production also formed work teams to oversee work in urban factories, battle corruption, and identify class enemies. The work teams had the authority to investigate, discipline, and punish locals. They had considerable discretion and in some cases resorted to physical violence and torture during investigations.[48]

To accentuate the threat posed by domestic class enemies was to break with the predominant message of the mid-1950s that the rehabilitation of the exploitative classes was on the right path and, consequently, that the class system itself was becoming increasingly irrelevant to Chinese society.[49] By contrast, class status became central to the evaluation of cadre integrity in the 1960s. Cadres were divided into a "good" or "relatively good" majority and a small minority of "degenerate" and "alien class elements," who had managed to reach positions of influence. Issues such as minor graft or lack of enthusiasm in the workplace were consequently interpreted as isolated errors if the cadre had a "good" class status, but could be construed as proof of a failure to reform reactionary thinking if the status was "bad."

The obsession with class was part of a more general concern with public memory that permeated Chinese politics and culture in the 1960s. The history of class struggle and the injustice of "old society" were narrated in cinema, literature, and in newly established museums.[50] The Four Cleanups' most important contribution to this restructuring of the past was the reexamination of class labels and the compilation of class archives to systematize knowledge on individual class backgrounds.[51] Just like the Four Cleanups in general, class reexamination was initially and largely a rural affair. However, in the summer of 1963, the CCP Hubei Provincial Committee convened to discuss a pilot project that would assign class statuses in the cities.[52] When Wuhan set up work teams to join the Four Cleanups in the latter half of 1964, the review of class statuses thus became one of their tasks.[53] In the spring of 1965, the work team in charge of Bai's coal shop compiled a class archive on him. The compilation of this thin file was seemingly conducted with minimal effort. It contains a simple autobiography, a four-point list of issues to investigate in order to answer the question of Bai's class status, and finally a form reviewing the current situation of his capitalist status. There was no serious investigation of his socio-economic background, nor was there a critical evaluation of his assigned class status. The conclusion makes no reference to Bai's documented efforts to reform himself, but simply states that because he had lived off of the surplus value produced by other people's labor and still received a small dividend from the state acquisition of his business, his capitalist class status should be upheld. The conclusion cites a draft by the provincial Party committee on the standards of urban class division, presumably a result of the 1963 meeting, together with the still authoritative 1950 decision on rural class status. Despite the Hubei pilot project, the criteria for determining capitalist class status seem to have remained vague. Even more problematic for people like Bai was the priority given to identifying hidden class enemies, which would have created incentives to change "good" class statuses into "bad" rather than the other way around.

The Party branch committee of the coal shop received a first indication that Bai may have been unsuitable to continue in the capacity of assistant manager in June 1964, when it received a letter from one of its workers. The letter denounced "Bai Tieshang (capitalist)" as having cynically taken advantage of the iron shortage during the Great Leap Forward to make a personal profit. Using a permit obtained by his wife, he had secretly produced galvanized iron in his home and when confronted by the workers he had denied the accusations and ignored their warnings that he was "walking the backward path of capitalism."[54]

In line with the goals of the Four Cleanups, the following "investigation" carried out by the coal shop's own Socialist Education work team was didactic rather than investigatory. In contrast to the 1950s, there was no outline with pre-defined questions that the investigators sought to answer. There were also fewer recorded testimonies than in both earlier and later investigations. A testimony from Jiang Qifa, a former neighbor and short-time business partner of Bai, later became important because of Jiang's connections to the GMD, but in 1965 the investigators ignored such problems of political history. Despite the superficiality of the investigation, the two folders with Four Cleanups materials are still the thickest in Bai's file. They consist mainly of detailed life stories and self-criticisms written by Bai himself.

Over a total of forty-nine pages, written on four separate occasions between April and June, Bai confessed to a wide range of transgressions. The confessions constitute an almost perfect negative to the ambitious goals of personal reform that Bai had set out for himself during the Great Leap Forward. According to his confession, he had indeed spent evenings and Sundays engaged in production, but he had done so for personal gain. Not only had he disrespected the leadership of the CCP, but he had also tried to "seize power" over production. Moreover, he confessed to having been guilty of "reactionary words and deeds" at six separate occasions and admitted in particular that his statements demonstrated his reactionary understanding of the great famine. He had, for instance, tried to blame the death of his ill mother during the food shortage in 1961 on the government. Even worse, he had claimed that the "three years of natural calamity" were not the result of natural causes, but the government having sold pork to the Soviet Union.[55]

In August, one of the Party committees overseeing the Socialist Education movement within the Wuchang District Coal Construction Company approved of the coal shop work team's suggestion to remove Bai from his post as assistant manager as a result of the investigation. Three reasons were given for this decision: (1) Bai had been guilty of "capitalist restoration activities" and "walking the backward path of capitalism" due to the illegal profits he had obtained by setting up a private business in his wife's name; (2) he had been guilty of small-time embezzlement involving food coupons; (3) he had taken advantage of his position within the work unit to take home small amounts of iron without permission. In addition to these errors, his overall conduct had been bad, his work lagged behind, and he continued to refuse his capitalist status![56] Bai stayed on in the coal shop as a repairman after his demotion.

The focus of the Four Cleanups investigation was on current behavior, rather than wrongdoings committed in the pre-revolutionary past. However, corruption and reactionary conduct were considered to be residual phenomena from the earlier class society. In this respect, the Four Cleanups was an attempt at radical personnel reform to disassociate the bureaucracy from the taint of "old society." As such, it sought to exclude class enemies and other "suspicious elements" from power while promoting ideals of proletarian leadership. This appeared all the more urgent in relation to the perceived danger of revisionism and the CCP's promotion of conspiracy theories of capitalist restoration. Ultimately, Mao Zedong would conclude that the screening carried out during the Socialist Education movement was insufficient to deal with "people in positions of authority within the Party who take the capitalist road."[57] Mao was calling for an even more radical upheaval to deal with opponents of socialism within the bureaucracy.

Third Review: Cleansing the Ranks

On August 19, 1966, the director of the CCP Central Organization Department An Ziwen and his eight deputies were officially suspended from their positions.[58] The top officials in charge of cadre examination in the 1950s now had their own pasts scrutinized, not by Party institutions but by rebels in the universities.[59] In the summer of 1966, Red Guards joined the agents of the newly established Central Case Examination Group in searching the archives for evidence to support charges against those already branded as enemies.[60] Cold case reviews had become a potent weapon in factional conflicts and for attacks on the bureaucracy. Before and after a brief period in 1966–1967, the power to conduct investigatory work had been exclusively held by the Party-state. Now, amateur detectives were allowed to investigate, detain, and pass judgment with revolutionary zeal as their only legitimation. The state's monopoly on enforcing norms and punishing transgression was suspended.

In October 1968, at the Twelfth Plenum of the Eighth CCP Central Committee, the Central Case Examination Group presented the results of its investigation into the disgraced Liu Shaoqi.[61] It branded him "a renegade, hidden traitor, and a scab." One of the primary charges against him was that he had "turned renegade" (*panbian*) and "surrendered to the enemy" (*touxiang diren*) during the war. As shown above, similar charges had been brought against Bai Tieshang, but because he no longer held any position of influence, Bai was unaffected by the unfolding storm of Party inquisition and amateur investigation. Because he was a "capitalist," Red Guards raided his home in September 1966. They seized jewelry, silk clothing, government bonds, and scrap metal.[62] In connection with the raid, Bai turned informer as he was made to testify against his former cohabitant and business partner, the "reactionary" Jiang Qifa, who had, Bai wrote, sold weapons to the GMD.[63] Bai's own case was not reopened until two years later, not by Red Guards but under the authority of the military control committees carrying out a terror campaign known as the Cleansing of the Class Ranks.

In the wake of the factional fighting that had wreaked havoc in Wuhan in the summer of 1967, the new leadership of the Wuhan Military Region pledged to protect the leadership of the revolutionary committees.[64] This was the local setting for the Cleansing of the Class Ranks, a nationwide campaign to suppress any lingering opposition to the newly established power structures. It did not exclusively target members of competing factions, but also the PRC's usual suspects: people with "bad" class status, former GMD members, and the social outcasts collectively referred to as "bad elements." It was a campaign carried out by decree under the military's close watch; radio broadcasts and newspapers constantly reminded everyone to "take note of policy" (*zhuyi zhengce*) as it progressed.[65] At this point, the Party and military bureaucracy had restored hierarchical control over investigations. Previous "outsourcing" had ceased with the disbandment of the Red Guards and the assimilation or suppression of worker rebels. New policies restricted access to archival material and banned the use of investigations in factional conflict.[66]

Once again, Bai got into trouble with the authorities following a game of mahjong. One evening in late September 1968, the police caught him gambling with some factory workers. Bai knew the drill by now. He confessed that his continued gambling was a sign of his "very deep bourgeois-exploitative mentality" and constituted a "serious violation of social order." He helpfully suggested that the police consult his personnel file to learn more about his dodgy past, to which he added: "if there are any concealed historical circumstances to which I have not confessed, I ask the organization to examine them and handle the situation according to the Party's law [*dang de falü*]."[67] However, in sharp contrast to how class had dominated the process three years earlier, accusations of gambling and "bourgeois mentality" now failed to raise further interest. Instead, the investigators went back to the subject of the 1958 cadre examination: Bai's time with the New Fourth Army from 1941 to 1945.

Despite the fact that the men behind the earlier cadre examination had been utterly discredited, there was no radical break with the methods of investigating historical problems they had developed. At a lecture in Jilin in early 1968, the senior inquisitor of the CCP, Kang Sheng, singled out "the question of people having surrendered [*zishou*], the question of turning against the Party [*panbian*], and the question of people having been arrested or captured [*beibu*]" as particularly difficult to investigate.[68] In this respect, he was in complete agreement with the assessment of his disgraced predecessors. Of course, Kang Sheng stressed that providing the enemy with information was tantamount to treason, but he cautioned investigators to analyze each situation carefully with the specific circumstances in mind. To reach a correct conclusion, investigators were to draw from three sources of wisdom: Mao Zedong Thought and the dialectical method, class analysis, and CCP policy. These basic principles, Kang Sheng let his audience know, had not been upheld in the past, which was why new investigations had to be carried out.

In November 1968, a month after Bai had been apprehended, the coal shop's revolutionary committee requested that he write a new confession. This time, the topic was his time with the New Fourth Army. The content of this confession more or less resembled the autobiographies of 1958, but it did incorporate some additional details from the earlier investigations. The most significant change, and the focus of the 1968 investigation, was new information on his relation to the GMD arms supplier Jiang Qifa. Bai wrote that he had known of Jiang's relations with the GMD and even that his wife had, by mistake, burned a certificate proving Jiang's collaboration with the enemy. Bai admitted to "serious mistakes" and asked to receive "education."[69] As the newly installed revolutionary committee of the Wuchang coal shop was looking for targets for the Cleansing of the Class Ranks, this previously neglected piece of information became a reason to reinvestigate Bai's time in captivity. Once again, most of the actual investigation was delegated to Hong'an County. The questions were similar to those posed ten years earlier: Had Bai betrayed the revolutionary organization? Had he betrayed his comrades? Why had the enemy forces released him?[70] To answer these questions, the revolutionary committees in Wuchang and Hong'an collected testimonies from seventeen witnesses, including the majority of the fourteen persons heard in 1958.

What happened next is not completely clear. The authorities seem to have concluded that there was evidence of serious crimes. An undated and unsigned draft concludes that Bai had indeed "sold out" his comrades. In contrast to the 1958 investigation, historical errors were considered in connection to his reactionary and bourgeois mentality. Gambling and idleness were seen as aggravating circumstances, indicating unwillingness to reform. The conclusion was harsh: "[Bai Tieshang has] seriously violated social order and disturbed public security. Based on his conduct before and after liberation, he must receive a criminal sentence and be delivered to the masses for supervision and reform."[71] This draft is included in his file, but does not seem to have been followed by any formal action. Instead, almost five years passed before the investigation could be formally concluded. The final decision was approved in June 1973 and stamped with the official seal of the coal shop revolutionary committee. In a matter-of-fact style, the decision resumes the events of 1941–1956 without making any mention of Bai's gambling habit or unwillingness to reform. The conclusion reads:

> During the Cleansing of the Class Ranks, this person already confessed to the problems described above, [the confession] basically matches an investigation of the facts. Wanting to save his own neck, Bai sold out the organization and his comrades. The nature [of this issue] is rather serious, but his admission of guilt is quite good. No other crimes have been discovered thus far. In line with the spirit of the Party's policy of 'leniency to those who confess and severity to those who resist,' the Party branch [has concluded] after deliberation that the nature of this issue is one of political history [and that] Bai Tieshang will be exempted from punishment.[72]

Problems of political history continued to be a cornerstone of administrative investigation until 1978. The last major investigation of pre-revolutionary crimes was that of the alleged Gang of Four. Circulated as inner-Party propaganda in March 1977, the second of three collections of evidence against the Gang tells of treachery, collaboration with the enemy, and sordid class backgrounds.[73] Yet, the 1980 indictment against the ten members of the "Lin [Biao], Jiang [Qing] Counterrevolutionary Cliques," which was based largely on the three collections of evidence, was inseparably linked to the Cultural Revolution.[74] Both the decision to conduct a trial and the charges brought against the accused reflected the CCP's new view on the past and its own historical role. In the new era, the relevance of pre-revolutionary positions and conduct was diminishing, as a more immediate past became associated with historical injustice. The violence and abuse that had taken place during the tumultuous decade of the Cultural Revolution now became more relevant for the assessment of integrity than wartime activities and class status. When Party and state organs reviewed cases involving political history and class status in the 1980s, it was not to punish or exclude but more frequently to determine whether the person in question had been wrongfully accused, a victim of leftist excesses.

Fourth Review: Insufficiently Capitalist

In the autumn of 1973, shortly after the decision to treat Bai leniently, a majority of the possessions that had been confiscated from his home in 1966 were returned to him.⁷⁵ Both his lenient treatment and the return of property can be understood in the context of the CCP's gradual return to a less contentious relationship with members of the national bourgeoisie. Following the upheavals of 1966–1968, the Party introduced a series of measures that aimed to reintegrate capitalist elements and other targets of the united front policy. The orthodox view that united front work was suspended throughout the ten-year Cultural Revolution requires serious qualification. Although there was a lack of nationwide coordination, both institutions and operations resumed to varying degrees in the early 1970s.⁷⁶ It began with a gradual recovery of the Central United Front Work Department, which was followed in 1972 by the establishment of local groups for united front work under the new revolutionary committees.⁷⁷ The decision to exempt Bai from punishment and return his property was taken in the months following the restoration of the CCP Wuhan Municipal United Front Work Department in the winter of 1972–73.⁷⁸

In 1977, Bai's class status once again came up for review. In contrast to the assessment of the Socialist Education movement, the explicit motive this time was to identify people who had been assigned a capitalist class status, but who were in fact "insufficiently capitalist" (*bu gou zibenjia*). In these cases, the work units were to provide them with a more appropriate status, one that reflected that they were "living from their own labor." The review of capitalist class status, which was expanded in the early 1980s, has received little scholarly attention. This omission makes for a more straightforward story, according to which 1978 represents a paradigmatic shift in official class theory. Yet, by tracing these reviews back to their origins, it is possible to detect an early relaxation of class struggle coinciding with the consolidation of the Cultural Revolution in the early 1970s.

The resumption of united front work in the early 1970s gave a push to the policy to return property confiscated in the summer of 1966 to its original owners.⁷⁹ The implementation of this policy was uneven, however, and local administrators put caps on the extent of compensation. During Deng Xiaoping's brief return to power in 1974–75, further measures were taken to return property, raise salaries, and improve social policy for the "national bourgeoisie."⁸⁰ These policies continued after Mao's death under the leadership of Hua Guofeng. Chairman Hua did not wait long before declaring that the Cultural Revolution had been "successfully completed" and that a time of "peace and unity" was upon China. He would not go so far as to abandon class struggle completely, but at the Eleventh National Congress, he announced that the struggle had now entered a more peaceful phase. He opened up for letting "the majority of the petty bourgeoisie, the majority of the bourgeois intellectuals, and people among the nationalist bourgeoisie willing to accept socialist transformation" join the struggle at the side of the proletariat.⁸¹

In October 1977, two months after Hua's declaration, the Wuchang District Party Committee gave its approval to a decision that Bai no longer be considered a capitalist. The review of Bai's class status came at a relatively early stage. It was not until November 1979 that the CCP Center approved a report on "differentiation work" (*qubie gongzuo*) signed by the CCP Central United Front Work Department, together with six other Party organs and government ministries.[82] The report suggested that the pilot projects set up the previous year to separate "former industrialists and merchants" from members of the toiling masses be extended to the whole country. It also provided some general criteria and guidelines. Differentiation work radically decimated the capitalist population and, as a consequence, redefined what it meant to be part of this category. By 1981, only a fifth of a population of 860,000 was still classified as capitalists.[83] In Bai's province, Hubei, only 7,135 people—twenty percent of the original population—were still considered to be capitalists after differentiation work had been completed.[84]

Already in the spring of 1969, Mao Zedong had approved a circular carrying a report from the Beijiao Lumber Mill, one of the famous "six factories and two schools" (*liu chang er xiao*), which sketched out how to reclassify those who were "insufficiently capitalist," i.e. had possessed little or no capital in the "old society" and relied mainly on their own labor.[85] However, it was only in late 1979 that the CCP took measures to carry out a systematic and general review of capitalist class status.[86] Bai's review predated this turn and thus represents a belated continuation of Maoist policies, spurred by the reconciliatory line pursued by Hua Guofeng. The conclusion of his review still cites the same passage from the 1950 decision on rural class status, supplemented by a 1975 document from the municipal section of the United Front Work Department. The review materials included: a new autobiography, testimonies from two former business partners, four pages detailing his share in the business and the value of dividends, a record from a meeting where workers had been brought in to discuss his case, and a conclusion approved by the Wuchang District Party Committee. The decision to relieve Bai from his capitalist label was taken only a day after the meeting of worker representatives. The language was that of a parole hearing, highlighting efforts of individual change while carrying warnings to remain vigilant. One worker remarked:

> This person has participated in the main production [i.e. manual labor], his conduct has been relatively good and he has been serious and responsible in his work. [I] recommend that he is withdrawn from the ranks of capitalists and assigned the class status of a petty merchant. This "judgment" embodies the generosity of Chairman Mao's revolutionary line and the Party's policy. Bai Tieshang himself must recognize this point and he must recognize his own exploitative activities and exploitive mentality to improve the strengthening of his self-awareness in ideological transformation.[87]

Bai thanked the masses for their "assistance" and the Party for its "affectionate attention" throughout the personal transformation that had finally enabled him to leave his capitalist identity behind. The final decision stated that Bai had "always been considered a capitalist," but that his conduct had been "relatively good" and that he had shown willingness to reform.[88] The sudden decision to change Bai's status illustrates the irony of the capitalist figure and the dilemma of reform. While the capitalist status was said to designate a population that needed to reform their reactionary thinking, no formal procedures were put into place to re-assign those who had made sufficient progress; a temporary status thus became an inescapable stigma. When reclassification finally did take place, it was in response to new policies from above and not the conduct of the individual.

The 1977 review was the last to evaluate Bai's position and activities in the pre-revolutionary past. A decision to raise his pension three years later made no reference to his capitalist label or revolutionary activities; it was based on state regulations applying to workers. Around the same time, the political stigma of the capitalist status disappeared from Party discourse. The term "former industrialist and merchant" was substituted for the negatively connoted "capitalist." The new term referred to a much smaller population of aging specialists. As the Democratic National Construction Association and the Federation of Industry and Commerce resumed activities, aging members of the national bourgeoisie regained institutional representation within the socialist state. The most influential members spent their last years as public officials, trade consultants, and managers of state enterprises.

Post-Revolutionary Integrity

The investigations of Bai Tieshang were primarily administrative, despite intermittent involvement by public security officers. The suggestion in 1968 that he should receive criminal punishment never materialized and the file used for this study is a personnel file rather than a criminal case file. Such a dossier was a versatile resource that work units and other authorities could make use of in a variety of situations. The investigative materials therein are accompanied, among other things, by salary documents and a decision on retirement. Read for the purpose of vetting, the personnel file became a repository of potentially incriminating data on Bai's conduct and background. To reconstruct Bai's past, the investigators relied heavily, if not uncritically, on his own testimony and earlier investigations. When initiating an investigation, they used the personnel file to retrieve data about his past, which provided the basis for a counterfactual interrogation about the narrative within the file.[89] They would proceed by reframing the past according to their own understanding of what had happened and in line with a shifting verdict on history. Influenced in this way, they formed an investigative hypothesis that in turn constrained the interpretation of testimonies and evidence. What is crucial here is that the official representation of the past changed radically between different political moments. Even if we allow for a conceptual resilience on the part of the investigators, they expertly adapted charges to new circumstances whether they believed in them or not. They proved able and willing to reach conclusions that were in line with the political priorities of the time. In each investigation, Bai's spotted past seemed to match the dangers outlined in the latest Party directive. In 1958, the cadre examination office discovered proof of disloyal conduct during the war. In 1960, Bai was obliged to enroll in a political school, not as the result of an investigation, but because of resistance toward an arbitrary yet authoritative decision on what his class identity in the "old society" had been. In 1965, his problematic class status was reaffirmed. What might otherwise have been considered minor offences were taken as signs of bourgeois and reactionary conduct. In 1968, the revolutionary committees, backed by the military, were once again more interested in his relation to the GMD than his class status. What they found was not substantially different from what had been discovered ten years earlier. However, at a time when the cadre examinations of the 1950s were criticized for having let hidden enemies slip through the net, Bai was able to escape a criminal sentence only because the final decision was delayed long enough for yet another political shift to take place. Finally, in 1977, the political leadership in Beijing was talking about unity and local officials were quick to adapt to the spirit of the time. Bai's colleagues and superiors agreed that he had broken sufficiently with his bourgeois ways to be included in the community of workers.

The aim of the investigation campaigns was to dissociate the administration from the pre-revolutionary past, but through the constant unveiling of new enemies and further evidence of reactionary conduct, they paradoxically worked to sustain the relevance of the past for the socialist present. This changed abruptly around the time of Bai's retirement, in the final years of the 1970s, when a new political agenda made the period in time before the founding of the PRC largely irrelevant for the assessment of integrity. It was not that the weight of the past had gradually diminished, as illustrated by the fact that Bai's historical errors were interpreted as far more severe in 1968 than in 1958, but rather the result of a new understanding of the revolutionary movement and socialist state building. The tragedy of the Cultural Revolution had displaced the nightmare vision of the "old society" as the main referent of historical injustice. Background checks were no longer conducted to identify "alien class elements" or "reactionaries" among the cadre ranks after 1978. At a time when half of the Party members had been recruited after 1966, the goal was instead to weed out those who had profited from the crimes and excesses of the Cultural Revolution.[90] Although the veterans at the highest echelon of the CCP continued to vaunt their revolutionary experience to justify their own position, the majority of the Party bureaucracy was too young to have any meaningful connection to the war. The CCP cleared up any confusion among young cadres by standardizing recent history in a way that brought forth the achievements of the revolution and branded the ten-year Cultural Revolution as an aberration in the history of Chinese socialism. As the final review of Bai's class status makes clear, the epoch of the "old society" was by now far removed from lived experience. Likewise, in the countryside, some women were found to use the term to refer to the period up to the Great Leap Forward, rather than to China before 1949, and others took it as meaning all history up to the agricultural reforms of the early 1980s.[91] By historicizing the revolution, the CCP amplified the diminishing significance of pre-revolutionary society in public memory. Without calling into question the motives or means of the revolution, the new leadership severed it from the present by confining it to a foundational but completed juncture in the intertwined genealogies of Party, state, and nation.[92] In sharp contrast to the previous thirty years, the threat from domestic class enemies was downplayed, which in turn meant that integrity was no longer considered in pre-revolutionary categories. While the Cultural Revolution has continued to serve as a cautionary tale for the Party elite until this day, the "old society" no longer has an immediate bearing on the present.[93] As the Party has left the revolution behind, integrity is no longer a question of alignment with the revolutionary enterprise, but one of loyalty to the Chinese nation, the socialist state, and its ruling elite.

Notes

1 Zhang Jishun's study of Shanghai following the CCP takeover reveals the extent to which the Party relied on politically and socially suspect individuals to govern and reform the city, *Yuanqu de dushi: 1950 niandai de Shanghai* [A City Displaced: Shanghai in the 1950s] (Beijing: Shehui kexue wenxian chubanshe, 2015), 21–82. Jeremy Brown makes a similar point regarding the takeover of Tianjin, documenting how technically skilled urbanites were generally privileged over ideologically trustworthy veterans from the countryside, *City Versus Countryside in Mao's China: Negotiating the Divide* (New York: Cambridge University Press, 2012), 15.

2 Toward the end of the Civil War, the CCP compiled and circulated a list accusing the leaders of the GMD of war crimes and generally portrayed them as more deserving of war trials than Japanese troops. On the latter point, see Kerstin von Lingen and Robert Cribb, "Justice in Time of Turmoil: War Crimes Trials in Asia in the Context of Decolonization and Cold War," in Kerstin von Lingen, ed., *War Crimes Trials in the Wake of Decolonization and Cold War in Asia, 1945–1956* (London: Palgrave Macmillan, 2016), 20. The communists were not content to indict the political leadership, but

claimed that the entire capitalist (and feudal) order was illegitimate, thus Mao Zedong spoke of "lawless" landlords in his "Report on an Investigation of the Peasant in Hunan" (March 1927), in *Selected Works of Mao Tse-Tung*, vol. 1 (Beijing: Foreign Languages Press, 1965), 25.
3   I am grateful to Daniel Leese for making this item from his personal collection available to me.
4   The classic study on the subject is Frederick Teiwes, *Politics & Purges in China: Rectification and the Decline of Party Norms, 1950–1965* (New York: M.E. Sharpe, 1979).
5   "Zhou Enlai dui Qu Qiubai de pipan" [Zhou Enlai's Criticism of Qu Qiubai], August 30, 1966, in Song Yongyi, ed., *The Chinese Cultural Revolution Database* (Hong Kong: Universities Service Centre for China Studies, 2006).
6   Yang Kuisong explores the consequences of the *guomin–renmin* distinction in *"Bianyuan ren" jishi: Ji ge "wenti" xiao renwu de beiju gushi* [People on the Margins: The Tragic Stories of Several "Problematic" Individuals] (Guangzhou: Guangdong renmin chubanshe, 2016), 1–35.
7   Aminda Smith, *Thought Reform and China's Dangerous Classes: Reeducation, Resistance, and the People* (Lanham: Rowman & Littlefield, 2012), 55.
8   David Shearer describes similar challenges facing the new administration after the Russian Revolution, see *Policing Stalin's Socialism: Repression and Social Order in the Soviet Union, 1924–1953* (New Haven: Yale University Press, 2009), 38.
9   With the exception of public figures, all personal names appearing in this chapter have been replaced with pseudonyms.
10 "Zizhuan" [Autobiography], June 19, 1956.
11 "Ganbu lülishu" [Cadre Résumé], May 12, 1960.
12 These provisions closely resemble the two outlines for autobiographical writing (from 1956 and 1958) featured in Michael Schoenhals, "Social History of China: 1949–1979," http://projekt.ht.lu.se/rereso/sources/life-stories/, accessed January 18, 2018.
13 Andrew Walder makes the same observation with regard to Party membership in *China under Mao: A Revolution Derailed* (Cambridge, MA: Harvard University Press, 2015), 112–13.
14 Gail Hershatter, *The Gender of Memory: Rural Women and China's Collective Past* (Berkeley: University of California Press, 2011), 38.
15 Jin Zhenbao, "Jianguo chuqi Zhongguo gongchandang zhaokai de liang ci quanguo zuzhi gongzuo huiyi" [Two Organization Work Conferences Convened by the CCP in the Early Period of the PRC], *Dangshi zongheng*, no. 3 (1990): 30–34.
16 Zhonggong zhongyang, "Guanyu shencha ganbu de jueding" [Decision on the Examination of Cadres], November 24, 1953, in Zhonggong zhongyang zuzhibu ganshenju, ed., *Ganshen gongzuo zhengce wenjian xuanbian* [Selected Policy Documents on Cadre Examination Work], vol. 1 (Beijing: Dangjian duwu chubanshe, 1993), 161–65. Available in the Maoist Legacy Database (MLD), item no. 1362.
17 Gao Hua, "1940 nian Yan'an shen'gan" [Yan'an Cadre Examination in 1940], *Yanhuang chunqiu*, no. 3 (2012): 21–27; see also, by the same author, *How the Red Sun Rose: The Origin and Development of the Yan'an Rectification, 1930–1945*, trans. Stacey Mosher and Guo Jian (Hong Kong: Chinese University Press, 2017).
18 Zhonggong zhongyang zuzhibu and Zhonggong zhongyang dangxiao dangshi yanjiushi, eds., *Zhongguo gongchandang zuzhi shi ziliao* [Materials on the Organizational History of the CCP], vol. 5 (Beijing: Zhonggong dangshi chubanshe, 2000), 9.

19 Ibid.
20 Zhonggong zhongyang, "Pizhuan Zhongyang zuzhibu guanyu quanguo shencha ganbu gongzuo huiyi qingkuang de baogao (jielu)" [Approved and Commented CCP Central Organization Department Report Regarding the Situation of the National Conference for Cadre Examination Work (Excerpt)], *Zhongfa (1957) hai* no. 51, December 23, 1957, in *Ganshen gongzuo zhengce wenjian xuanbian,* vol. 1, 205–9. Available in MLD, item no. 1397.
21 In fact, close collaboration between cadre examination offices and the small groups in charge of the investigation of hidden revolutionaries had been official policy since 1955, see Zhonggong zhongyang, "Guanyu shen'gan gongzuo tong sufan douzheng jiehe jinxing de zhishi" [Instructions Regarding the United Progression of Cadre Examination Work and the Struggle to Purge Counterrevolutionaries], *Zhongfa (1955)* no. 224, October 24, 1955, in *Ganshen gongzuo zhengce wenjian xuanbian,* vol. 1, 174–76. Available in MLD, item no. 1379.
22 "Tanwu daoqie weifa xingwei diaocha dengjibiao" [Form for the Investigation of Corruption, Theft, and Illegal Conduct], 1957.
23 "Suyao zhengming cailiao tigang" [Outline of Wanted Evidence Material], June 3, 1958.
24 Chen Yeping, ed., *An Ziwen zhuanlüe* [Biographical Sketch of An Ziwen] (Taiyuan: Shanxi renmin chubanshe, 1985), 126–27.
25 An important reason for this variation was undoubtedly the differences in regional experiences during the war. In the area where Bai had been active, the communist commanders had made some concessions regarding what could be divulged due to "tense" relations with the GMD. See Zhonggong zhongyang zuzhibu, "Guanyu chuli yuan Zhongyuan jiefangqu de dangyuan zishou wenti gei Hubei shengwei de xin" [Letter to the Hubei Provincial Committee on Handling the Problem of Party Members of the Former Central Plains Liberated Area Turning Themselves Over], June 1, 1957, in *Ganshen gongzuo zhengce wenjian xuanbian,* vol. 1, 196–97. Available in MLD, item no. 1387.
26 "Guanyu XXX de qingkuang" [On XXX's Situation], June 29, 1958.
27 "Jingguo xiangxi jingli" [Detailed Account of Past Experiences], June 5, 1958.
28 "Shencha jielun" [Conclusion of Cadre Examination], August 28, 1958.
29 The tension between due process and the need of thorough personnel reform in the wake of conflict is a well-documented problem. See, for example, the case of UNMIBH screening of Bosnian police, Pablo De Greiff and Alexander Mayer-Rieckh, eds., *Justice as Prevention: Vetting Public Employees in Transitional Societies* (New York: Social Science Research Council, 2007), 190. On a similar note, Andrew Rigby criticizes the lustration process in post-communist Czechoslovakia for having failed to respect the presumption of innocence, as those who could not prove that they had not worked for the secret police or as communist officials were purged, *Justice and Reconciliation: After the Violence* (Boulder: Lynne Rienner, 2001), 104.
30 The earliest record of the phrase *tanbai congkuan, kangju congyan* is from a directive drafted by Mao Zedong in March 1952, see *Selected Works of Mao Tse-Tung,* vol. 5 (Beijing: Foreign Languages Press, 1977), 66. However, the practice has roots in a system dating back to the Qing dynasty, see Jiang Zhengyang, "The System of 'Turning Oneself In' in Qing and Contemporary China: Some Reflections on Legal Modernism," in *The History and Theory of Legal Practice in China,* eds. Philip C.C. Huang and Kathryn Bernhardt (Leiden: Brill, 2014), 269–305.

31 I borrow this distinction from Roman David's classification of personnel reform, which distinguishes between inclusive, exclusive, and reconciliatory systems, see *Lustration and Transitional Justice: Personnel Systems in the Czech Republic, Hungary, and Poland* (Philadelphia: University of Pennsylvania Press, 2011).
32 For an institutional analysis of the class status system, see Jean-Francois Billeter, "The System of Class Status," in *The Scope of State Power in China*, ed. Stuart Schram (London: School of Oriental and African Studies, 1985), 127–69.
33 The "decision" consisted of three parts. The first two were slightly edited versions of documents adopted by the Jiangxi Soviet in 1933. To these were attached a complementary set of guidelines compiled in July under the direction of Liu Shaoqi. See: Zhonggong zhongyang wenxian yanjiushi, ed., *Liu Shaoqi nianpu* [Chronological Biography of Liu Shaoqi], vol. 2 (Beijing: Zhongyang wenxian chubanshe, 1996), 129.
34 In August 1952, for example, a central document provided a short definition of "capitalist agents." Nine years later, the Central United Front Work Department made an attempt to distinguish between "capitalists" and "peddlers." Both documents are quoted in "Guanyu huafen zibenjia he xiaoshang xiaofan de ji ge wenti" [Some Issues Regarding Dividing Class Statuses among Capitalists as well as Petty Merchants and Peddlers], in Zhonggong Minyang diwei zuzhibu, eds., *Jilü jiancha gongzuo wenjian xuanbian* [Selected Documents on Discipline Inspection Work] (Minyang, August 1977). Available in MLD, item no. 2000.
35 Mao Zedong, "The Chinese Revolution and the Chinese Communist Party" (December 15, 1939), in *Selected Works of Mao Tse-Tung*, vol. 2 (Beijing: Foreign Languages Press, 1965), 320.
36 Golfo Alexopoulos makes a similar observation concerning the ambiguities of identifying "the disenfranchised" in the Soviet Union, see *Stalin's Outcasts: Aliens, Citizens, and the Soviet State, 1926–1936* (Ithaca: Cornell University Press, 2003), 46–49.
37 Sheila Fitzpatrick, *Tear off the Masks! Identity and Imposture in Twentieth-Century Russia* (Princeton: Princeton University Press, 2005), 5.
38 To view the socialist class taxonomy in this perspective opens up a range of illuminating comparisons. For example, it allows for a more fine-grained comparison between Stalin's Russia and Hitler's Germany, in line with the proposal in Jörg Baberowski and Anselm Doering-Manteuffel, "The Quest for Order and the Pursuit of Terror: National Socialist Germany and the Stalinist Soviet Union as Multiethnic Empires," in *Beyond Totalitarianism: Stalinism and Nazism Compared*, eds. Michael Geyer and Sheila Fitzpatrick (Cambridge: Cambridge University Press, 2009), 180–227. The authors stress that classification ironically produced the very ambiguity that it was intended to eliminate and suggest an affinity between how class and ethnicity were understood when empires re-organized into nation-states. The ambiguities of the CCP's ethnic classification in Yunnan are the subject of Thomas Mullaney, *Coming to Terms with the Nation: Ethnic Classification in Modern China* (Berkeley: University of California Press, 2011). As Mullaney's study indicates, the techniques and patterns of this type of categorization are particular to the modern state and legacies of a colonial past, a point that is further illustrated by the analogous development of racial categories in the U.S. censuses, see Paul Schor, *Counting Americans: How the US Census Classified the Nation* (New York: Oxford University Press, 2017).
39 "Ganbu shencha jielunbiao" [Conclusion Form for Cadre Examination], July 21, 1958.
40 Following nationalization in 1956, Party and mass organizations published many books, leaflets, and articles on the subject of individual reform. A notable example is Li Peizhi and

Guo Zhen, *Zibenzhuyi gongshangyezhe de geren gaizao* [The Personal Reform of Capitalist Industrialists and Merchants] (Shanghai: Shanghai renmin chubanshe, 1956).

41   Li Weihan, *Huiyi yu yanjiu* [Recollection and Deliberation], vol. 2 (Beijing: Zhonggong dangshi ziliao chubanshe, 1986), 846–47.

42   "Wuchang duanqi zhengzhi xuexiao diyi qi xueyuan XXX xuexi qingkuang" [The Study Situation of the First Semester Student XXX at the Wuchang Short-term Political School], August 26, 1960.

43   "Duanqi zhengxiao xuexi tihui" [Short-Term Political School Learning Experience], August 25, 1960.

44   "Geren xingdong guihua" [Plan for Individual Action], March 18, 1960.

45   This was the essence of a sixty-four-page document circulated by the CCP Central Committee General Office, see "Mao Zedong on Investigation and Research," *Zhongfa* (1961) no. 261, April 4, 1961, trans. Michael Schoenhals, http://prchistory.org/links-and-resources/, accessed January 18, 2018.

46   This was one of the four "good texts" attached to Zhonggong zhongyang, "Guanyu muqian nongcun gongzuo zhong ruogan wenti de jueding (cao'an)" [On Some Issues in Current Work on the Countryside (Draft)], *Zhongfa* (1963) no. 347, May 20, 1963, in Song, ed., *The Cultural Revolution Database*.

47   At the center of this unlikely conspiracy theory was United States Secretary of State John Forster Dulles' formulation of "peaceful evolution." This rather inconsequential phrase took on a life of its own in the Chinese context. Bo Yibo recalls it being a major influence on the strategy of the top CCP leadership in the early 1960s, see *Ruogan zhongda juece yu shijian* [Reflections on Certain Major Decisions and Events], vol. 2 (Beijing: Zhonggong zhongyang dangxiao chubanshe, 2008), 799.

48   Brown, *City Versus Countryside,* 125–26.

49   In 1956, Deng Xiaoping stated that the class status system "had lost or was losing its importance," quoted in Billeter, "The System of Class Status," 131.

50   On the establishment of new museums for "class education" in the mid-1960s, see Denise Ho, *Curating Revolution: Politics on Display in Mao's China* (Cambridge: Cambridge University Press, 2018), 138–73.

51   Jeremy Brown lays out the policy background and process of rural class reexamination in "Moving Targets: Changing Class Labels in Rural Hebei and Henan, 1960–1979," in *Maoism at the Grassroots: Everyday Life in China's Era of High Socialism*, eds. Jeremy Brown and Matthew Johnson (Cambridge, MA: Harvard University Press, 2015), 58–62.

52   "Zhonggong Hubei shengwei chengshi huafen jieji chengfen shidian zuotanhui wenjian" [Documents from the CCP Hubei Provincial Committee Forum on the Pilot for Urban Division of Class Status], July 1963, Hubei Provincial Archive, SZ 1-3-383.

53   Wuhan difangzhi bianzuan weiyuanhui, ed., *Wuhan shizhi: Dashiji* [Wuhan Municipal Chronicle: Chronology of Major Events] (Wuhan: Wuhan daxue chubanshe, 1990), 240.

54   The permit obtained by Bai's wife had been issued at a time when limited free market activities were allowed as part of an emergency response to the famine. On this topic, see Feng Xiaocai, "Yijiuwuba nian zhi yijiuliusan nian Zhonggong ziyou shichang zhengce yanjiu" [Research on the Free Market Policies of the CCP from 1958 to 1963], *Zhonggong dangshi yanjiu*, no. 2 (2015), 38–53.

55   "Guanyu yixie lishi wenti" [Concerning some Historical Issues], June 20, 1965.

56   "Guanyu chexiao zibenjia XXX fu zhuren zhiwu baogao" [Report on the Dismissal of Capitalist XXX from the Position of Assistant Manager], July 29, 1965.

57 Quoted in Roderick MacFarquhar, *The Origins of the Cultural Revolution*, vol. 3 (Oxford: Oxford University Press, 1997), 428.
58 Roderick MacFarquhar and Michael Schoenhals, *Mao's Last Revolution* (Cambridge, MA: The Belknap Press of Harvard University Press, 2006), 95.
59 Nie Yuanzi boasted about being responsible for exposing An Ziwen and his "black gang," *ibid.*, 96. Zhou Enlai instead credited a student at Nankai University with having discovered the evidence, see "Zhou Enlai dui Qu Qiubai de pipan."
60 Michael Schoenhals, "Outsourcing the Inquisition: 'Mass Dictatorship' in China's Cultural Revolution," *Totalitarian Movements and Political Religions*, no. 1 (2008): 3–19; and by the same author, "The Central Case Examination Group, 1966–79," *The China Quarterly*, no. 145 (1996): 87–111.
61 Zhongyang zhuan'anzu, "Guanyu pantu, neijian, gongzei Liu Shaoqi zuixing de shencha baogao" [Examination Report Concerning the Crimes of the Renegade, Hidden Traitor, and Scab Liu Shaoqi], in *Wuchan jieji wenhua da geming wenjian huibian* [Collection of Documents from the Great Proletarian Cultural Revolution], Hubei shengwei geming weiyuanhui, ed., vol. 3 (Wuhan: Hubei shengwei geming weiyuanhui, 1968), 1128–41.
62 "Tuihuan chachao caiwu qingdan" [Inventory for the Return of Confiscated Possessions], September 19, 1973.
63 "Ta shi Guomindang fandongpai junxu" [He is a Reactionary Provider of Military Material for the GMD], September 6, 1966.
64 Xu Hailiang, *Wuhan "qi-er-ling" shijian shilu* [The True Record of the Wuhan July 20 Incident], (Hong Kong: Zhongguo wenhua chuanbo chubanshe, 2010), 403–4.
65 Wang Guangzhao, *Zheli nashi chaoqi chaoluo: Wuhan guolu chang wenge jishi* [The Flood and Ebb in this Place at that Time: Chronicle of the Cultural Revolution at the Wuhan Boiler Factory] (Hong Kong: Zhongguo wenhua chuanbo chubanshe, 2013), 163.
66 Vivian Wagner, *Erinnerungsverwaltung in China: Staatsarchive und Politik in der Volksrepublik* (Köln: Böhlau, 2006), 222–23.
67 "Jiantaoshu" [Self-Criticism], September 8, 1968.
68 Kang Sheng, "On Case Examination Work," translated in *China's Cultural Revolution, 1966–69: Not a Dinner Party*, ed. Michael Schoenhals (Armonk: M.E. Sharpe, 1996), 118.
69 "Tanbaishu" [Confession], November 3, 1968.
70 "Guanyu zibenjia XXX zhengli waidiao tigang" [Outline for an External Investigation into the Capitalist XXX's Political History], November 29, 1968.
71 "Guanyu XXX wenti diaocha baogao" [Investigatory Report on the Issues of XXX], n.d.
72 "Shencha jielunbiao" [Conclusion Form for Examination], June 23, 1973.
73 Zhonggong zhongyang, "Yinfa 'Wang-Zhang-Jiang-Yao fandang jituan zuizheng (cailiao zhi er)' de tongzhi, [Notification Distributing "Evidence of the Crimes of the Wang-Zhang-Jiang-Yao Anti-Party Clique (Material II)"], March 6, 1977.
74 Alexander Cook, *The Cultural Revolution on Trial: Mao and the Gang of Four* (New York: Cambridge University Press, 2016), 58.
75 "Tuihuan chachao caiwukuan shouju" [Receipt of the Return of Possessions and Money], September 19, 1973.
76 Gerry Groot lists a few "significant moves towards re-establishing united front work" in *Managing Transitions: The Chinese Communist Party, United Front Work, Corporatism and Hegemony* (New York: Routledge, 2004), 99–100.
77 *Zhongguo gongchandang zuzhi shi ziliao*, vol. 5, 72.

78 Zhonggong Hubei shengwei zuzhibu, Zhonggong Hubei shengwei dangshi ziliao zhengji bianyan weiyuanhui, Hubei sheng dang'anguan, eds., *Zhongguo gongchandang Hubei sheng zuzhi shi ziliao* [Materials on the Organizational History of the CCP in Hubei Province], (Wuhan: Hubei renmin chubanshe, 1991), 581.
79 Zhonggong zhongyang, "Zhuanfa Zhongyang guojia jiguan tongzhan xitong junguan zuzhi dui zai Jing bufen tongzhan duixiang bei chachao caiwu de chuli yijian" [Transmission of the Military Control Organization of the Central State Organs United Front System's Opinion on Handling Possessions Confiscated from United Front Targets in the Capital], *Zhongfa* (1971) no. 12, February 7, 1971, East China Normal University Center for Contemporary Documents and Historical Material, EN 0351-204-172.
80 See, for example, Shanghai Municipal Revolutionary Committee United Front Group, "Guanyu qu Beijing canjia zhongyang tongzhan zuotan youguan zibenjia chachao caiwu, gaoxin, tuixiu deng zhengce wenti de yijian de qingshi baogao" [Report with Opinions on Going to Beijing to Discuss Confiscated Possessions, High Salaries, Retirement, and Other Policy Issues Concerning Capitalists], October 12, 1975, Shanghai Municipal Archive, A33-4-100-13.
81 See *People's Daily*, August 23, 1977, 1.
82 Zhonggong zhongyang, "Pizhuan Zhonggong zhongyang tongzhanbu deng liu bumen guanyu ba yuan gongshangyezhe zhong de laodongzhe qubiechulai wenti de qingshi baogao" [Approved and Commented Report from the CCP Central United Front Department and Six Other Departments Concerning the Issue of Differentiating Laborers from the Former Industrialists and Merchants], *Zhongfa* (1979) no. 84, November 12, 1979, in *Ganshen gongzuo zhengce wenjian xuanbian*, vol. 2, 1127–31. Available in MLD, item no. 60.
83 Zhonggong zhongyang bangongshi, "Zhuanfa 'Guanyu ba yuan gongshangyezhe zhong de laodongzhe qubiechulai de gongzuo zongjie baogao'" [Transmission of a "Summary Report on the Work to Differentiate Laborers from the Former Industrialists and Merchants"], November 3, 1981, in *Ganshen gongzuo zhengce wenjian xuanbian*, vol. 2, 1144–50. MLD, item no. 66.
84 Zhonggong Hubei shengwei dangshi yanjiushi, Zhonggong Hubei shengwei tongzhanbu, eds., *Zhongguo zibenzhuyi gongshangye de shehui zhuyi gaizao: Hubei juan* [The Socialist Transformation of China's Capitalist Industry and Commerce: Hubei volume] (Beijing: Zhonggong dangshi chubanshe, 1993), table 24.
88 Zhonggong zhongyang, "Guanyu 'Beijing shi Beijiao mucaichang renzhen luoshi dang dui minzu zichanjieji de ge xiang zhengce' de tongzhi" [Notice Regarding "Beijing Municipality Beijiao Lumber Mill's Conscientious Fixing of the Party's Policies Toward the National Bourgeoisie and the Petty Bourgeoisie], *Zhongfa* (1969) no. 20, May 8, 1969, in MLD, item no. 2079.
86 Yin Zhijun and Song Penglin, "Yijiuqiba nian zhi yijiuqijiu nian: luoshi dang dui minzu zichanjieji zhengce" [1978 to 1979: Fixing the Party's Policies Toward the National Bourgeoisie], *Zhonggong dangshi yanjiu*, no. 11 (2011): 88.
87 "Guanyu dui XXX de chengfen qunzhong daibiao tizhi jilu (zhaiyao)" [Notes by the Representative Organization of the Masses on the Class Status of XXX (Summary)], September 10, 1977.
88 "Ba bugou zibenjia de huachulai de jielun shenpibiao" [Approval Form for the Conclusion on the Differentiation of the Insufficiently Capitalist], September 11, 1977.
89 Cf. Martin Innes and Alan Clarke, "Policing the Past: Cold Case Studies, Forensic Evidence and Retroactive Social Control," *The British Journal of Sociology*, no. 3 (2009): 543–63.

90 The portion of Party members recruited after 1966 is cited in "Hu Yaobang tongzhi guanyu jiaqiang zhengzhi duwu de yijian" [Comrade Hu Yaobang's Opinions on Strengthening Political Reading Materials], April 4, 1979, Shanghai Municipal Archive, A22-4-295-1.
91 Observations from interviews conducted by Gail Hershatter and Wang Guohong, see *The Gender of Memory*, 25–26.
92 Yves Chevrier, "La Chine aujourd'hui: la nation sans la démocratie," in *La démocratie: histoire, théories, pratiques,* eds., Jean-Vincent Holeindre and Benoît Richard (Auxerre: Editions sciences humaines, 2010), 276.
93 As the Bo Xilai affair unfolded in early 2012, Premier Wen Jiabao warned that the historical tragedy of the Cultural Revolution could occur again, see "China Premier Wen Jiabao's Comments at NPC Press Conference," *Reuters*, March 14, 2012, accessed January 18, 2018, http://www.reuters.com/article/china-npc-highlights-idUSL4E8EE11K20120314. The same trope was used in a *People's Daily* commentary on the fiftieth anniversary of the May 16 Notification to celebrate the reform era, see Ren Ping, "Yi shi wei jian shi weile genghao qianjin" [The Purpose of Using History as a Mirror is to Make even Better Advancements], *People's Daily*, May 17, 2016, 4.

Jeremy Brown
5 A Policeman, His Gun, and an Alleged Rape
Competing Appeals for Justice in Tianjin, 1966–1979

Zeng Huizhen and Mou Jingguan fundamentally disagreed about what happened between them.[1] According to Zeng, Mou raped her at gunpoint in a field in late 1958, a few weeks after she moved to the city of Tianjin from her home village. Zeng, who was eighteen at the time, said that over the following months Mou forced her to have sex eight or nine other times. Mou, a police officer and distant relative of Zeng's who was thirty-seven in 1958, disputed Zeng's account. He claimed that they had a consensual relationship. Mou acknowledged that there was a gun present during their first encounter, but he argued that it was simply a required part of his police uniform.

For the next eight years, what happened between Zeng and Mou remained secret. But in September 1966, with Tianjin's Cultural Revolution in full swing, Zeng tearfully told her husband her side of the story. Her husband immediately wrote a denunciation letter, which led to Mou's arrest; he was held for more than two years in a detention center. In 1969, the military control committee in charge of public security in Tianjin labeled Mou a "bad element" who had committed "rape at gunpoint." The following year he was deported to his native place, a village in Hebei Province, "to be handed over to the poor and lower-middle peasants for supervision and reform."[2]

Throughout the 1970s, Mou repeatedly asked Tianjin authorities to revise and correct what he eventually came to call his "unjust, false, and mistaken case." His appeal strategies mirrored the shifting politics of the decade and responded directly to the Communist Party's piecemeal attempts to deal with the arbitrary or uneven application of justice between 1966 and 1970. Mou's superiors and colleagues in the Tianjin Public Security Bureau neither ignored nor protected him. On at least five different occasions, municipal police officials reinvestigated the rape allegations against Mou. Over time, they slightly adjusted his verdict and punishment, but Mou was never satisfied and continued to appeal.

Zeng's allegations against Mou, as well as Mou's multiple appeals, came to light when I found a dossier about the case in a flea market in Tianjin. The file contains transcripts of police interviews of Zeng about the alleged rape, Mou's handwritten appeal letters, and the results of multiple reinvestigations. The legal case against Mou arose because of the unique political and legal environment of the Cultural

---

For their helpful comments and assistance with sources, I am grateful to Daniel Leese, Puck Engman, Jennifer Neighbors, Michael Schoenhals, Amanda Shuman, and Xu Lizhi.

Revolution, which encouraged ordinarily voiceless or marginalized individuals to accuse people in positions of power of long-hidden wrongdoings. Many of these accusations were exaggerated or fabricated. Some may have revealed actual crimes.

This chapter builds on Xu Lizhi's argument in this volume that criminal justice and public security during the Cultural Revolution were not, in fact, suspended or in a state of anarchy for ten full years. The *Comprehensive History of the Legal System of the People's Republic of China* asserts that criminal justice during the Cultural Revolution allowed the "basic functioning of society" and maintained "rudimentary order."³ The case of Zeng Huizhen versus Mou Jingguan shows that such words as "basic" and "rudimentary" understate the legal avenues available to victims and convicted criminals alike. In fact, the events of 1966 presented a new opportunity for police oversight. Zeng may not have been entirely satisfied with Mou's punishment, but without the Cultural Revolution, it is unlikely that Mou would have been punished at all. Moreover, after 1971 "bad elements" such as Mou had the opportunity to demand reinvestigation and restitution. Criminal justice during the Cultural Revolution was flawed, but it was a complex system that evolved over time and sometimes functioned as it was intended.

The File

In the file about Mou Jingguan's alleged rape of Zeng Huizhen, Mou's voice rings much louder than Zeng's. The file contains 227 pages and includes twenty-four postmarked envelopes that originally held Mou's appeal letters, all bound together by two metal clasps and covered with heavyweight brown butcher paper. It centers on his appeal, not her complaint. The handwritten title on the front cover reads, "Mou Jingguan's Appeal Materials." No author or organization is listed on the title, nor is there a table of contents, but the file appears to have been compiled by the Tianjin Public Security Bureau in 1979, involving cadres from the municipal PSB's Political Department (*zhengzhibu*), Security Protection Section (*zhi'an baoweichu*), the PSB's Communist Party Branch Organization Department, as well as its ad hoc Fixing Cadre Policy Office (*Luoshi ganbu zhengce bangongshi*).⁴ Original documents in the file date from 1972 through July 1979. They also include handwritten copies of earlier materials dating from 1966, 1967, and 1969.

Zeng's Side of the Story

Although Mou Jingguan's appeal letters make up the bulk of the file, Zeng Huizhen's voice is audible. In October 1975, a public security clerk from the rural county in Hebei Province where Mou had been deported gained access to and copied transcripts of police interviews of Zeng that had been conducted in 1966, 1967, 1969, and 1972. These copies made their way back to the city and into Mou's appeal dossier because in November 1978, two comrades from the Tianjin PSB traveled to the Hebei county where Mou had lived in the 1970s to investigate his appeals and to request relevant materials. Apparently, it was easier for the city investigators to get copies from the countryside than to track down the original documents. This cooperation between rural and urban police made Zeng's side of the story available to city investigators in the 1970s (and to historians today).[5]

Zeng retold her story at a neighborhood police station in Tianjin on the evening of March 13, 1967. This was the third time she had met with investigators to discuss Mou Jingguan since her husband wrote a letter to the Tianjin PSB on September 24, 1966, accusing Mou of rape. Zeng's interviewer asked her about events in 1958, when she was eighteen.[6] Zeng did not recall the exact date of her move to Tianjin but remembered that it was autumn, when the weather was "about to turn cold." She had left her rural home to join her husband, who had recently started a job at a factory. Zeng's husband was living at his factory dormitory so she stayed with relatives in the city, specifically with her husband's great-aunt. The great-aunt's son, thirty-seven-year-old police officer Mou Jingguan, also lived in the home where Zeng was staying. A few days after she arrived in the city, Zeng's great-aunt urged her to ask Mou to help her find a job.

Zeng recalled that Mou agreed on the spot, saying, "put on some clothes and we'll go to sign you up" for a job. Mou was wearing his police uniform and hat when they went out. Sometime after 7 p.m., they were walking in a remote area and ended up at a grassy field. According to Zeng, Mou then said: "How about right here?" Zeng replied: "Aren't we going to sign up for a job?" Mou said: "Right here." Zeng recounted what happened next:

> I started to walk away and he grabbed me. He grabbed me with one hand and he took out his gun with the other hand. He unholstered his gun from his belt, pointed it at me, and said: "Stay still or I'll kill you." I was scared and didn't dare to speak. He pinned me down, undid my belt, and pulled down one of my pant legs. He pulled his pants down halfway. Ordinary [sex] position. After five or six minutes, at most ten minutes, it was over. I said: "You had me come out to sign up for a job, what are you doing? What am I going to say when I get home?" Mou told me to say that nobody was at the factory.

Zeng continued her story, saying that two or three days later, Mou raped her again, "grabbing me with one hand and touching his gun with the other hand." "[Sexual] relations happened" several more times after that, including once at the police station where Mou worked; each time, Zeng claimed, Mou threatened to kill her.

After telling her police interviewer what happened in 1958, Zeng skipped ahead in her story to a much more recent interaction with Mou. In May 1966, she said, Mou dropped by her home and wanted to know if anyone had asked her about what had happened between them. Zeng said, "No, how could I tell people about it, isn't it humiliating enough already?" Mou then "guaranteed" that if she did say anything, he would deny it. He wondered what she would do if someone held a knife to her neck and asked about the two of them. "I still wouldn't say anything," Zeng responded.

Zeng's story remained quite consistent throughout the nine or ten times she spoke to the police. Police wanted to know where and how the sex happened and were especially interested in Mou's gun and his threatening language. They did not dwell on minor inconsistencies in Zeng's account. Perhaps they had a sense, ahead of their time, that trauma can affect memory and that, as one study noted in 2013, "inconsistencies should not be confused with a false report."[7] A more likely explanation for the investigators' treatment of Zeng is that their main task was to evaluate the extent of Mou's "badness," not to question Zeng's credibility.

Sometimes police let Zeng tell her story uninterrupted. Other times they asked specific questions: "When did you come [to Tianjin]? Who arrived first, you or your mother-in-law? ... Why did you stay at Mou's house? ... What did he say to you after sex? ... Did he have a holster for his gun? ... What happened next? ... How did the sex happen? ... Then what? ... Who pulled down your pants?"[8] Zeng's interrogators were most concerned about how to characterize Mou Jingguan's actions. They did not care, or were not aware, that repeated questioning by different interviewers might traumatize Zeng.[9]

Rape, Power, and Influence in the Mao Zedong Era

Had Zeng's complaint against Mou occurred in China before 1949, or in Taiwan thereafter, the Criminal Code of the Republic of China (ROC) promulgated in 1935 would have applied. Article 228 of the ROC Criminal Code lists a specific crime for cases in which a rapist abuses a position of authority. "Someone who uses his power and influence (*liyong quanshi*) to rape or molest a person under his supervision because of a family, doctor-patient, charitable, government, or professional relationship," the ROC code rules, "can receive a maximum sentence of five years."[10] If two people willingly consented to illicit sex in a relationship in which one person's disproportionate "power and influence were completely irrelevant," then the sex could be considered adultery, but should not be prosecuted as rape using power and influence, according to a compilation of court interpretations of cases published in Taiwan in 1972.[11] If it had been heard in an ROC court, Zeng's case against Mou might have hinged on questions of consent and whether Mou was actually "supervising" Zeng. She may not have been directly under Mou's familial or professional supervision, but she was in a subordinate position in his household, sought employment help from him, and seemed affected by his status as a police officer.

These questions were moot because the crime of rape using power and influence was not enshrined in the laws of the PRC after 1949. Some PRC officials abused their power for sexual purposes during the 1950s, 1960s, and 1970s. They were punished in various ways.[12] The lack of laws as specific as those found in the ROC Criminal Code, however, meant that the courts and police, as well as the disciplinary organs of the CCP, had latitude in dealing with people in positions of power who had been accused of rape. Jerome Cohen has noted the "absence of any published legislation relating to the major common crimes, such as murder, rape, and robbery," and that "unpublished regulations define murder, rape, arson, and many other common crimes and set forth the maximum and minimum penalties for each."[13] The officials investigating Mou Jingguan seemed appalled by his alleged abuse of power, but they did not have clear legal guidance about how to punish him for it. This lack of clarity affected the handling of Mou's case from the moment he was accused in 1966 through the multiple reinvestigations that followed. It also gave Mou space to appeal and encouraged him to focus on the contested details of his encounter with Zeng rather than addressing his status as a police officer and family member.

Although a patchwork of regulations, rather than laws, dictated how security officials dealt with rape cases during the Mao Zedong era, police still took the crime seriously. As shown in Table 1, the Ministry of Public Security (MPS) compiled a nationwide annual count of criminal cases, including murder, arson, poisoning, rape, robbery, theft, and fraud (the collection of crime statistics stalled between 1964 and 1970, leaving a major gap in the data). These numbers reflected the number of cases reported to the MPS by provincial security officials and shed light on how local authorities prioritized different types of crime. After rape cases reached 7.01 percent of the total number of criminal cases in 1963, the tally climbed even higher the following year, when the Supreme People's Procuratorate reported in *Prosecution Work Situation Report* that by the second quarter of 1964, rape had risen to first place among all types of crime. In November 1964, the MPS circulated the procuratorate's report in *Public Security Construction,* commenting that the "raping of women and young girls is a type of criminal activity that severely disrupts social order and violates personal rights. Each locality must firmly uphold the guiding principle of striking hard at this type of criminal activity and dealing with it severely, no matter when it occurs and no matter who perpetrates it."[14]

Table 1: National Rape Case Data Compiled by the MPS, 1952–75

Year	Total Criminal Cases	Rape Cases	Rape Cases as Percentage of Total	Place of Rape Cases Among Seven Categories of Criminal Cases
1952	243,003	1,795	0.74	6
1953	292,308	2,782	0.95	5
1954	392,229	4,246	1.08	5
1955	325,829	8,221	2.52	4
1956	180,075	5,562	3.09	3
1957	298,031	15,488	5.20	2
1958	211,068	13,453	6.37	2
1959	210,025	8,469	4.03	2
1960	222,734	5,912	2.65	3
1961	421,934	4,235	1.00	5
1962	324,639	6,781	2.09	3
1963	251,226	17,622	7.01	2
1964	215,352	NA	NA	NA
1965	216,125	NA	NA	NA
1966–1970	NA	NA	NA	NA
1971	323,623	17,142	5.30	2
1972	402,573	18,869	4.69	2
1973	535,829	27,924	5.21	2
1974	516,419	29,295	5.67	2
1975	475,432	31,976	6.73	2

Source: Figures compiled from year-end data recorded in *Jianguo yilai gongan gongzuo dashi yaolan, 1949 nian 10 yue–2000 nian* [General Survey of Important Events in Public Security Work since the Founding of the People's Republic, October 1949–2000] (Beijing: Qunzhong chubanshe, 2003). The percentages in column four come from my own calculations, not from the MPS.

One goal of the MPS's directive to "strike hard" against rape was to "frighten enemies and educate the masses" through public trials in areas where rape was especially rampant. One such event in Beijing drew a crowd of more than 5,000 that watched the sentencing of eight criminals.[15] An unintended consequence of the vigorous anti-rape drive of late 1964 and early 1965, however, was that police in some places traumatized rape victims. According to a "Notice Forbidding Hymen Inspection" authored by Hunanese legal authorities and circulated nationwide by the Supreme People's Court, Supreme People's Procuratorate, and MPS on March 11, 1965, hymen inspection had become the primary rape investigation method in some jurisdictions. Even worse, police in certain localities "unscrupulously did coercive inspections, and some inspectors even took advantage of the situation to molest women, having an extremely bad effect on the masses." The notice prohibited hymen inspection of rape victims and ruled that the results of such inspections could not be used as evidence.[16] We do not know if Mou Jingguan read or reflected on these directives about how to properly investigate rape in the context of severely punishing rapists in late 1964 and early 1965. He was aware, however, that he remained vulnerable to charges of rape. A year-and-a-half after the MPS launched its anti-rape push, Mou visited Zeng Huizhen at home and told her to stay quiet. As it turned out, his worries were not unfounded.

The Cultural Revolution, Police, and Sex

After 1958, life and work continued normally for Mou Jingguan, but for one blemish on his record. By his own admission, he had an affair with a married woman in 1962. When his Party committee at work discovered this affair the following year, he was disciplined by being put "on probation within the Party" (*liudang chakan*) for two years.[17] According to the Tianjin PSB, Mou received this punishment because he had "used his official authority as a police captain to engage in illicit sexual relations with a female accountant."[18] When sanctioning Mou, his superiors seemed to consider the workplace power imbalance between Mou and the accountant. In 1964, Mou was transferred to a new job as cafeteria manager in a PSB-run mental institution.

Life changed dramatically for Mou and for many other residents of Tianjin in 1966. The Cultural Revolution encouraged ordinary citizens to criticize authority figures. For some people in Tianjin, neighborhood police officers offered an inviting target. One internal report from Tianjin's Hongqiao District reveals that local police were distressed by the events of September 1966, especially when Red Guards scrutinized their families' historical and political records. When the "masses" accused one police official named Ma of having illicitly sold ration tickets for cloth and bicycles, Ma stayed home from work, claiming that he was ill. His bosses at the police department called him in to the office to investigate after they learned that the "masses" were preparing to "struggle against" him. When

Ma denied having done anything wrong, the Hongqiao PSB deemed that he had "failed to honestly confess to the Party."[19]

This is the charged context in which Zeng Huizhen's husband denounced Mou Jingguan on September 24, 1966. District cadres in charge of guiding the Cultural Revolution in Tianjin's neighborhoods tried to discourage people from fixating on sexual transgressions, calling the criticism of a nurse who had a child out of wedlock an example of "insufficiently grasping the main focus of struggle in the movement."[20] Nonetheless, as Neil Diamant has shown, Red Guards considered "promiscuity, bigamy and the like" evidence of bourgeois decadence. Sexual misbehaviour was therefore fair game for criticism and punishment.[21] It was also one of the few concrete examples of supposedly bourgeois behaviour that directly affected the everyday lives of urban residents. Zeng Huizhen's husband was outraged at Mou Jingguan. In September 1966, the Cultural Revolution gave him a unique chance to vent his anger and seek justice.

By 1966, Zeng's husband was no longer a factory worker. He had become a security cadre at a local vegetable company.[22] In other words, Zeng's husband and Mou Jingguan were on opposite professional trajectories: while Mou had been demoted from his position directing a neighborhood police station, Zeng's husband's status had risen considerably. He began his letter by pointing out that Mou Jingguan had served as a police officer under the Nationalists before 1949 and had hidden his true class background of "landlord." The first accusation was accurate but the second did not stick; in 1978 the Tianjin PSB noted that Mou's class background was in fact "middle peasant." Zeng's husband explained that he first became suspicious that something was wrong in 1958 when he learned that Mou had taken his wife to sign up for a job in the evening and they did not return home until 9 or 10 p.m. The timing seemed wrong for job hunting. Zeng's husband kept asking her to explain, but she refused to speak about that night. This led to arguments and disunity in their marriage, Zeng's husband wrote, and once she even said she wanted a divorce.

Finally, on the evening of September 23, 1966, Zeng told her husband "about the entire situation in detail, crying bitterly" as she mentioned the desolate field, the gun, the death threat, and the rape. Zeng was so upset, her husband wrote, that she cried all night. She said that she wanted to lie down on the train tracks and commit suicide.

Zeng's husband concluded his letter with a formal request. Viewed simply as a "sexual affair," he wrote, what happened between his wife and Mou could be considered a "contradiction among the people," meaning that it could be solved through education rather than through the law. Zeng's husband advocated a different approach: "the law cannot permit Mou Jingguan, a police officer carrying a gun ... to commit rape all over the place and destroy my family harmony."

Punishing Mou

The Tianjin PSB found the argument of Zeng's husband persuasive enough to lock Mou up for "investigation" (*shencha*) in December 1966. Shortly thereafter, however, the public security bureaucracy in the city collapsed in the midst of factional conflict and was eventually put under military control. This upheaval meant that Mou Jingguan languished in detention until May 1969, when he was sent back to his work unit. Mou had been detained without charges for almost two-and-a-half years. Although the words "anarchy," "arbitrary detention," and "vigilante justice" do not accurately depict the entire "Cultural Revolution decade," they do come closer to describing how some people experienced the years between 1966 and 1969. Not surprisingly, Mou viewed his ordeal between December 1966 and May 1969 as punishment in and of itself. Had he been formally charged with rape and found guilty, it is possible that his sentence—either in prison or a labor camp—would not have exceeded two years. A "barefoot doctor" in a Guangdong village who confessed to molesting a twelve-year-old in 1968 was sentenced to two years of reform through labor the following year. Villagers expressed anger at the doctor's relatively light sentence, which local officials said was justified because he had proactively admitted to his crime during the Cleansing of the Class Ranks campaign.[23] Jerome Cohen has documented other cases of rape and attempted rape before the Cultural Revolution that resulted in sentences ranging from one to three-and-a-half years, depending on the class status of the offender, the severity of violence involved, and whether the assailant was drunk (intoxication was considered a mitigating factor in one case in 1958).[24]

Given these legal precedents, Mou might have thought that his long detention-without-charges was punishment enough and hoped that he could quietly return to work after his release in May 1969. He would be disappointed. His case became one of many during not only the Cultural Revolution, but also the entire Mao Zedong era, that was not handled by the courts.[25] On May 3, 1969, the Second Security Section of the PLA Tianjin Public Security Organs Military Control Committee, citing Mou's case of "rape at gunpoint," formally requested that he be labeled (*daimao*) as an enemy and handed over to the "masses for supervision and reform."[26] A month later, the decision to label Mou and place him under supervision was announced at a mass criticism meeting.[27]

Historian Yang Kuisong has written that during the Mao Zedong era the "definition of *huaifenzi*," or "bad element," was "broad, and the factors leading to conviction were numerous and complex."[28] According to Mao Zedong, bad elements were criminals who caused "serious harm to socialism," but whose nefarious deeds were less severe than those of "counterrevolutionaries" who directly opposed the Communist Party.[29] A central document defining different types of "bad elements" issued in 1956 did not specifically mention rape or rapists, but included two subcategories of bad elements that encompassed those who committed sexual crimes: "hooligan elements" (*liumang fenzi*) who were "habitual evildoers who refused to mend their ways despite repeated disciplinary action," plus "degenerate elements of extremely vile character," who only made up approximately five percent of all "bad people."[30]

In November 1970, the Tianjin Heping District public security organ issued detailed definitions for how to identify and label political enemies, including bad elements. Even though the Heping instructions were published after Mou's case had been decided, they still illuminate how the labeling process worked during the 1970s, when Mou's status was repeatedly reinvestigated. Most bad element cases dealt with "graft and embezzlement, hooliganism and rape, and profiteering and fraud." In "defining and handling" people who had committed such transgressions, the document continued, it was necessary to weigh whether the individual was a "bad person doing bad things, or a good person making mistakes," a habitual or first-time offender, a "hooligan by nature" or someone engaging in "ordinary hooligan behaviour," and whether he had committed "rape versus ordinary sexual relations." Those who fit the second part of each binary could be "educated to prevent recidivism," while those who were bad to the bone could be labeled as bad elements and "brought to justice."[31]

In a report dated August 10, 1969, Tianjin security officials deemed that Mou needed to be declared a bad element. As a police officer in Tianjin under the old regime between 1942 and 1949, Mou had "enthusiastically served the enemy" and "suppressed the student movement." After liberation, he pretended to support the Communists and sneaked his way into the Party. Mou's main problems, the report asserted, were his "corrupt morals" and "habitual hooliganism." Back in his home village, when he was young, he had repeatedly molested a girl and "after liberation, he had used his identity as a public security officer, along with other various tricks, to molest and rape as many as five women."[32] In October 1969, Mou was expelled from the Communist Party on the same grounds.[33] In April 1970, he was deported to his birthplace in Hebei Province.

More than 40,000 residents of Tianjin were deported (*qiansong*) from the city to the countryside between 1966 and 1970. This number includes political enemies who were deprived of urban residency as punishment, along with their family members. It does not include people who moved to the countryside as sent-down youth, as part of the civil defense evacuations of 1970 and 1971, or as part of the Third Front industrial push. Bad elements like Mou Jingguan, who purportedly harmed socialism and threatened women through sexual predation, were dumped—without a formal trial and without a fixed sentence—in impoverished villages that did not want them. This practice lays bare the reality of the rural-urban divide in Mao's China: cities were considered privileged proletarian space that needed to be cleansed of impurities. City officials treated the countryside as part prison, part garbage dump.[34]

Mou's Side of the Story

Mou Jingguan clearly recognized the reality of China's rural-urban divide. For a decade following his designation as a bad element and his deportation to a village, he dedicated himself to appealing the judgment against him. He wanted to regain his city residency and his job. Above all, he wanted his name to be cleared so that he could "return to the side of the people" (*huidao renmin yibian*).[35]

Mou's self-advocacy began timidly when he was required to sign off on the formal decision labeling him as a bad element. In acknowledging that his "mistakes" had harmed the Party and the people, he pledged to reform himself and accept the supervision of the poor and lower-middle peasants. He accepted the decision that labeled him a bad element, admitting to various historical problems including having served as a police officer under the Nationalists before 1949 and to many instances of sexual misconduct. But there was one detail he could not accept: he disputed the conclusion that he had raped Zeng Huizhen.[36]

Each time Mou wrote an appeal letter during the 1970s, he retold his version of what had happened in 1958. What follows is an account he penned in April 1979. When Mou first met Zeng, he claimed that she was "eagerly attentive and solicitous," making eyes at him. He interpreted this as romantic interest. He explained:

> I wanted to follow up on it but there were always people at home and it was very inconvenient, so one night I took her to a small casting factory to look for work. She waited outside the factory gates and I went inside but everyone had already left, so the job search was unsuccessful. On the way home...we stopped at a field to talk. I stroked her braid and worked up the nerve to ask if she wanted to have sex. All she said was, "I'm scared that I'll be disgraced if people find out," but she did not show any negative reaction. After she consented, she pulled down her own pant leg (I remember that it was the left leg) and that's how we had sex for the first time. Then we went home together. Later, I did get her a job at the XX factory and we often had improper sexual relations over the course of a year.[37]

After their affair ended, Mou wrote, they both agreed to never tell anyone about it, so when he got in trouble in 1962 for having an adulterous relationship with a different woman, he did not mention the earlier affair he had had with Zeng. He admitted that he was wrong to have concealed his time with Zeng, but he said it was illogical to use the term "rape at gunpoint" for an affair that lasted almost a year. Mou also argued that he was required to carry the gun as part of his police uniform. He never touched it, never unholstered it, and never used it in a threatening way around Zeng, he wrote. He could not accept the idea that the gun was relevant in any way. Beginning in 1970, Mou contested the charge of "rape at gunpoint" (*chiqiang qiangjian*) and asked that it be corrected.

Mou's Appeals between 1970 and 1975: Heard with Unsympathetic Ears

In 1972, Mou received the correction he had asked for. After what he called "intense requests to the Party to clarify right and wrong,"[38] a reinvestigation by the Tianjin Municipal People's Protection Bureau Party Committee slightly revised the official characterization of Mou's crime. In a July 25, 1972 ruling, "rape at gunpoint" was changed to "raped his nephew's wife Zeng Huizhen while carrying a gun." Otherwise, security officials ruled, the original verdict stood. Because Mou was an "impenitent hooligan by nature who had caused extremely adverse effects among the masses," his bad element label still applied. He was required to remain in his native place, laboring under the supervision of the poor and lower-middle peasants.[39]

Investigators had offered Mou a concession by altering a single Chinese character. They granted that perhaps he had not threateningly wielded a firearm (*chiqiang*), but he had still committed rape while carrying a gun (*xieqiang*). Judging by Mou's increasingly feverish appeals after 1972, this small victory felt like defeat. He was not at all satisfied, but he sensed an opening and kept pushing.

Mou accurately felt one shift in the political climate in the early 1970s. Many deportees had their cases reevaluated in 1972 as part of a broader effort to "fix policy" (*luoshi zhengce*). This vague phrase represented an admission that some policies had been ignored or arbitrarily applied between 1966 and 1970, an adjustment that was politically justified by scapegoating Vice-Chairman Lin Biao after his shocking death in September 1971. The investigations of 1972 offered the possibility of genuine change for deportees: while some had their verdicts upheld, others were rehabilitated and regained their urban residency and jobs.[40]

A parallel shift in the policing realm also affected the handling of Mou's case. It ensured that his appeals would be heard, but suggested that they would be viewed unsympathetically. A national public security conference held from December 11, 1970 to February 11, 1971, led to a partial restoration of pre-1966 investigation methods and reporting of crime statistics. The central document circulated after the conference seemed to encourage appeals and complaints from lower levels of the security bureaucracy, criticizing the "severe mistake of the MPS in recent times closing the door to subordinates, not being in charge or keeping others informed, and having the organs of dictatorship keep its eyes and ears shut."[41] As a former member of the local security apparatus, Mou would have been heartened by this adjustment. He might have been troubled, however, by other parts of the post-conference document, which criticized purged officials Liu Shaoqi, Peng Zhen, and Luo Ruiqing for having overseen a major removal of labels of the "Four Types of Elements," including bad elements. This implied that it would not be an easy or automatic matter for such bad elements as Mou Jingguan to seek redress. The central document also excoriated officers who distanced themselves from the masses by acting superior, enjoying special privileges, beating, cursing, and even firing their guns to threaten people. This admonition against police abuse of authority—and especially its specific mention of firearms—could not have helped Mou's appeal, which centered on the presence of a handgun.

The policy changes of the early 1970s meant that Mou's appeal would be heard, considered, and formally adjudicated. Heightened attention to sexual crimes, however, suggested that investigators in the 1970s were less likely to help a police officer who had been convicted of raping an eighteen-year-old, even if the alleged offense had occurred years earlier. Cadres accused of sexual predation faced increased scrutiny beginning in 1970, as central authorities became aware of local officials who raped and demanded sex from young women sent to the countryside. As Michel Bonnin writes, female sent-down youth were "generally defenseless against such harassment and arbitrary decisions. That was especially true in the case of rape by these cadres, which explains why it was so widespread."[42]

In May 1970, the CCP Center called for those who raped sent-down youth to be "punished according to the law" and mandated that "cadres who abuse their official position to commit evil should be dismissed, investigated, and dealt with."[43] In spite of this attention from top leaders in Beijing, the problem persisted. A national conference on sent-down youth work in 1973 targeted "criminals who use fascist methods to brutally persecute sent-down youth and rape female sent-down youth."[44] Following the conference, Party Center excoriated assailants who threatened victims and took revenge on whistle-blowers, and even called for "resolutely killing" the worst offenders. In response, the Tianjin Party Committee ordered the city's public security and justice agencies to reinvestigate all cases of rape against female sent-down youth that had been tried in previous years; if they had been improperly handled they were to be readjudicated.[45]

The policy of harshly punishing cadres who raped young women in the countryside did not apply to Mou's offense, which had taken place fifteen years earlier. But the recipients of Mou's appeal letters in the 1970s may well have interpreted the case's details (gun, police uniform, teenage victim) in light of top Party leaders' tough stance toward officials who preyed on young women. In this context, Mou's appeals had very little chance of success. Tianjin public security investigators had nothing to lose by upholding the original verdict. Not surprisingly, a new reinvestigation of Mou in December 1975 resulted in no changes: he was to remain in the countryside as a bad element.

Correcting "Unjust" Cases in the Late 1970s

Undeterred, Mou continued to appeal. He was especially busy in early 1976, writing at least ten letters and statements ranging from two to eight pages. He wrote to such offices as the Tianjin PSB Fixing Policy Office and the PSB Organization Department, and he also addressed letters to specific individuals, including San Renzheng, who led the city PSB. Later, waves of letters hit the desks of Tianjin officials in October 1977 and in April and May 1979.

Mou's correspondence strategy perplexed and exasperated Tianjin security officials. Annoyed by having "received him many times," a Tianjin PSB cadre ruled in September 1977 that his case did not merit reopening because multiple investigations had verified Mou's crimes. But "given Mou's recent good behavior" in the countryside, the PSB cadre suggested that his label could possibly be removed; Mou should not, however, be allowed to return to the city. A PSB section head did not comment on this casual proposal to offer amnesty to Mou, writing only, "Do not deal with this again."[46]

Mou, however, proved impossible to ignore. Not only did he keep writing appeal letters, he apparently moved back to Tianjin without permission, as indicated by the return address he used. When Wang Jianzhi, another PSB section head, received a five-page appeal from Mou in October 1977, he scribbled his response at the bottom of Mou's obsequious cover letter: "I don't know this guy... how does he know I'm at 1 Anshan Road? Why is he writing me? I'm baffled by this." Wang directed two comrades to look into whether Mou's problem needed any further attention.[47]

The mere existence of Mou's many appeals mattered more than the details of their contents, which were extremely repetitive. Each letter triggered a response: reinvestigation or passing the case along to another office or exhaustedly scrawling "we have already dealt with this multiple times." Throwing Mou's letters in the garbage or punishing him for overzealous petitioning (an offense known as "unreasonably causing trouble," or *wuli qunao*)[48] may have crossed the minds of his recipients, but there is no evidence that anyone pursued these options.

Official responses depended not on Mou's petitioning strategies but on the changing political context. Mao Zedong's death in September 1976 and the arrest of Jiang Qing and her allies a month later opened up the possibility of going beyond earlier efforts to "fix policy." Nonetheless, case revisions proceeded in a limited and halting fashion in 1977. As Daniel Leese has described, Hu Yaobang's leadership of the CCP Central Organization Department beginning in December 1977 led to more thorough reinvestigations in 1978, but it was only after the Third Plenary Session of the Eleventh Central Committee in December 1978 that widespread revision of verdicts began at the grassroots.[49]

As Table 1 illustrates, following the revival of public security statistical work in 1971, the number of rape cases reported to the MPS by local authorities climbed every year between 1971 and 1975. Some men convicted of rape, however, did win complete exoneration and rehabilitation during the 1970s. The treatment of Zhou Jigui, who was convicted of "rape at gunpoint" in Anhui Province and given a five-year sentence in June 1970, shows what Mou Jingguan might have hoped for. After his conviction, Zhou Jigui was sent to a farm in Yunnan Province for labor reform. Zhou "persistently appealed," leading to an inconclusive reinvestigation in 1974. Three years later, Yunnan court personnel traveled to Anhui to initiate a second reinvestigation. They found that Zhou had been framed by a political rival. Zhou had confessed under torture to raping a woman at gunpoint. In June 1977, a county-level court in Yunnan reversed Zhou's verdict and restored his political reputation; his old work unit reinstated him to his job and compensated him for lost wages. His accuser was arrested and sentenced for "fabricating false charges and framing a good person." Zhou's case was publicized in *People's Judiciary* in early 1978 and again in March 1979 as a model for how to revise verdicts.[50]

Mou Jingguan could not have known that Zhou Jigui had been completely cleared of rape at gunpoint, but Mou's letters from 1979 reveal his awareness of the national transitional justice project.[51] His renewed appeals in 1979 were sparked by Party Center's approval of the Supreme People's Court report about "correcting unjust, false, and mistaken verdicts, and diligently fixing Party policy," circulated nationwide on December 29, 1978, and publicized in *People's Daily* in 1979.[52] Mou was also encouraged by the results of another official reinvestigation of his case in November 1978.[53] This reinvestigation, which was likely prompted by a system-wide review of Cultural Revolution cases rather than by Mou's relentless appeals, determined that the basis of his original verdict was factual. "Mou is genuinely morally corrupt," Tianjin PSB investigators wrote, "his actions were indecent. In enforcing the law he violated the law" by molesting as many as five women.

The reinvestigation report then directly addressed the discrepancy between Mou's claims and Zeng Huizhen's version of what happened in 1958. Zeng's oral testimony on ten different occasions "confirmed that Mou had tricked her into going to a field, threatened her with a gun, and raped her." Mou denied that he had done anything threatening but admitted to having planned to take Zeng to the field. He also admitted to having a gun during the act. Even though Mou disagreed about the details, investigators still found him guilty: "Because both parties are maintaining their points of view, we cannot take sides in believing one over the other. But we can say for certain that Mou, who was the director of a police station at the time, had bad morals and used trickery to seduce a young woman."

Tianjin security authorities therefore concluded that the original verdict should stand, but they tried to close the case by offering Mou a seemingly attractive package:

> Based on the Party's policy of giving a way out and on Mou's rather good behavior after his deportation, and because of his economic difficulties living alone in the village, we believe that his bad element label can be removed. He can return to Tianjin and be given a level twenty-three desk job with a monthly salary of 49.50 yuan.

Far from placating Mou, however, this decision drove him to initiate a new round of appeals, this time explicitly presenting his case as a mistaken verdict that needed to be corrected.

Mou did not learn of the Tianjin PSB Party Committee's latest ruling until March 1979. In a subsequent petition, he complained that his label had not in fact been eliminated and that a comrade at the Security and Protection Section's Fixing Policy Office had told him to "resign due to illness" (*bingtui*) instead of giving him the job he had been promised.[54] What disappointed him even more, however, was that the verdict against him remained unchanged. "Removing my label and resettling in Tianjin are entirely different from fixing policy and correcting unjust, false, and mistaken verdicts," Mou wrote. Then he directly quoted Party Center's policy: "Because my verdict was mistakenly determined, it should be corrected based on the principle of 'every wrong will be righted.'"[55] This principle had appeared in the pages of *People's Daily* thirty-one times between being issued by Party Center on December 29, 1978, and the writing of Mou's appeal on April 26, 1979.

Mou's other appeals in April 1979 adopted the language of the time, criticizing Lin Biao and the Gang of Four for destroying the legal system, praising Hua Guofeng as a "wise leader," and complaining that he had been "treated unjustly" (*yuanwang*).[56] One letter that Mou sent directly to the Tianjin Municipal Organization Department's Fixing Cadre Policy Office prompted a response that was equally couched in the season's tone. Someone at the Organization Department attached a cover page redirecting Mou's letter to the PSB and asking comrades there to "please firmly grasp and diligently research, fix policy, and provide an answer to him."[57]

This request from the Organization Department obliged the PSB to take yet another look at the case, but security cadres could only review the same stack of testimony, appeal letters, and previous reinvestigations that they had already examined. There was nothing new. When Mou stopped by the Security Protection Section on July 11, 1979, to check on his appeal, he was furious at what he learned. A comrade there allowed him to read and hand copy the latest "Opinion on the Reinvestigation of Mou Jingguan's Problems." This new opinion—the final official decision that appears in Mou's file—repeated the conclusions of the reinvestigation report of November 1978. It stated that Mou had tricked Zeng into going with him for the purpose of raping her. It noted that Mou was carrying a gun in his possession at the time.[58] Anyone reading it could only conclude that Mou's conduct had been bad, even if the removal of his bad element label was a step toward political rehabilitation.

Mou titled his anguished response "My Opinion on the Opinion on the Reinvestigation of my Problems." He complained that instead of being exonerated as he had hoped, he had been accused of an entirely new charge, "rape by trickery" (*pianjian*). He argued that accusation material and testimony from the early phase of the "Cultural Revolution," meaning the period of his detention between December 1966 and May 1969, should not be considered evidence in a post-Cultural Revolution reckoning. He asserted that his mistakes were ancient history, pointing out that eleven years had passed between his alleged offense and the approval of his bad element label. He pointed to his good behavior, writing that he "had not committed any similar mistakes since being punished in 1962." Mou concluded his plea by asking investigators to "reconsider my problems and make a just resolution."[59]

Conclusion

The file in my possession concludes with Mou's appeal of July 21, 1979. I do not know what happened next. Nationwide investigations into "unjust and mistaken" cases continued well into the 1980s. It is possible that Mou eventually received the full exoneration he so desperately wanted. It is also possible that the paper trail indeed ended on July 21, 1979; perhaps the authorities decided that Mou's case had been handled in a satisfactory manner and they refused to consider further appeals. Difficult as it is to imagine, maybe Mou himself realized that after thirteen years of detention, deportation, and dogged petitioning, it was time to move on.

Even if I knew how the case developed after 1979, many open questions would remain. The biggest puzzle is the one that investigators in Tianjin confronted when weighing Zeng's testimony against Mou's in November 1978, when they admitted that they could not "take sides in believing one over the other." Scholarship about the Cultural Revolution shows that many people, including elite officials, suffered persecution based on false accusations.[60] Many top cadres who enjoyed power and privilege before 1966 were brutalized and humbled during the Cultural Revolution.[61] The violence they suffered was terrible. If they survived, many would later benefit from a reversal of verdicts. Many returned to positions of authority in the 1970s, 1980s, and beyond. The stories of elites—first persecuted, then rehabilitated—dominate the narrative of how China recovered from the trauma of the Cultural Revolution and give the impression that most accusations were maliciously false. Many accusations were indeed false, but when examining such non-elites as Zeng and Mou, scholars should be open to the possibility that some complaints may not have been based on fabrications.

A separate body of scholarship focusing on a very different context—North America and Europe over the past three decades—suggests that false accusations of rape make up an exceedingly low proportion of the total number of rapes reported. In other words, false allegations of rape do exist but are rare.[62] This finding pushes me to believe that Zeng was telling the truth. Conventional wisdom about widespread false accusations during the Cultural Revolution pushes in the other direction.

Even if the standard narrative of the Cultural Revolution is correct that the event gave rise to many baseless allegations, historians would be unwise to ignore the everyday human reality of murder, rape, and other crimes that remained part of Chinese society during the Mao years. Some of these crimes went unreported or were covered up until the advent of a political movement that encouraged people to accuse others of wrongdoing.[63] It therefore makes sense to think of 1966 as a year that provided ample space for accusations, many of which were trumped up but some of which must have been factual.

As much as I want to believe Zeng, I can only reach the same conclusion as the investigators who examined the case. Like them, I cannot know who was telling the truth. For the historian, however, weighing Zeng's credibility against Mou's is less significant than analyzing the details of how the case unfolded. The file containing Mou Jingguan's materials reveals how competing appeals for justice functioned in practice at the grassroots and how the Chinese legal system evolved over time between 1966 and 1979; from encouraging accusations, detaining defendants without charges, and labeling and reporting, to dealing with waves of appeals and reinvestigations.

Above all, the file shows that the police officials investigating the case did their best with the information available to them in an uncertain and rapidly changing situation. This may sound like a superficial truism but it stands in stark contrast to scholarly accounts of criminal justice and policing in Mao's China that prioritize "politics" and downplay the unique process that led to many cases being handled outside a courtroom.[64] Even though the Tianjin public security cadres who handled Mou's case in the 1970s administered a politicized system meant to identify and isolate individuals harmful to society, they were responsive and careful. On multiple occasions, the authorities looked at the surrounding circumstances, admitted that they did not know for sure what had happened, and concluded that Mou was in the wrong for having sex with a teenager twenty years his junior while wearing his police uniform and carrying a gun. The punitive and rehabilitative tools that officials had access to—deportation and the bad element label—certainly reflected the spoken ("hand over to the poor and lower-middle peasants for supervision and reform") and unspoken (dump urban problems in the countryside) political norms of the time, but they did not preclude cautious investigative work. This grassroots police work calls into question stereotypes about the Cultural Revolution as an anarchical, hyperpoliticized hell. It also shows an example of a transitional justice effort that meticulously questioned and verified evidence rather than automatically overturning a verdict.

Notes

1. I have used pseudonyms to protect the privacy of the individuals mentioned in this case.
2. Zhongguo gongchandang Tianjin shi geming weiyuanhui renmin baoweibu san zu weiyuanhui, "Guanyu dui huaifenzi Mou Jingguan de fucha baogao" [Report about the Reinvestigation of Bad Element Mou Jingguan], July 25, 1972, *Mou Jingguan shensu cailiao* [Mou Jingguan's Appeal Materials, hereafter abbreviated as MJS].
3. Han Yanlong, ed., *Zhonghua renmin gongheguo fazhi tongshi* [Comprehensive History of the Legal System of the People's Republic of China], vol. 2 (Beijing: Zhonggong zhongyang dangxiao chubanshe, 1998), 636.
4. "Fixing policy" (*luoshi zhengce*) is a euphemism that, in the context of addressing and handling mistakes during and after the Cultural Revolution, refers to reinvestigating, rehabilitating, and offering restitution to officials who had been punished.
5. Tianjin shi gonganju, "Diaocha zhengming cailiao jieshaoxin" [Introduction Letter for Investigating Testimony Materials], November 11, 1978, MJS.
6. Material in this and the following two paragraphs is from X xian gonganju, "Chaolu Mou Jingguan anjuan bilu cailiao" [Copy of Recorded Material from Mou Jingguan's File], March 13, 1967, copied on October 10, 1975, MJS.
7. Human Rights Watch, *Improving Police Response to Sexual Assault*, January 2013, 20, https://web.archive.org/web/20180118173901/https://www.hrw.org/sites/default/files/reports/improvingSAInvest_0.pdf.
8. Questions from nine of Zeng's statements to police, dated October 10, 1966; November 8, 1966; March 13, 1966; August 2, 1967; January 28, 1969; February 24, 1969; April 8, 1969; October 9, 1969; May 16, 1972, copied in October 1975, MJS.

9   Human Rights Watch, *Improving*, 5.
10 Guo Wei, ed., *Xiuzhen xin liufa quanshu* [Comprehensive Pocket Volume of the Six Laws], vol. 1 (Shanghai: Huiwentang xinji shuju, 1947), 334. This law remains in effect in Taiwan today. See also Tao Baichuan, ed., *Zuixin liufa quanshu* [Latest Comprehensive Volume of the Six Laws] (Taibei: Sanmin shuju, 1986), 845.
11 Xinlu shuju bianjibu, ed., *Zhonghua minguo xingfa panjie shiyi quanshu* [Comprehensive Volume of Interpretations of the Republic of China's Criminal Code] (Taibei: Xinlu shuju, 1972), 625.
12 See, for example, Cao Shuji and Yang Bin, "Cadres, Grain, and Sexual Abuse in Wuwei County, Mao's China," *Journal of Women's History* 28, no. 2 (2016): 33–57.
13 Jerome Alan Cohen, *The Criminal Process in the People's Republic of China, 1949–1963: An Introduction* (Cambridge, MA: Harvard University Press, 1968), 22, 317.
14 *Jianguo yilai gongan gongzuo dashi yaolan, 1949 nian 10 yue–2000 nian* [General Survey of Important Events in Public Security Work since the Founding of the People's Republic, October 1949–2000] (Beijing: Qunzhong chubanshe, 2003), 279.
15 Ibid.
16 Ibid., 285.
17 Mou Jingguan, "Guanyu zhengzhi wenti de shensu" [Appeal about my Political Problem], December 5, 1973, 2, MJS.
18 Tianjin shi gonganju zhibaochu yundong lingdao xiaozu, "Guanyu dui Mou Jingguan wenti de fucha baogao" [Reinvestigation Report about Mou Jingguan's Problems], November 21, 1978, 1, MJS.
19 Zhonggong Tianjin shi Hongqi quwei wenhua geming bangongshi, "Gongan Hongqi fenju bufen ganjing dui qinshu bei chudong hou de fanying" [Reactions of Security Cadres and Police from the Hongqi PSB toward their Families being Shaken Up], *Tianjin shi Hongqi qu wenhua geming jianbao* [Hongqi District Cultural Revolution Bulletin], no. 12 (September 17, 1966): 2, Hexi District Archive (Tianjin), 1-6-33C.
20 Zhonggong Tianjin shi Hongqi quwei wenhua geming bangongshi, *Wenhua geming qingkuang ribao* [Cultural Revolution Situation Daily], no. 1 (September 6, 1966): 2, Hexi District Archive, 1-6-33C. Michael Schoenhals has shown that Red Guards flouted and excoriated earlier injunctions against writing about sexual behavior in big-character posters; Michael Schoenhals, "Sex in Big-Character Posters from China's Cultural Revolution: Gendering the Class Enemy," in *Gender Politics and Mass Dictatorship: Global Perspectives*, ed. Jie-Hyun Lim and Karen Petrone (New York: Palgrave Macmillan, 2010), 240.
21 Neil J. Diamant, *Revolutionizing the Family: Politics, Love, and Divorce in Urban and Rural China, 1949-1968* (Berkeley: University of California Press, 2000), 307.
22 The following three paragraphs are from *Chao Zeng Huizhen zhi fu XXX jianju Mou Jingguan de xin* [Copy of Zeng Huizhen's husband reporting on Mou Jingguan], September 24, 1966, hand copied in 1975, MJS.
23 Anita Chan, Richard Madsen, and Jonathan Unger, *Chen Village: Revolution to Globalization*, third ed. (Berkeley: University of California Press, 2009), 176–77, 181.
24 Cohen, *The Criminal Process*, 266–68, 347, 415–16.
25 Klaus Mühlhahn, *Criminal Justice in China: A History* (Cambridge, MA: Harvard University Press, 2009), 195.
26 Tianjin's PSB had been dissolved and put under military control earlier in the Cultural Revolution. "Zhi er chu chengqing daimao anjian pishibiao" [Second Security Section

Approval Form Petitioning for the Application of a Label], May 3, 1969, hand copied in 1975, MJS.
27 Mou Jingguan letter to Tianjin Municipal Office to Fix Policy, April 27, 1979, MJS.
28 Yang Kuisong, "How a 'Bad Element' Was Made: The Discovery, Accusation, and Punishment of Zang Qiren," in *Maoism at the Grassroots: Everyday Life in China's Era of High Socialism*, ed. Jeremy Brown and Matthew D. Johnson (Cambridge, MA: Harvard University Press, 2015), 20.
29 Mao Zedong, "Guanyu zhengque chuli renmin neibu maodun de wenti" [On the Correct Handling of Contradictions among the People], February 27, 1957, in *Mao Zedong xuanji* [Selected Works of Mao Zedong], vol. 5 (Beijing: Renmin chubanshe, 1977), 366, cited in Yang, "How a 'Bad Element' Was Made," 19. See also Yang Kuisong, *"Bianyuan ren" jishi: Jige "wenti" xiao renwu de beiju gushi* [People on the Margins: The Tragic Stories of Several "Problematic" Individuals] (Guangzhou: Guangdong renmin chubanshe, 2016).
30 "Zhongyang shiren xiaozu guanyu fangeming fenzi he qita huaifenzi de jieshi ji chuli de zhengce jiexian de zanxing guiding" [Central Ten-Person Small Group's Temporary Regulations on Policy Demarcations Explaining and Handling Counterrevolutionary Elements and Other Bad Elements], May 10, 1956.
31 Zhongguo renmin jiefangjun Tianjin gongan jiguan junguanhui Heping qu junguanzu, "Guanyu dingxin gongzuo de jidian zuofa" [A Few Methods for Labeling Work], *Jingyan jiaoliu cailiao* [Materials for the Exchange of Experiences] (Tianjin: Tianjin shi geming weiyuanhui renmin baoweibu zhengce xuexiban, December 1970), 6.
32 Zhongguo renmin jiefangjun Tianjin gongan jiguan junguanhui zhi er chu junguanzu, "Guanyu Mou Jingguan de chuli jueding" [Decision on Dealing with Mou Jingguan], August 10, 1969, hand copied in 1975, MJS.
33 Zhonggong Tianjin shi gonganju junguanhui linshi dangwei, "Guanyu kaichu huaifenzi Mou Jingguan dangji de jueding" [Decision on Expelling Bad Element Mou Jingguan from the Party], October 31, 1969; "Chaolu Mou Jingguan anjuan cailiao," hand copied in 1975, MJS.
34 For more on the deportation of political enemies from Tianjin, see Jeremy Brown, *City Versus Countryside in Mao's China: Negotiating the Divide* (New York: Cambridge University Press, 2012), 137–168.
35 Mou Jingguan, "Guanyu zhengzhi wenti de shensu" [Appeal about my Political Problems], December 5, 1973, MJS.
36 "Benren qianzi" [Signature of the Accused], March 13, 1970, appended to "Guanyu Mou Jingguan de chuli jueding," August 10, 1969, hand copied in 1975, MJS.
37 Mou Jingguan, "Wo de shensu" [My Appeal], April 26, 1979, 3–4, MJS.
38 Mou Jingguan letter to Tianjin Municipal Office to Fix Policy, April 27, 1979, MJS.
39 Zhongguo gongchandang Tianjin shi geming weiyuanhui renmin baoweibu san zu weiyuanhui, "Guanyu dui huaifenzi Mou Jingguan de fucha baogao," July 25, 1972.
40 Brown, *City Versus Countryside*, 152–53.
41 "Zhongyang pizhuan 'Di shiwu ci quanguo gongan huiyi jiyao' de tongzhi" [CCP Center Notice Approving and Circulating "Summary of the Fifteenth National Public Security Conference"], *Zhongfa* (1971) no. 20, March 2, 1971, https://web.archive.org/web/20180129215307/http://communistchinadoc.blogspot.com/2015/02/1971226.html.
42 Michel Bonnin, *The Lost Generation: The Rustication of China's Educated Youth (1968–1980)* (Hong Kong: Chinese University Press, 2013), 296.
43 "Zhonggong zhongyang zhuanfa guojia jiwei jundahui guanyu jinyibu zuohao zhishi qingnian xiaxiang gongzuo de baogao" [CCP Center Circulates the State Planning

Commission Military Representative Committee's Report on Improving Work on Educated Youth Sent to Villages], *Zhongfa* (1970) no. 26, May 12, 1970.

44 Zhonggong Tianjin shiwei, "Guanyu guanche Zhonggong Zhongyang [1973] 30 hao wenjian de yijian" [Opinion on Implementing Central Document Number 30 of 1973], August 25, 1973, in *Zhishi qingnian shangshan xiaxiang gongzuo wenjian xuanbian* [Collected Documents on Sent-down Youth Work], ed. Tianjin shi zhishi qingnian shangshan xiaxiang bangongshi (Tianjin, 1973), 102.

45 Ibid.

46 Tianjin shi gonganju zhibaochu zhengzhichu, "Laixin laifang chengpidan" [Submission and Approval Form for Letters and Visits], September 1 and 5, 1977, MJS.

47 Letter from Mou Jingguan to Wang Jianzhi, October 15, 1977; Wang's margin notes dated October 17, 1977, MJS.

48 For the story of a persistent petitioner trying to regain urban residence who received this label in 1963, see *City Versus Countryside in Mao's China*, 101.

49 Daniel Leese, "Revising Political Verdicts in Post-Mao China: The Case of Beijing's Fengtai District," in *Maoism at the Grassroots*, 102, 107.

50 Xinan zhengfa xueyuan xingfa jiaoyansuo, ed., *Yuan jia cuo an xuanbian* [Selection of Unjust, False, and Mistaken Cases] (1979), 96–97, trans. Menghan Yan, "Five Injustices – From Small-Character Posters to Wrongful Execution," *The Maoist Legacy*, January 21, 2016, https://web.archive.org/web/20180118174230/http://www.maoistlegacy.uni-freiburg.de/en/2016/01/21/five-injustices/.

51 Alexander Cook argues that the term "transitional justice" can be effectively applied to China after 1976. Alexander Cook, *The Cultural Revolution on Trial, Justice in the Post-Mao Transition* (New York: Cambridge University Press, 2016), 21–24.

52 Zhongyang pizhuan Zhonggong zuigao remin fayuan dangzu "Guanyu zhuajin fucha jiuzheng yuan, jia, cuo'an renzhen luoshi dang de zhengce de qingshi baogao" [CCP Center Approves and Circulates the Supreme People's Court Party Group's "Report Asking for Instructions about Firmly Grasping Reinvestigating and Correcting Unjust, False, and Mistaken Verdicts and Diligently Fixing Party Policies], *Zhongfa* (1978) no. 78, December 29, 1978, https://web.archive.org/web/20180129215602/http://www.reformdata.org/index.do?m=wap&a=show&catid=301&typeid=&id=16516.

53 Details in this and the following two paragraphs are from Tianjin shi gonganju zhibaochu yundong lingdao xiaozu, "Guanyu dui Mou Jingguan wenti de fucha baogao," November 21, 1978, MJS.

54 Letter from Mou Jingguan to leading comrades at the Tianjin Municipal Office to Fix Policy, April 27, 1979, MJS.

55 Mou Jingguan, "Wo de shensu," April 26, 1979, 2, MJS

56 Mou Jingguan, "Shensu cailiao" [Appeal Materials], April 12, 1979, MJS.

57 Zhongguo gongchandang Tianjin shi weiyuanhui zuzhibu luoshi ganbu zhengce bangongshi cover memo to PSB luoban, May 17, 1979, MJS.

58 Zhibaochu, "Dui Mou Jingguan de wenti fucha yijian" [Opinion on the Reinvestigation of Mou Jingguan's Problems], hand copied by Mou Jingguan on July 11, 1979, MJS.

59 Mou Jingguan, "Guanyu wo de wenti fucha yijian de yijian" [My Opinion on the Opinion on the Reinvestigation of my Problems], July 21, 1979, MJS.

60 The most prominent false allegation may have been about the "Counterrevolutionary May 16 Conspiracy," investigations of which targeted ten million people nationwide. The conspiracy was later determined to have never existed. Roderick MacFarquhar and

Michael Schoenhals, *Mao's Last Revolution* (Cambridge, MA: The Belknap Press of Harvard University Press, 2006), 221.

61 Liu Shaoqi and Deng Xiaoping were among the most prominent victims. The trial of the Gang of Four in 1980 largely focused on falsified charges by Jiang Qing, Kang Sheng, and others against other prominent Party leaders. See Cook, *Cultural Revolution on Trial*, 60.

62 Philip N.S. Rumney, "False Allegations of Rape," *Cambridge Law Journal* 65, no. 1 (March 2006): 128–158.

63 I argue that political movements during the Mao years brought to light previously concealed industrial accidents in Jeremy Brown, "When Things Go Wrong: Accidents and the Legacy of the Mao Era in Today's China," in *Restless China*, ed. Perry Link, Richard Madsen, and Paul G. Pickowicz (Lanham, MD: Rowman & Littlefield, 2013), 15.

64 Such accounts include Michael Dutton, *Policing Chinese Politics* (Durham, NC: Duke University Press, 2005), and Mülhahn, *Criminal Justice in China*, 175–283, which leaves the mistaken impression that labor camps dominated the criminal justice system under Mao.

Zhang Man
6 From Denial to Apology

Narrative Strategies of a "Perpetrator" after the Cultural Revolution

Xu Hexin, a rebel leader and by 1972 deputy director of Shanghai's Number Five Silk-Weaving Plant (*Shanghai diwu sizhichang*), would hardly have expected that he would be dismissed from this leading position and expelled from the CCP just a few years later. However, after the arrest of the alleged "Gang of Four" in October 1976, the political environment changed quickly. Reflecting on this period two years later, Xu stated that he had not been as happy about the arrest of the Gang as his factory colleagues. In fact, he had disagreed with it.[1] Soon, Xu faced interrogations in the factory, as an immediate result of his political actions during the Cultural Revolution. He was held responsible for one person's death and two suicide attempts. As a consequence, Xu was demoted in 1979 and excluded from the plant leadership in 1982. He thus lost everything he had gained as a result of the Cultural Revolution.

Xu's experience was not unique. The process of demoting or expelling "leftist" cadres like Xu was part of the official process of dealing with the legacies of the Cultural Revolution. In Party terms, it became known as "bringing order out of chaos" (*boluan fanzheng*). The practice of demoting and expelling former rebels was carried out through launching a series of related campaigns, most importantly the movement to Expose, Criticize, and Investigate (*jie pi cha yundong*), the Double-Blow movement (*shuangda yundong*),[2] the trials against the "counterrevolutionary cliques" of Lin Biao and Jiang Qing,[3] and the campaign to Cleanse the Three Types of People (*qingli san zhong ren*).[4]

Simultaneously, the Party indicated clearly that all resentment from cadres, Party members, and the masses should be directed at the Gang of Four and Lin Biao.[5] The term "Gang of Four" and all those associated with it came to symbolize "perpetrators" throughout the country. It thus also referred to those who could be listed as accomplices or alleged collaborators and came to be sanctioned or purged in the aftermath of the Cultural Revolution on these grounds. In Shanghai, 5,388 people were investigated for being involved in conspiratorial activities related to the Gang of Four, of whom 1,072 were punished.[6] Moreover, those who received the most severe punishments were "new cadres" (*xin ganbu*), who had been promoted during the Cultural Revolution, and many of whom had been former rebel leaders. For example, from October 1976 to late 1978, as many as 560 of these new cadres at the factory level[7] in Shanghai's textile sector were demoted, in comparison to just fifty "old cadres" (*lao ganbu*).[8] Likewise, in the Shanghai

Silk Industry Company, twelve old cadres were promoted and two were demoted, while none of the new cadres were promoted and twenty-seven were demoted.[9] In addition, those who were now said to have "rushed to join the Party" (*tuji rudang*) during the Cultural Revolution were also examined. As many as 390,000 Party members were investigated nationwide and over 30,000 of them were expelled.[10] The phrase *shuangtu* came to refer to those who had either risen as new cadres during the Cultural Revolution (*tuji tigan*) or who had "rushed to join" the CCP and were thus in need of renewed investigation.[11] Xu, who had been promoted to a cadre position and joined the CCP during the Cultural Revolution, belonged to this category of *shuangtu*.

In this paper, I rely on archival records to reconstruct the fate of a single worker rebel. The records were compiled by Shanghai's Number Five Silk-Weaving Plant.[12] The whole set of documents spans from 1969 to 1984 and contains forty-two volumes covering the history of the plant from the 1950s to the 1980s. This case study specifically relies on two volumes that center on the investigations into Xu's past behavior. The first volume is entitled "Investigation and Handling of the Errors Committed by Xu Hexin during the Cultural Revolution."[13] It includes fifty-seven documents, 141 pages in total. The documents can be categorized into four types: (1) copies of confessions from victims who participated in so-called "study classes" held at the factory under Xu's guidance in 1969 and 1970; (2) meeting minutes of the plant Party committee between October 1969 and September 1978; (3), testimonies from twenty-eight additional witnesses; (4) investigation reports compiled by the local Party committee. The reports document the procedure of investigating Xu's case and include Xu's "ideological understanding" (*sixiang renshi*). This volume is more or less complete in encompassing the narratives of all parties involved. The other volume, dating from 1984 onwards, bears the title "Investigation of the Situation Regarding the Errors Committed by Xu Hexin during the Cultural Revolution." According to its index, it should contain eighteen documents; however, seven documents are missing.[14] I also rely on information from other volumes in this set that contain several references to this case.

Based on these records and a close narrative analysis, I intend to show how the "confessional scripts" of a former rebel changed according to different political contexts after the Cultural Revolution. In her work on perpetrators' confessional performance, Leigh Payne coined the concept of "confessional scripts" to denote a reinvention of the past to fit a particular political moment or personal need.[15] Campaign targets in the PRC also used such confessional scripts as narrative strategies to retell the past. The most common type of confessional scripts of "perpetrators" were self-criticisms (*ziwo piping*) and self-examinations (*ziwo jiancha*). They were usually meant to show their transformation. Confessional scripts were thus never solely or even primarily employed to simply retell past events. They were narrative strategies that linked individual experience to general political discourses. In this chapter, I do not argue that Xu became sincerely remorseful and apologized for his former deeds as a result of the changes in his statements. Rather, by analyzing Xu's statements for their confessional scripts, including self-criticisms, self-statements, and self-understandings written in three different periods, I conclude that the changing political contexts significantly altered the way he narrated his past.

The chapter starts by tracing Xu's career during the Cultural Revolution and his subsequent downfall following its end. Then, by looking at three different later periods, when he had to narrate his previous actions to investigative bodies, the chapter demonstrates how Xu changed his narrative strategies each time in order to either defend, justify, or protect himself.

Promotion and Persecution: Xu's Fate during the Cultural Revolution

The role of worker rebels during the Cultural Revolution in Shanghai has been covered in meticulous detail by previous research. Elizabeth Perry and Li Xun have chronicled the rise and decline of these worker rebels in Shanghai, who came to garner nationwide attention in November 1966 by staging the Anting Incident.[16] Rebel workers in Shanghai intercepted a train en route to Beijing in order to complain about the Shanghai Municipal Committee. The Anting Incident led to the official acknowledgment of the first workers' organization, the Shanghai Workers' Revolutionary Rebel Headquarters, and accelerated the establishment of other workers' organizations all over the country. After the January Power Seizure in 1967, the lines of conflict changed.[17] The focus shifted from struggles between radical and conservative factions to frictions among the radicals.[18] The conflicts became increasingly fierce and eventually led to armed struggles, especially in the textile industry where several rebel leaders hailed from.

Shanghai's Number Five Silk-Weaving Plant was one of the factories that became heavily affected by the turmoil of the early period of the Cultural Revolution. The majority of its workers split into two competing rebel factions. One faction, called *Luzhi*, was led by Wang Dehao. It received support and was attached to the Luwan District Headquarters of the Red Guards formed on September 5, 1966. The other faction called itself *Luzong*. It was supported by the Luwan District Liaison Station of Shanghai Workers' Revolutionary Rebel Headquarters that was formed on November 15, 1966.[19]

There were two main reasons that caused the split in the plant. The first reason was related to pre-existing conflicts. Shanghai's Number Five Silk-Weaving Plant, located in Luwan District, had been established in 1965 by merging two factories: the Futian Silk Factory and the Jiuchang Silk Factory. It was supervised by the Shanghai Silk Industry Company. Once the Futian Silk Factory was closed down and the staff was transferred to the Jiuchang Silk Factory, conflicts arose between the two former factories.[20] According to statements made by the former secretary of the plant committee, Cai Guangjin, and the former vice director, there were at least three conflicts.[21] First, leaders in the Jiuchang Silk Factory were opposed to merging with Futian. The leadership in each factory held each other in contempt and both were reluctant to build the new factory together. Second, there were conflicts over personnel appointments. The cadres and workers of the Futian Silk Factory demanded that their former general secretary be made one of the leaders in the plant. The fact that the company ignored this demand caused discontent. Third, after the merging of the two factories in 1965, people from the two factories had quarrels with each other due to different work systems and work conditions in their respective factory.[22] In order to resolve this issue, in May 1966 a work team was sent by the company to the plant.[23] However, people from the former Jiuchang Silk Factory objected to the work team, as they believed that it was partial to the former staff of the Futian Silk Factory. After less than three months, some youths from Jiuchang drove the work team from the plant.[24] Soon thereafter, another work team arrived at the plant and also left. In October 1966, the Textile Industry Bureau had to send a third work team that was later considered by the rebels to have pursued a "bourgeois reactionary line."

The other reason why the plant split into two factions was related to so-called "political and historical issues" of plant Party secretary Cai Guangjin.[25] The first work team labeled Cai a capitalist-roader immediately after the Cultural Revolution started.[26] However, significant divergences existed in the plant: people of *Luzhi* defended and supported Cai, while people belonging to *Luzong* denounced Cai as a counterrevolutionary revisionist. This is also why the faction *Luzhi* was deemed "conservative" by *Luzong*. Two of Cai's major "issues" were subject to investigation: the first was related to allegations that his Party membership was fake and the other to suspicions that he had collaborated with spies (*tong te xianyi*).[27] Three rounds of investigations unfolded. The first one was conducted from late 1967 to early 1968 by the Rebel Team of Shanghai's Number Five Silk-Weaving Plant, which was mostly composed of rebels from *Luzong*.[28] This investigation suggested that Cai had not joined the Party and may have been a spy.[29] However, the other side remained unconvinced. Thus, the Shanghai Silk Industry Company, the direct superior of the plant, carried out a second investigation in June 1968. The company came to a different conclusion. The plant committee decided to reinvestigate again in March 1969, but the two factions were not able to reach an agreement on staffing the investigation team. In the end, the Shanghai Textile Bureau intervened and dispatched its own investigation team.³⁰ Cai was "liberated," which meant that the criticism ceased and he was reinstated as a cadre in the autumn of 1969.³¹

Promotion

Xu did not belong to either of the two factions. In December 1966, he established an organization called the People's Commune of the New Shanghai Number Five Silk-Weaving Plant. Xu was one of its leaders until February 1968.³² During the first half of 1967, Xu and his colleagues forced cadres in the plant to confess their problems by having "conversations." Xu was particularly active. As some cadres involved in these "conversations" later recalled, they had been ordered to write confessional materials.³³ Based on how they are described in the case files, these "conversations" resembled interrogations. Moreover, according to a work team in Shanghai's Number Five Silk-Weaving Plant, Xu was also involved in factional conflicts. As per one report, "[Xu] often used *Luzong* to suppress *Luzhi*. For example, when *Luzhi* was convening a session to criticize the Cultural Revolution Work Team, Xu, in the name of the commune, took over the meeting place and announced that *Luzhi* was a conservative faction and not qualified to hold criticism sessions. This seditious speech only aggravated conflicts between *Luzhi* and *Luzong*."³⁴

As far as the archival records reveal, Xu was not deeply involved in the factional activities during the early stages of the Cultural Revolution. When armed battles between *Luzhi* and *Luzong* occurred between late 1967 and early 1968, Xu's commune faction was not strong enough to carry out large-scale activities. On the contrary, during an armed battle in December 1967, Xu was asked by *Luzong* to mediate between the two factions because he commanded respect and had worked in the plant for over fifteen years.

In October 1967, the CCP Center called upon the different factions to unite in what came to be called "great revolutionary alliances" or "revolutionary three-in-one combinations." Members of the revolutionary masses, the military, and the revolutionary cadres were to jointly take over leadership positions. In this situation, Xu's faction formed an alliance with *Luzong* in February 1968. The two main factions, *Luzong* and *Luzhi*, did not form an alliance or establish a revolutionary committee until October 1968. At this point, Xu was included in the plant's revolutionary committee as a representative of the rebels and assumed the position as head of the plant's rebel team. It is noteworthy that neither the rebel leaders in *Luzhi* nor in *Luzong* were able to obtain the highest position within the revolutionary committee. Rather, the director of the revolutionary committee had been assigned to the plant by its superior in December 1968, when the fiercest factional struggles had already ended. It seems that Xu's limited involvement in factional battles contributed to his sudden rise to a leadership position.

In February 1972, Xu was promoted to deputy director of the revolutionary committee and chairman of the plant trade union. Three months later, he joined the CCP. Xu's career reached its peak. After successive promotions, Xu became a leader in the plant, but he had been deeply involved in the political persecution against those singled out during the previous political campaigns.

Persecution

As Andrew Walder has shown, the majority of victims during the Cultural Revolution suffered due to the actions of state actors, especially during the campaign to Cleanse the Class Ranks launched in 1968, and the One Strike, Three Antis campaign that started in 1970.[35] In Shanghai's Number Five Silk-Weaving Plant, a key component of both these campaigns were the study classes, which targeted people with alleged political, historical, or financial "issues." According to the archival documents, targeted participants of the study classes were forced to provide self-examinations, confess to "issues" or "crimes," accept criticism, and "expose" others. If they chose not to confess, they would be subjected to full-scale struggle sessions. Hence, forced confessions were sometimes induced by torture.[36] In both campaigns, Xu was assigned by the Party and revolutionary committees to carry out and take charge of study classes. In other words, he was carrying out the committees' orders, which would become a prominent argument in his later defense.

In the campaign to Cleanse the Class Ranks, which lasted from March 1968 to September 1970 at the plant, seventy-four people were forced to participate in study classes.[37] Xu's part in these classes included interrogating the targets, reproaching them, or commanding those who would not confess to kneel down on the floor. Having suffered from the psychological pressure and physical torture of these intensive interrogations, two people attempted suicide.

The first person to attempt suicide was Wang Bingkui, who was suspected of having been a member of the GMD and the Shanghai Workers' Welfare Committee, an organization set up to provide intelligence on labor movements in the Republican period.[38] He was taken into the study class on October 10, 1969. As Wang did not confess, his study class lasted longer than that of others. When recollecting the study class in 1980, Wang said:

> Xu criticized me by name every day and said that I was crafty and dishonest. Once he held a note and told me it was my son's words telling me to confess. If I would not confess, my family would disown me. And if I continued refusing to confess, I would be locked up alone.[39]

After being interrogated for more than a month, on November 24, 1969, Wang attempted suicide. He hit his head against a screw in the ground, but survived.

Sun Fengqu, the other person who attempted suicide, was also investigated in study classes on the suspicion of having been a member of the GMD and the Workers' Welfare Committee. On January 6, 1970, he escaped from his study class. He then bought a rope and tried to hang himself, but some workers on patrol found him and sent him to a local police station. He was taken back to the factory afterward and said, "[I can] answer the first questions, but not the rest of them. [I] do not know what to do. I am better off dead. Today I got a chance, so I escaped and tried to commit suicide."[40]

Meanwhile, in the One Strike, Three Antis campaign that began in March 1970, and aimed to solve economic issues and strike at counterrevolutionaries, forty-nine people in total were investigated in over twenty study classes held at the plant.[41] The Party and revolutionary committees decided to hold three types of study classes in October 1970. Eleven people were targeted in the first study class on grounds of so-called "political issues," including the vandalism of portraits of Party leaders. Nine other people attended study classes due to problems in the economic realm. Another twenty-nine people were sent to study classes because of "ideological issues," such as listening to enemy broadcasting stations, slandering, and sabotaging the sent-down movement.[42]

In these study classes, Chai Xinjin, a worker at the supply and marketing section of the plant, was one of the targets. Chai was brought into a study class because of alleged financial issues. In 1978, Xu gave the following reason for why Chai had been singled out:

> Chai was not the main target of the study class, but when Chai was in the study class, he was timid and fearful. Thus more emphasis was put on him because it was easier to make him confess and find more clues for class struggles in the supply and marketing section.[43]

Chai poisoned himself on the second day of the study class. A study class leader later recalled the interrogations of Chai: "The interrogations were intense and Chai could not answer the questions they asked him. Chai was very nervous and his hands trembled all the time."[44] Following his death, Chai's wife began to suffer from cranial nerve atrophy and died a year later.[45] Xu had been in charge of the study classes. Whether he had directly caused Chai's death or not, he was partly responsible for it. Causing Chai's death became one of the main accusations against Xu after the Cultural Revolution.

However, the above activities cannot fully explain Xu's demise after the Cultural Revolution because he was not the only one involved in persecution. His actions during the Criticize Lin Biao and Confucius campaign[46] in 1974 also significantly contributed to his downfall. He criticized old cadres by name in the meetings of the plant Party committee. For example, he denounced Chen Damei, the secretary of the plant at that time, for forcing everything to go through her for approval, and for having made new cadres mere figureheads. He was discontent about new cadres being suppressed in the name of eliminating factionalism and reshuffling leadership.[47] After the Cultural Revolution, Chen maintained leadership power as a deputy secretary of the plant Party committee, while Xu was subjected to criticism and investigation.

By tracing Xu's fate throughout the Cultural Revolution, it is clear that Xu seized the opportunity of rebellion to improve his political status from worker to cadre. After being included in the leadership, Xu played a leading role and took part in enacting a series of political campaigns. However, once the radical faction at the CCP Center lost its power and was criticized nationwide, it was unavoidable that Xu, having benefitted from the Cultural Revolution, would be deprived of his leading position and subjected to criticism and investigation. Based on a close reading of his "confessional scripts" at three separate stages, each occurring in a different political context, the following three sections of this chapter analyze the narrative strategies employed by Xu.

1978: Self-Criticism as Self-Defense

The arrest of the Gang of Four in October 1976 triggered a movement that criticized and investigated the Gang and its accomplices. Most of those who were singled out were former rebels. In each region, once alleged accomplices had been identified, all criticism was directed at them. Moreover, in order to criticize the Gang of Four, as well as to reorganize local leadership, a nationwide rectification movement was launched in 1977 and 1978.

Meanwhile, in June 1978, the Shanghai Textile Bureau reappointed the leadership and replaced both the secretary and director of the plant. Xu was able to keep his position as deputy director, but was dismissed from the post as director of the plant's trade union. Furthermore, he lost a significant amount of the power he once had as deputy director, as he was no longer in charge of production but was responsible for the staff's living situation.[48] He continually requested to be put in charge of production again, but to no avail.[49]

In this situation, Xu had to make self-criticisms about his work ethics and his adherence to the Gang of Four during the Cultural Revolution. According to the archival documents, Xu made at least two self-criticisms: on September 2 and 27, 1978. His self-criticisms were mainly concerned with three aspects of his behavior during the Cultural Revolution. First, he stated that he had criticized and struggled against old cadres in the plant at the early stages of the movement. Second, he had followed the Gang of Four and carried out their policies. He stated that he had been "deeply poisoned" by their ideology. Lastly, he criticized his bad actions and thoughts, including his individualistic thinking, arrogance, and loathing of his colleagues.

Xu put more emphasis on the latter two aspects while downplaying his role in the study classes. Xu's narrative in this period sounded more like self-defense than self-criticism:

> In the movement, I did not provoke factional struggles and was not involved in beating, smashing, and looting, even though I had factionalist thoughts. Regarding Cai [Guangjin], I neither imposed struggles on him nor offered him any protection. I only criticized him for the errors that he had made.[50]

Xu also tried to downplay the consequences of the study classes. He described all of his activities in just three sentences, amounting to approximately 300 Chinese characters or roughly ten percent of the entire self-criticism. In fact he did not mention the study classes, Chai's death, or Sun's and Wang's attempted suicides at all. Instead, in the self-criticism he argued that his actions had been in line with the campaign to Cleanse the Class Ranks, which had aimed to "sort out those people who had joined the Workers' Welfare Committee and the Nationalist Party." Also, he used "rather be on the Left than on the Right" (*ning zuo wu you*) to justify conducting "conveyor belt" interrogations—a method involving investigators energetically taking turns to constantly interrogate a person until they became exhausted, stressed, or even disoriented. Xu admitted he was responsible for these interrogations and had "damaged his comrades' enthusiasm."

Clearly, the reason that Xu did not mention anything about the study classes was not a lack of knowledge about their serious consequences. Before Xu's self-criticism, the plant had already investigated the death of Chai, and Xu had been questioned twice on August 14 and on December 24, 1978, respectively. In his August account, Xu explained that there were some people who had exposed Chai's historical and economic problems after the One Strike, Three Antis campaign began. Therefore, Chai was sent to the One Strike, Three Antis study class even though he was not the main target.[51] Moreover, Xu described the whole event as a third party and did not express any regrets or guilt over Chai's death. He did not articulate the reason for Chai's death and only cited the verdict of the revolutionary committee of Shanghai's Number Five Silk-Weaving Plant to indicate that the suicide was the result of Chai's own ignorance of policies. Xu even stated that Chai's wife and children were quite content with the arrangement made by the committee at that moment in time.[52] Xu was clearly trying to use the verdict of the plant committee to clear himself of the responsibility for Chai's death and thereby vindicate himself.

In his statement dated December 24, 1978, however, Xu's narrative changed slightly. For the first time, he blamed Chai's death on the influence of the Gang of Four and expressed his grief over Chai's death: "[I was] affected by the 'Gang of Four,' so [I] had a certain responsibility. [I] did not properly engage in ideological work and this caused Chai's death, which could have been avoided. I feel so sad. Therefore, [Chai] should be rehabilitated."[53] The change in Xu's narrative might have resulted from the acceleration of case reversals in connection to the Third Plenum of the Eleventh Central Committee, which reversed several prominent cases. One such example was the verdict on the so-called Tiananmen Incident of April 1976, when public mourning of Zhou Enlai had been used to voice grievances, including criticism against Jiang Qing and her allies. This caused many people, singled out as followers of the Gang of Four, to draw a clear line between themselves and the Gang. Although Xu acknowledged a certain amount of responsibility for Chai's death, he still stressed that enrolling Chai in the study class was discussed and decided on by the plant's Party committee. In other words, Xu was just following orders, meaning that he should not be held entirely responsible for Chai's death.

Xu's statements frequently use Party language to deny, excuse, or downplay his behavior. For example, he uses the term "conversation" to describe the action of criticizing old cadres; "rather be on the Left than on the Right" and "interrogation" to justify his behavior in the study classes; and "poisoned by the 'Gang of Four'" to excuse his errors. Xu's scripts can be compared to that of alleged perpetrators elsewhere. According to scholarship on comparable cases where policy has been used to address a traumatic past, under new regimes, perpetrators often evoke the vocabulary they were taught by the previous regime to deny, justify, excuse, or legitimate their past actions.[54] In this way, they downplay or cover up their own acts.

Xu's self-criticism and his statements on Chai's death show how he attempted to vindicate himself from atrocities committed during the Cultural Revolution and portray himself as a victim of the Gang of Four. Making self-criticisms was a coping strategy that downplayed his accountability and served to acquire a lenient verdict from the Party.[55] Xu refused to take responsibility for holding study classes or for Chai's death.

In January 1979, a new plant committee was elected. One month later, Xu was transferred to a workshop (*daizhi xiafang*), although he still nominally occupied the position of vice manager until 1982.⁵⁶ During the Cultural Revolution, many workers had been promoted to leading positions, but their salaries and *bianzhi* did not change. *Bianzhi* refers to the system of ascribing a total number of personnel in a unit or organization and the concomitant categorization of each position in urban factories as either "cadre" or "worker." During the Cultural Revolution, regardless of whether people were promoted or demoted, their *bianzhi* remained in the original category. Even after being promoted to the position of deputy director, Xu still had a worker's *bianzhi*. Therefore, if previous worker rebels in positions of leadership committed mistakes or were assigned back to the factories, it meant that they became ordinary workers once again.⁵⁷ Hence, Xu was effectively demoted to the position he had held prior to the Cultural Revolution and was marginalized in leadership circles. Even though he was discontent with this reassignment and argued with the Party committee, he was unable to reverse the decision. However, he was able to maintain his Party membership and did not receive any substantial punishment.

1980 to 1982: Denial and Self-Victimization

As the official process of dealing with the legacy of the Cultural Revolution unfolded, the exclusion of former rebels from Party and state leadership took full force. The CCP Center established the Leading Group to Investigate the "Two Cases" of Lin Biao and the Gang of Four in July 1979. Following the trials in November 1980, the process of larger-scale investigations and trials of their alleged followers accelerated at lower levels. Whereas in earlier years Xu simply made self-criticisms in the plant Party committee and revolutionary committee, his case was now formally investigated by the Shanghai Silk Industry Company's Party Committee, which supervised Shanghai's Number Five Silk-Weaving Plant. Xu's self-written narratives in this period show how he reacted to being identified as a "perpetrator" by former victims and the plant leadership.

The investigations of Xu began in early 1980. After over two years of investigations, on May 15, 1982, the Shanghai Silk Industry Company's Party Committee submitted a request to the Shanghai Textile Bureau asking for instructions on dealing with mistakes committed by Xu during the Cultural Revolution. The Shanghai Silk Industry Company Party Committee also clarified that Xu belonged to the category of *shuangtu*; he had rushed to join the Party and had been promoted to a leading position during the Cultural Revolution. He was classified as having committed serious mistakes in connection to the two suicide attempts and the death of Chai Xinjin. The company's Party committee suggested dismissing

Xu from his post of vice manager, demoting him to the workshop floor as an ordinary worker, and revoking his Party membership.

The report has three other documents attached. The first document is an "Investigation Report on Xu's Problems during the Cultural Revolution," which lists Xu's three main mistakes, including having been promoted to a cadre and recruited into the Party thanks to his activism during the Cultural Revolution; having obtained confessions through force when in charge of study classes; and having caused Chai's death and two attempted suicides. The report also states that Xu disagreed with his demotion to an ordinary workshop position. Additionally, the report finds Xu's attitude toward his mistakes committed during the Cultural Revolution unacceptable, despite the fact that he had apparently received "help and education" several times.[58] The second document illustrates Xu's mistakes. The last is Xu's "ideological understanding" of his actions during the Cultural Revolution.[59] Xu wrote this document on June 16, 1982, in which he explained, or rather defended, his actions. The document reveals the dominant script Xu was to employ toward the accusations leveled by the victims and the plant leadership.

Regarding the "conversations" with former cadres of the Futian Silk Factory in the early period of the Cultural Revolution, Xu claimed:

> It was very common to "talk" with cadres in the initial stages of the Cultural Revolution. If the Cultural Revolution had not been launched, we would not have "talked" with [these] cadres. Now I realize that it was not necessary at all. It should be up to the organization to talk with those cadres. I must learn from it.

These words show that Xu still considered his actions a result of the Cultural Revolution. "Not necessary" and "learn from it" indicate that Xu was disappointed and felt cheated. As for holding study classes, Xu says that "the study classes were arranged by the Party committee. The decision to put me in charge of the study classes was made by the Party committee through collective discussion."

In short, Xu deflected the blame onto the Party committee by stating that they—and not him—were ultimately responsible. It had been the committee's decision to put him in charge of the study classes. In his view, he should thus not be held responsible for the consequences of this decision.

Furthermore, in Xu's ideological understanding, he also stresses that Sun, who had attempted suicide in the study class, admitted to having been a member of the Shanghai Workers' Welfare Committee. In other words, Xu continued to insist that he had actually discovered a hidden enemy. The last part of Xu's ideological understanding states that he had exposed "contradictions" during the Criticize Lin Biao and Confucius campaign:

[The Party committee] demanded I give a speech. The plant Party committee decided to expose contradictions and the leadership had to take the lead. What I said was not meant to attack or slander anyone, but to put forward my own opinions based on the objective reality. Now when I think about it, I realize that I should not have attended the meeting. I was duped.

Xu also wrote a statement on June 13, 1982 that included more details on his activities during the Cultural Revolution. In this statement, he insisted that he had not obtained confessions by force. He wrote:

The Cultural Revolution was launched by Chairman Mao, and Mao guided the Cleansing of the Class Ranks. The Cleansing of the Class Ranks was deemed significant to safeguard the Central Committee, to safeguard Chairman Mao, and to defend the red regime. The organization gave me no choice but to hold [the study classes]... I was duped and misled.[60]

Xu used the authority of Mao Zedong to legitimate his actions during the Cultural Revolution. Moreover, he continually used words like "duped" to deflect responsibility. He also attached a note at the end of his statement to profess his loyalty to the Party. In this note he stated: "I think it over again and again and feel that I have not done anything for which I need to beg forgiveness from the people and the Party. I believe that eventually the organization will figure things out and make the right verdict."[61] In other words, Xu believed that he was treated wrongly and unjustly; that he too was a victim of the Cultural Revolution.

From Xu's words above, it is hard to assess whether his accounts related any "truths" about the past, or even whether or not this is how he truly felt about his past actions. Nevertheless, it is obvious from his statement that Xu sought to consistently emphasize the role that the plant Party committee had played during the Cultural Revolution. He was just someone who had followed orders from his superiors. It is worth noting that Xu's language is similar to a January 1979 central document dealing with the January Power Seizure of 1967. This central document declared that mass organizations and the masses themselves had been deceived by Lin Biao, Chen Boda, and the Gang of Four and were therefore not to be held responsible for their actions.[62] The document was distributed to the county level. Xu, a deputy manager, had most likely read it. He thus employed official language to prove his innocence and construct a self-narrative of victimhood. Moreover, when comparing his accounts with those of the victims, we can see how Xu tried to shift the blame away from himself and onto higher authorities.

According to the files, the investigation team at the Shanghai Silk Industry Company interviewed twenty-eight people and recorded thirty-two testimonies in this case (some people were interviewed on several occasions). Among these interviewees, thirteen can be seen as "victims," meaning that they or their family members had been sent to study classes. Ten people (including Xu), all of whom had been in charge of or conducted investigations for the study classes, can be considered "perpetrators." The roles of the remaining five are less clear-cut. Among the thirteen victims, twelve testified that they had experienced different kinds of physical abuse, such as "conveyor belt" interrogation. Among the five who can be classified as neither victims nor perpetrators, two reported similar experiences. In contrast, the ten "perpetrators" all announced that there had been no physical abuse in the study classes. It seems that both sides tried to utilize contemporary political language in their own favor. The "victims" accused the "perpetrators" of torture in order to, on the one hand, emphasize their suffering during the Cultural Revolution, and on the other hand, to have the "perpetrators" punished. The "perpetrators" denied the use of torture to avoid receiving harsher punishments.

Differences between testimonies also existed concerning specific details. In 1980, for example, the "victim" Wang described his suicide attempt in 1969 as follows:

> They interrogated me every day and [the interrogations] lasted until very late. As I was not allowed to sleep, I could not bear it anymore... I thought about suicide. I hit my head on a screw, but I was held back immediately by others. My head was bleeding. Xu said I could die if I wanted to, but [told me] not to threaten them (i.e., him and the others leading the class); if I died, [then] all members of my family would be [labelled as] counterrevolutionaries.[63]

Xu, in contrast, described the same event in 1982 as follows:

> Wang was a student of a GMD spy... He confessed that he used to be an executive member of the GMD's district subsection. He felt guilty. So he kneeled down on the ground and his head hit the floor in the name of asking Chairman Mao's pardon. His head swelled, but it was fine after applying mercurochrome. [His] head [was] not wounded or bleeding... My colleagues told me about this event because I was not there. Afterward, Wang expressed his gratitude and thanked us for helping him.[64]

Xu did not acknowledge that Wang had attempted suicide. Instead, he described the event in a way that portrayed Wang repenting to Chairman Mao for his past as a member of the GMD.

When comparing the above two narratives of the same event, it is evident that Xu's narrative strategy differed from those of the victims. First, he stressed that Wang knelt down and hit his head on the floor out of guilt, while Wang said that he was trying to commit suicide. Moreover, Xu said that Wang had not seriously hurt his head, while Wang stated that his head had cracked and was bleeding. Finally, Xu indicated that he was not on the scene when Wang tried to commit suicide, but in Wang's description Xu was not only there—he had even threatened Wang. These differences between two conflicting narratives about what had happened show how each party chose to describe the event in a way most conducive to his own benefit.

The committee's report tended to adopt the standpoint of the victims. For example, even though the connection between Wang's suicide attempt on November 24, 1969 and Xu's role in it was difficult to assess, the report did determine that Xu had attended Wang's interrogations and signed the interrogation report on November 17, 1969. This one detail gave the impression that Xu's participation in the interrogation led to Wang's suicide attempt. It is not difficult to understand why the Party committee was partial; they were simply following the "spirit" of the instructions from higher levels. During the search for "accomplices," to declare a former rebel leader innocent invited criticism.

Certainly, the committee did not believe everything that the witnesses reported. For example, Cai Guangjin, the former secretary of the plant Party committee, accused Xu of having slapped him once when Xu asked him to confess to having pursued a bourgeois reactionary line. The committee questioned the former members of the New Shanghai Number Five Silk-Weaving Plant People's Commune several times regarding this specific issue. It found that Cai was the only one who claimed that Xu had slapped him. The witnesses and other members of the commune all confirmed that no one had beaten Cai. Additionally, no one in the commune reported that people had been beaten during the Cultural Revolution. Xu had not beaten anyone; on the contrary, the investigation found that he had been slapped once but never slapped back. The committee concluded in its investigation report that there was no other evidence to corroborate Cai's accusation, which was deemed false.[65] Nevertheless, it is worth noting that all the witness names mentioned by Cai were also members of Xu's faction. Thus, there exists the possibility that these witnesses were unwilling to expose Xu for fear of potential future repercussions.

Through analyzing and comparing Xu's scripts with those of the victims, we can see how they changed between 1978 and 1982. In 1978 Xu made a self-criticism, in which he generally examined his work ethics and personal shortcomings, but failed to discuss the study classes or Chai's death. He utilized this self-criticism as a strategy to protect himself. Beginning in 1980, following the start of the investigations, Xu directly confronted the accusations coming from victims by applying the official language at the time to transfer responsibility to the Party committee.

1984: Remorse and Apologies

At the end of 1982, the CCP under Deng Xiaoping carried out a rectification movement to cleanse the "Three Types of People" from the Party, which included the reinvestigation of former rebels. Deng felt that the two previous screenings of the Gang's followers had not been thorough enough. For those who had committed "serious mistakes" (*yanzhong cuowu*), "due measures" would follow.⁶⁶ Nevertheless, the CCP Center also emphasized that those who had committed "general mistakes" (*yiban cuowu*) should be exonerated and the material related to these mistakes was to be removed from their dossiers.⁶⁷ In July 1984, the CCP Center further explained that people who had been affected by "leftist" ideology and had participated in "radical actions of general nature" (*yiban guoji xingwei*) were only guilty of "general mistakes" and should therefore be exempt from punishment. Those who were verified as having committed "general mistakes" were to be informed and the verdict was to be announced in the respective unit.⁶⁸ The units were instructed to no longer target these smalltime offenders for criticism or investigation. The policies for handling and punishing people who had committed "serious mistakes" were considerably harsher. Hence, Xu continued appealing to the plant committee and refused to accept the 1982 verdict that he had committed "serious mistakes." If Xu could manage to get his verdict revised, then he would have a greater chance of escaping punishment and improving his political situation.

Xu had continually appealed to the plant Party committee and the company since 1982. In 1984, the Shanghai Party Rectification Office and the Verifying "Three Types of People" Team released a notification stipulating that all content of written material and verdicts against cadres who had committed "serious mistakes," should be communicated to the offenders. This provided an opportunity for the accused to express disagreement to the new authorities. Furthermore, the notice stipulated that cadres' opinions on their verdicts be heard and in the event of any discrepancies with the verdicts, the facts were to be investigated again.⁶⁹ Xu wrote six documents in July to explain and express his opinions on Chai's death and the study classes.⁷⁰ In light of his clear disagreement with the earlier verdict and the petitions that followed, the Shanghai Number Five Silk-Weaving Plant Party Committee reviewed Xu's case between June and November 1984.

The review mainly focused on the death of Chai. A critical figure related to this issue was Song Xiaoming, one of Xu's colleagues who, according to the files, had conducted the study class on Chai and had been sent to pressure him into confessing on the day he committed suicide. In statements from witnesses, Song was considered instrumental in having caused Chai's suicide. He was questioned several times and continually insisted that he had just been following Xu's orders. Song emphasized that Xu was the one making decisions in the study classes.⁷¹ Song thus tried to shift the blame onto Xu; unsurprisingly, Xu refused to take the blame. Instead, Xu said that he had been trying to have Chai released from the study class. Xu also noted that the plant Party committee did not approve a release and preferred to have Song talk with Chai.⁷² After investigating this issue in 1984, the company committee noted in its report that it was Song's bad attitude that led to Chai's suicide. Nevertheless, Xu, as leader of the study class, still held a degree of responsibility for Chai's death.[73] The fact that no one wanted to accept responsibility for the tragedy shows a problematic aspect of state violence. The state attempted to shift the blame onto named individuals, who, in response, fended off accusations made by the state and tried to evade responsibility and transfer blame onto others, both superiors and subordinates.

In addition to the steps outlined above, the company committee also re-examined other parts of the 1982 investigation report. The review covered five aspects of the case. The first four parts dealt with the conclusions reached in 1982 with regard to Xu's mistakes. The review clarified that the first accusation of "having had conversations with old cadres" at the beginning of the Cultural Revolution, and the last, of criticizing the cadres during the Criticize Lin and Confucius campaign, were consistent with the facts. However, the review indicated that the second and third charge, namely, forcing confession through torture and causing one suicide and two attempted suicides, were incompatible with the facts. For example, the original report in 1982 stated that Xu was responsible for having "extorted confessions and believed in them" (*bi gong xin*). By contrast, the 1984 review stated that it was false to say that Xu had brought up the idea of holding a study class for Chai because the decision to hold such classes had in fact been made by the enlarged meeting of the plant revolutionary committee.[74]

The 1984 review carried out by the Shanghai Number Five Silk-Weaving Plant Party Committee reached a conclusion in Xu's case that was markedly different from the 1982 report. The final review report demonstrated that the original verdict on Xu had not clarified his main mistakes and responsibilities. In other words, Xu was not to be held completely accountable for the consequences of the study classes, although he did hold a certain responsibility (as a leader) for the interrogations and Chai's death. The report also stated that the conclusion of the previous report, which stated that Xu had an "awful" attitude and had failed to acknowledge his mistakes, was based on "flimsy foundation and could not be affirmed." The new report suggested that Xu had only committed "general mistakes" during the Cultural Revolution. It thus changed the original verdict to revoke Xu's Party membership into a decision to let him "remain and receive education within the Party" (*liudang jiaoyu*). Xu was thereby reinstated into the Party.

Another intriguing aspect of this review is the apparent change in Xu's attitude toward his past actions during the Cultural Revolution. Instead of denial, excuses, or shifting blame to others, he confessed, expressed remorse, and apologized for what had happened. Whereas in 1982 he emphasized that he had not agreed to hold study classes and blamed other leaders, he began his 1984 ideological understanding by admitting that he had committed mistakes (including holding study classes) in enacting the "leftist" line during the Cultural Revolution. Xu also adopted a very different narrative strategy when describing his actions during the study classes. For the first time, he acknowledged that the study classes had involved the forceful extraction of confessions. He also described Wang hitting his head on the ground as a suicide attempt instead of claiming that Wang was asking Chairman Mao for forgiveness for past mistakes. Moreover, Xu no longer stated that Wang and Sun had been grateful for the "help" received during the study classes. He also directly acknowledged his responsibility for Chai's death, saying,

> Although [Chai's family] received financial subsidies and one of his children was recalled to Shanghai from Xinjiang, it is still not enough to make up for the family's loss. There was no reason to enroll Chai in the study class. It was we who carried out the "leftist" line that killed people [like Chai]. I am really guilty.

Finally, Xu expressed remorse for Sun's and Wang's suicide attempts and Chai's death, stating: "There was also no reason to hold study classes against the 'old masters' (*lao shifu*) Sun Fengqu and Wang Bingkui [or] to investigate them. I owe Chai's family an apology, and owe Wang, Sun, and their families apologies." This is the only time that Xu used the title "master"—a sign of reverence and high esteem—when addressing Sun and Wang, and it was the first time he offered apologies to the victims. In 1982 Xu had tried to distance himself from his actions by claiming that it was the plant Party committee that had made all the decisions, but in 1984 he was suddenly willing to accept the blame, along with a mild form of punishment.

As for criticizing the old cadres in the early stage of the Cultural Revolution, Xu still insisted that he had been cheated. Only this time, it was the Gang of Four instead of the plant Party committee that had deceived him. This modification was adapted to reflect the broader discourse of criticism against the Gang of Four. What is noteworthy is that Xu offered his apologies to cadres he had criticized, especially to Chen, who still remained in the plant leadership since its rearrangement in 1979.[75] The possibility of Xu receiving a more lenient verdict was thus dependent on his expression of remorse to a cadre he had criticized during the Cultural Revolution but who had now been reinstated in the leadership. At the end of his self-understanding, Xu humbly added, "due to my poor writing skills, I am unable to express myself thoroughly. [I] beg the organization and comrades to forgive me and provide comments or criticism. I appreciate [your] help."

This was dramatically different from the last part of his 1982 statement, in which he had insisted that he had not done anything regrettable to the Party or the people. Although we cannot tell if this is how he sincerely felt in 1984, we do see that his narrative changed significantly following his loss of political power and stature. Xu was no longer officially a cadre and was thus not able to narrate himself or act like a cadre. This partly explains why Xu's narrative changed in 1984. He needed to show the Party his transformation from an "awful" attitude to a "good" one. Otherwise, it would have been impossible for him to shift responsibility for his past actions onto the Party organization or to ask for leniency.

Conclusion

Xu's self-criticism in 1978, his statements in 1982, and his ideological understanding in 1984 show how his account changed depending on the political context of the time. Xu's narrative shifted from self-defense, denial, and self-victimization to remorse and apology. At first, the authorities labeled him a perpetrator, but Xu claimed that he was duped and contended that he was also a victim. The later reviews of his case demonstrate the problems associated with the attempt to shift the responsibility for state violence from the regime to specific individuals who claimed to have acted on state orders. Meanwhile, at the beginning of the process of addressing the legacies of the Cultural Revolution, many people were still unsure of how to interpret these unexpected political changes. Cadres were now often attacked for the same behavior that had earlier been necessary to retain one's position and "This laid the ground for serious disenchantment on the part of basic-level officials who felt unjustly singled out for criticism when they had done their best to implement the onerous policies in force."[76] This partly explains why Xu refuted the accusations made against him. After a series of political movements, most former rebels were removed from leading positions. There was no longer an easy way for them to regain the political power they had lost. Xu therefore altered his previous statements to that of remorse in a last ditch effort to regain the Party's trust. In this way, the Party rectification movement in 1984 created an opportunity for Xu to appeal to the authorities and show his transformation. By expressing remorse and rephrasing his statements, he was successful in having his Party membership restored.

Apart from continuing to stress the importance of "cleansing" the leadership and the Party, in December 1982, the CCP Center also stipulated that those who had been removed from leadership positions during the "Three Types of People" campaign be given the chance to correct their errors, reform themselves, and begin anew.[77] Those whose conduct had been good (*biaoxian lianghao*) were given a second chance. The investigation report in 1984 pointed out that Xu's understanding of his errors had improved compared to before. His conduct had also been good since his demotion to his former position as a worker in 1982. It is understandable that, given the official policies, Xu not only acknowledged his errors, but also expressed deep regret and apologized to the victims and the plant leaders. He had to convince the authorities that he had become a new man, and that he was ready to devote himself to the modernization agenda of the reform period. For this reason, he employed the narrative strategy of expressing remorse while simultaneously admitting his past errors. Regardless of whether or not Xu had a real change of heart, he knew that such a statement was probably the only way he could have the earlier decision revised and try to improve his situation.

Notes

1   "Dangwei xiaozu xuexi taolun" [Study and Discussion of the Party Committee Small Group], September 2, 1978, Maoist Legacy Collection (MLC), Arch. 8, G102. Throughout this chapter, names have been changed to pseudonyms to protect the privacy of the individuals mentioned.
2   In some places, it was also called the One Criticize, Double Blow movement, which referred to criticizing the Gang of Four, while striking against sabotage by class enemies and against grafters, thieves, speculators, and profiteers.
3   *A Great Trial in Chinese History: The Trial of the Lin Biao and Jiang Qing Counter-Revolutionary Cliques, Nov. 1980 – Jan. 1981* (Beijing: New World Press, 1981); Alexander C. Cook, *The Cultural Revolution on Trial: Mao and the Gang of Four* (Cambridge: Cambridge University Press, 2016).
4   The "Three Types of People" referred to those who (1) had rebelled during the Cultural Revolution and gained power by following the Lin Biao and Jiang Qing Counterrevolutionary Cliques; (2) had been severely influenced by factionalist thinking; and (3) had indulged in beating, looting, and smashing. Zhonggong Zhongyang, *Guanyu qingli lingdao banzi san zhong ren wenti de tongzhi* [Notification on the Issue of Cleansing the "Three Types of People" from within the Leadership], December 30, 1982, in Zhongyang zuzhibu ganshenju, ed., *Ganshen gongzuo zhengce wenjian xuanbian* [Selection of Policy Documents on the Work of Cadres Examination], vol. 2 (Beijing: Dangjian duwu chubanshe, 1993), 1369–1374. Available in the Maoist Legacy Database (MLD), item no. 79. All in all, 480,000 people were investigated and 20,000 received prison sentences during the Expose, Criticize, and Investigate movement, the "Two Cases" trials, and the purge of people involved in "beating, smashing, and looting," see Gao Guangjing, "Qingli san zhong ren de qianqian houhou" [The Ins and Outs of Cleansing the Three Types of People], accessed January 18, 2018, http://www.hprc.org.cn/gsyj/yjjg/zggsyjxh_1/gsnhlw_1/d12jgsxslw/201310/t20131019_244911.html.
5   Several documents issued by the CCP Center and the Central Organization Department in 1978 and 1979 all stressed this point, see *Zhongfa* (1978) no. 48, *Zhongfa* (1978) no. 78, *Zhongfa* (1979) no. 59, *Zutongzi* (1978) no. 33, available in MLD, items no. 76, 73, 670, 392.
6   Shanghai tongzhi bianzuan weiyuanhui, ed., *Shanghai tongzhi* [Comprehensive Chronicle of Shanghai], vol. 1 (Shanghai: Shanghai shehui kexue chubanshe and Shanghai renmin chubanshe, 2005), 313.

7   This includes secretaries and directors of the Party committees, general Party branches, and Party branches.
8   According to a speech by Hu Yaobang, given to trainees in the second cadre training course of the Central Party School concerning cultivating young and middle-aged cadres, cadres between sixty and eighty years old were considered "old" cadres, those between forty and sixty years old as "middle-age," and those in their twenties to early forties as "young." *Dui zhong qing nian ganbu de yinqie xiwang* [Sincere Hope for the Middle-Aged and Young Cadres], July 20, 1982, in Tiedaobu zhengzhibu shen'gan bangongshi, ed., *Shen'gan gongzuo zhengce xuanbian* [Selection of Policies on the Work of Cadre Examination], vol. 4, 3–16. Available in MLD, item no. 1225.
9   Shanghai fangzhi gongyeju, *Fensui "sirenbang" qianhou changji ganbu bianhua qingkuang tongjibiao* [Statistical Table of Factory Level Cadre Changes around the Period of Smashing the Gang of Four], December 1978, Shanghai Municipal Archive (SMA), B134-3-1166.
10 Gao, *Qingli san zhong ren*.
11 Zhongyang zuzhibu, *Guanyu tuoshan chuli tuji fazhan dangyuan de yijian* [Suggestions on Properly Handling the Party Members Who Had Rushed to Join the Party], December 25, 1978, in Zhongyang zuzhibu ganshenju, *Ganshen gongzuo*, vol. 1, 1194–1197. Available in MLD, item no. 340.
12 These files were originally obtained by Daniel Leese and are now part of the Maoist Legacy Collection (MLC, Arch. 5–9). These personal dossiers are currently the only known available source for understanding individual cases in these Shanghai factories.
13 MLC, Arch. 8, G102.
14 The file itself does not appear to have been damaged or recompiled.
15 Leigh A. Payne, *Unsettling Accounts: Neither Truth nor Reconciliation in Confessions of State Violence* (Durham and London: Duke University Press, 2008), 19.
16 Elisabeth Perry and Li Xun, *Proletarian Power: Shanghai in the Cultural Revolution* (Boulder: Westview Press, 1997).
17 On the seizure of power in Shanghai, known as the January Storm or January Power Seizure, see Roderick MacFarquhar and Michael Schoenhals, *Mao's Last Revolution* (Cambridge: Belknap Press of Harvard University Press, 2009), 155.
18 Li Xun, *Geming zaofan niandai: Shanghai wenge yundong shigao* [An Era of Revolution and Rebellion: Draft History of the Cultural Revolution Movement in Shanghai], vol. 2 (Hong Kong: Oxford University Press, 2015), 853.
19 Shanghai shi Luwan quzhi bianzuan weiyuanhui, ed., *Luwan quzhi* [Luwan District Chronicle] (Shanghai: Shanghai shehui kexueyuan chubanshe, 1997), 48.
20 Zhu Zuxian, ed., *Shanghai sichou zhi* [Chronicle of Shanghai Silk] (Shanghai: Shanghai shehui kexueyuan chubanshe, 1998), 243.
21 *Cai Guangjin chenshu bilu* [Statements by Cai Guangjin], February 24, 1981, MLC, Arch. 8, G102; *Wo de jiefa* [My Exposure], February 24, 1967, MLC, Arch. 26, G109.
22 Ibid.
23 On work teams during the Cultural Revolution, see Huang Zheng, *Liu Shaoqi yuan'an shimo* [The Unjust Case of Liu Shaoqi: From Beginning to End] (Beijing: Zhongyang wenxian chubanshe, 1998), 10–19.
24 *Cai Guangjin chenshu bilu* [Statements by Cai Guangjin], August 15, 1980, MLC, Arch. 8, G102.
25 *Wo de jiancha jiaodai* [My Self-Examination and Confession], January 23, 1970, MLC, Arch. 5, G67.

26 *Cai Guangjin jiancha zhailu* [Excerpts from Cai Guangjin's Self-Examination], November 11, 1967, MLC, Arch. 6, G82, 2.
27 *Guanyu shenqing geli shencha Cai Guangjin de buchong baogao* [Supplementary Report on Applying for Isolating and Investigating Cai Guangjin], February 11, 1968, MLC, Arch. 6, G82, 5–6.
28 *Guanyu wuchang wudou de zhenxiang diaocha* [The Truth about the Armed Struggles in Shanghai's Number Five (Silk-Weaving) Plant], January 8, 1968, MLC, Arch. 7, G92, 1–4.
29 *Wo de jiancha jiaodai*, January 23, 1970.
30 Ibid.
31 *Cai Guangjin chenshu bilu*, August 15, 1980.
32 *Guanyu Xu Hexin tongzhi zai "wenhua dageming" zhong wenti de kaocha baogao* [Investigation Report on Comrade Xu Hexin's Issues during the "Cultural Revolution"], May 15, 1982, MLC, Arch. 8, G102.
33 *Guanyu wo bei jiuqu wuchang de qingkuang* [Situation Concerning My Being Seized by the Fifth Plant], June 3, 1982, MLC, Arch. 8, G102.
34 *Xu Hexin tongzhi qingkuang fanying* [A Report on Xu Hexin's Situation], December 12, 1978, MLC, Arch. 8, G102.
35 See Andrew Walder, "Rebellion and Repression in China, 1966–1971," *Social Science History* 38, no. 4 (Winter 2014): 513–539.
36 *Qingdui yundong he yida sanfan yundong gongzuo baogao* [Report on the Work of the Cleansing the (Class) Ranks Campaign and One Strike, Three Antis Campaign], 1970, MLC, Arch. 6, G87, 143.
37 Ibid, 138.
38 The Shanghai Workers' Welfare Committee was established by Lu Jingshi in June 1946. The primary purpose of this committee was to recruit GMD members in every factory, who would then provide intelligence on the labor movement to government authorities. See Elizabeth J. Perry, *Patrolling the Revolution: Worker Militias, Citizenship, and the Modern Chinese State* (Lanham: Rowman & Littlefield, 2007), 125–33.
39 *Zhai zi youguan Jingangcun xuexiban qingkuang Wang Bingkui de chenshu jielu* [An Excerpt of Wang Bingkui's Statements on the Situation Regarding the Jingangcun Study Classes], October 7, 1980, MLC, Arch. 8, G102.
40 *Sun Fengqu jiaodai bilu* [Records of Sun Fengqu's Confession], January 6, 1970, MLC, Arch. 8, G102.
41 *Qingdui yundong he yida sanfan yundong gongzuo baogao*, 138–39.
42 *Liangwei kuoda huiyi* [(Minutes of) Enlarged Meeting of Two Committees], October 5, 1970, MLC, Arch. 8, G102.
43 *Chenshu bilu (Zhai zi Shanghai diwu sizhichang Chai Xinjin de dang'an)* [Records (Excerpts from Chai Xinjin's File at Shanghai's Number Five Silk-Weaving Plant)], July 31, 1978, MLC, Arch. 8, G102.
44 Ibid.
45 *Xu de cuowu shishi* [Xu's Factual Mistakes], May 1982, MLC, Arch. 8, G102.
46 The Criticize Lin and Confucius campaign was launched in 1973 and transformed into a campaign to "criticize Confucianism, appraise Legalism" in 1974. But the ultimate target of the campaign was Zhou Enlai, see MacFarquhar and Schoenhals, *Mao's Last Revolution*, 366.
47 *Shanghai sichou gongye gongsi dangwei kuoda huiyi jilu* [Minutes of an Enlarged Meeting of the Shanghai Silk Industry Company's Party Committee], March 30, 1974, MLC, Arch. 8, G102.

48 Shanghai shi fangzhi gongyeju weiyuanhui, *Guanyu Shanghai diwu sizhichang lingdao banzi chongshi tiaozheng chongxin renming de pifu* [A Reply from the Shanghai Textile Industry Revolutionary Committee on Reinforcing, Adjusting, and Reassigning the Leadership of Shanghai's Number Five Silk-Weaving Plant], June 20, 1978, SMA, B134-3-1159-106.
49 *Dangwei xiaozu xuexi taolun*, September 2, 1978.
50 Ibid.
51 *Chenshu bilu (zhai zi Shanghai diwu sizhichang Chai Xinjin de dang'an)*, August 14, 1978.
52 According to one witness, after Chai died, the plant gave his family members financial support twice amounting to 350 yuan.
53 *Guanyu Chai Xinjin tongzhi siwang de qingkuang* [On the Situation of Comrade Chai Xinjin's Death], December 24, 1978, MLC, Arch. 8, G102.
54 Payne, *Unsettling Accounts*, 20.
55 See Philip E. Tetlock, Linda Skitka, and Richard Boettger, "Social and Cognitive Strategies for Coping with Accountability: Conformity, Complexity, and Bolstering," *Journal of Personality and Social Psychology* 57, no.4, (1989): 632–640.
56 After 1978, a factory manager responsibility system was reintroduced in factories in Shanghai. Names of positions changed accordingly.
57 Li, *Geming zaofan niandai* 1, 19–20.
58 *Guanyu Xu Hexin tongzhi zai wenhua da geming zhong suo fan cuowu de chuli qingshi baogao* [Request for Instruction on the Errors that Comrade Xu Hexin Committed during the Cultural Revolution], May 15, 1982, MLC, Arch. 8, G102.
59 *Wo de sixiang renshi* [My Ideological Understanding], June 16, 1982, MLC, Arch. 8, G102.
60 *Xu Hexin dui youguan wenge zhong qingdui ban xuexiban qingkuang huibao* [Report by Xu on the Situation of Study Classes in the Cleansing (Class) Ranks (Campaign) during the Cultural Revolution], June 13, 1982, MLC, Arch. 8, G102.
61 Ibid.
62 Zhonggong zhongyang, *Zhuanfa Shanghai shiwei guanyu jiejue suowei "yi yue geming" wenti de qingshi baogao de tongzhi* [Transmission of the CCP Shanghai Municipal Committee's Notice on How to Solve the Issue of the So-called "January Revolution"], January 4, 1979, in Zhongyang zuzhibu ganshenju, *Ganshen gongzuo* 1, 822–827, available in MLD, item no. 852.
63 *Zhai zi youguan jingangcun xuexiban qingkuang*, October 7, 1980.
64 *Xu Hexin youguan wenge zhong qingdui ban xuexiban*, June 13, 1982.
65 The files of Xu's case include these testimonies. They did say that beatings during conversations with cadres did not occur. See *Guanyu Xu Hexin da Cai Guangjin tongzhi yi erguang de qingkuang diaocha* [Investigations on the Issue of Xu Slapping Comrade Cai on the Face Once], April 8, 1981, MLC, Arch. 8, G102.
66 Hong Yung Lee, *From Revolutionary Cadres to Party Technocrats in Socialist China* (Berkeley: University of California Press, 1991), 245.
67 Zhonggong zhongyang, *Guanyu qingli lingdao banzi*.
68 Zhonggong zhongyang, *Guanyu qingli "san zhong ren" ruogan wenti de buchong tongzhi* [Supplementary Notice on Some Issues Related to Cleansing the "Three Types of People"], July 31, 1984, in *Ganshen gongzuo*, ed. Zhongyang zuzhibu ganshenju, 1375–1379. Available in MLD, item no. 74.

69 Zhonggong Shanghai diwu sizhichang weiyuanhui, *Guanyu Xu Hexin tongzhi zai wenge zhong de wenti chongxin hecha de diaocha baogao* [Investigation Report on Reexamining Comrade Xu Hexin's Issues during the Cultural Revolution], August 3, 1984, MLC, Arch. 8, G103.
70 Unfortunately, these documents are missing in the original file despite the titles being listed in the table of contents.
71 *Song Xiaoming guanyu Chai Xinjin tongzhi siwang qianhou de yixie huiyi* [Song Xiaoming's Recollection on the Situation of Comrade Chai Xinjin's Death], June 24, 1984, MLC, Arch. 8, G103.
72 *Wo de renshi* [My Understanding], October 30, 1984, MLC, Arch. 8, G103.
73 Zhonggong Shanghai shi sichou gongye gongsi weiyuanhui, *Guanyu gaibian Xu Hexin tongzhi wenge qijian cuowu xingzhi de hecha baogao* [Verification Report on Changing the Nature of Mistakes that Comrade Xu Committed during the Cultural Revolution], October 29, 1984, MLC, Arch. 8, G103.
74 Ibid.
75 Zhonggong Shanghai shi sichou gongye gongsi weiyuanhui, *Guanyu Shanghai diwu sizhichang dangweihui gaixuan hou zucheng renyuan de qingshi baogao* [Request for Instructions on the Reelected Members of Shanghai's Number Five Silk-Weaving Plant's Party Committee], January 3, 1979, SMA, B134-3-1396-20, 4.
76 Frederick C. Teiwes, *Politics and Purges in China: Rectification and the Decline of Party Norms, 1950–1965* (Armonk: M.E. Sharpe, 1979), 455.
77 Zhonggong zhongyang, *Guanyu qingli lingdao banzi*.

Song Guoqing
7 The Floating Fate of a Rebel Leader in Guangxi, 1966–1984

During the 1974 Criticize Lin Biao and Confucius campaign, Zhang Xiongfei, a former rebel from Guilin, informed a supporter of his activities: "Wei Guoqing is the leading figure in Guangxi, he should take primary responsibility for carrying out an incorrect line. We are now in the midst of a campaign [and] we must be clear about who the primary enemy that we should attack is."[1] When Zhang mobilized his supporters to attack Wei Guoqing, then first secretary of the Guangxi Party Committee, in February 1974, it had been six years since Guangxi's repression of rebel factions in 1968. This earlier oppression, conducted by the local leadership and the pro-Wei Guoqing faction known as the Guangxi United Command of Proletarian Revolutionaries, led to widespread killings throughout the region.[2] Many former rebels were subsequently held in custody before being assigned to new work units. As a rebel leader from the Guilin Song and Dance Troupe, Zhang's fate was similar. From September 1968 to June 1969, he was detained in the Huniushan Detention Center, fifteen kilometers west of Guilin. Between June 1969 and February 1973, he was held at the Guilin Normal School for Nationalities (*Guilin minzu shifan xuexiao*) and Aishantang Shelter, both in the city of Guilin, along with 200–300 other rebels and cadres who had supported them. In March 1973, Zhang was stripped of all positions in his former work unit, his Party membership and cadre status were revoked, and he became an ordinary worker in the Guilin Steel Works.[3]

In early 1974, the Criticize Lin and Confucius campaign swept through the entire country. From his case file, we can see that Zhang's experiences in this campaign undoubtedly played a very important role for his future career. During this period, Zhang resumed his former rebel standpoint from the early days of the Cultural Revolution by attacking Wei Guoqing and the local leadership. As a result, he was arrested in July 1975 and further criticized as a follower of the alleged Gang of Four in early 1977. Following a lengthy appeal process and significant political changes, which even included intervention from central departments, Zhang's verdict was reversed in January 1983. Zhang and his rebel supporters were rehabilitated by the Guangxi Party Committee in February 1984.

The author thanks Daniel Leese, Amanda Shuman, Man Zhang, and Puck Engman, who provided very helpful comments on earlier drafts.

https://doi.org/10.1515/9783110533651-008

By tracing Zhang's fate, this chapter reconstructs how and why the local leadership in Guilin labeled him a "counterrevolutionary" and later a follower of former political leaders of the Cultural Revolution, who by now had been officially designated as "perpetrators" (such as the Gang of Four), within a fluid political environment.[4] This historical case study specifically explores the interactions between (former) rebels, the local leadership, and the CCP Center at a time when the legal system and social policies in China were undergoing major reforms. I argue that the arrest and labeling of Zhang (in both 1968 and 1975) was consistently related to the local leadership's needs of suppressing potential political challenge and its interest in solely dominating the political landscape. This continued until the CCP Center decided in December 1978 to officially deal with "unjust, false, and mistaken cases" from the Cultural Revolution.[5]

Zhang's case also provides a window into understanding the complexity that existed as the Chinese leadership attempted to both distance itself from and deal with Maoist period injustices. In December 1978, at the Third Plenum of the Eleventh Central Committee, the CCP began to enact reform policies nationwide based on the concept of the Four Modernizations, which was reaffirmed by Deng Xiaoping. Current historical scholarship on case reversals in this period has focused on the rehabilitation (*pingfan*) of major persons at the central level,[6] as well as the procedures involved in the rehabilitation process itself.[7] However, as the case of Zhang Xiongfei reveals, this process varied according to specific circumstances and the political interests of the local leadership. This is evident, for example, by the fact that the timeline for dealing with his case did not reflect national policies. A close analysis of local level developments is therefore necessary.

This chapter begins with a discussion of Zhang's actions during the early Cultural Revolution between 1966 and 1968. It then concentrates on his activities during the Criticize Lin and Confucius campaign between 1974 and 1975, his arrest, sentencing, and related criticism between 1975 and 1977, before exploring the process of reversing his case after 1978. The chapter draws upon both official and unofficial material. Official sources include two sets of reference materials with criminal evidence issued by the Guangxi local leadership, various archival documents (including minutes from Guangxi Party Committee meetings that discussed Zhang's case, records of talks by the incumbent president of the Supreme People's Court concerning Zhang's case, and several relevant review and investigation reports) as well as newspaper articles. Unofficial material includes Zhang's unpublished memoir, manuscripts of appeals submitted both by him and his sister, and my own interviews with Zhang and several contemporary witnesses. The interviews revealed that the contention over how to interpret the experiences of the Cultural Revolution is still very much a matter of the present. This chapter, however, does not deal with the politics of memory in China, but reconstructs the fate of a local rebel leader in a turbulent political environment in order to gain a better understanding of how conflicts between the local leadership and the rebels developed, and how they came to be regulated through legal and administrative measures.

Rebelling: Becoming a Rebel Leader

Zhang had a very successful career prior to the Cultural Revolution. Although his father had worked under the famous Guangxi warlords Li Zongren and Bai Chongxi in the GMD era, his family apparently did not suffer political stigmatization.[8] He joined the PLA in 1949 as a member of the propaganda team at the age of twelve. In 1955, at eighteen, he became a member of the CCP. Ten years later, Zhang was demobilized and transferred to Guilin, where he assumed the position of captain of the opera ensemble and music conductor for the Guilin Municipal Song and Dance Troupe. This troupe, with fifty members in total, also included the famous film star Huang Wanqiu.[9] If not for the start of the Cultural Revolution, Zhang's career in entertainment would have probably continued.

In June 1966, heeding the call of Mao and the CCP Center, the first big-character poster entitled "Bombard the Guilin Municipal Party Committee" appeared on the campus of Guangxi Normal College (located in central Guilin), starting Guilin's Cultural Revolution.[10] At the time, Zhang and several of his colleagues were in suburban Guilin conducting the Four Cleanups campaign, and were asked by their unit leaders to return to defend the Guilin Party Committee. Initially, Zhang was a supporter of the local leadership and was criticized by the rebels in his work unit. Later, however, he joined the rebel faction in order to uphold Mao's theory of "continuing revolution under the dictatorship of the proletariat." In 2016, he explained his actions in the following way:

> At the beginning of the Cultural Revolution, I was [part of] the conservative faction, but through the influence of the [students] liaison teams [*chuanlian dui*] [from Beijing], my [political] standpoints became increasingly radical. Then I joined Guilin's rebel faction [called] "the Majority" because I agreed with a few new statements, such as "revolutionary rebellion," "opposing revisionism and preventing revisionism," and "striking down capitalist roaders,"[11] which were proposed by Chairman Mao and the CCP Center.

By emphasizing his ideological consent to Mao's call to rebel, Zhang might have overlooked the additional fact that, after the Guilin Party Committee withdrew its work teams from Guangxi Normal College and other schools in August 1966, most students and teachers in Guilin immediately answered the CCP Center's call and became rebels. Another former rebel observed that at that time, "Guilin's conservative organizations quickly collapsed ... it was a time when rebels felt proud and elated, Guilin's situation was truly excellent!"[12] In short, the change in Zhang's political viewpoints and affiliations was by no means extraordinary. The rebel group he joined even became literally known as *laoduo*—"the Majority."

In May 1967, various organizations supporting the former Guangxi leadership merged into a strong and united faction called the Guangxi United Command of Proletarian Revolutionaries (hereafter, United Command). United Command was supported by local PLA units and militia at all levels, and was loyal to Wei Guoqing—the former secretary of the Guangxi Party Committee, the chairman of Guangxi Zhuang Autonomous Region, and the political commissar of Guangxi Military District. The first clear-cut armed struggle recorded between United Command and the rebel faction opposing Wei Guoqing occurred in Guangxi's capital Nanning in June 1967.[13] At the time, the relationship between United Command and the rebel faction Majority in Guilin also increasingly deteriorated and more armed struggles took place. In the winter of 1967, Zhang Xiongfei, who up to that point had been a minor rebel chief for the Majority, joined an armed struggle with United Command for the first time. As he led a team to reinforce a rebel-controlled stronghold, he encountered and fought some United Command members. During this fight, he stabbed and wounded someone with a steel spear.[14]

Between May and August 1968, large-scale armed struggles between Majority and United Command took place.[15] In contrast to previous conflicts, Zhang and his team began using firearms to fight United Command. At the very beginning of this period, Zhang was appointed company commander, managing four platoons of infantry and forty other rebel combatants from the neighboring Lingui County. He was in charge of defending the "Western Front." Put simply, Zhang's task was to protect Ronghu Hotel and its surrounding strongholds from United Command attacks. The hotel and United Command forces were separated by a few bridges across a lake. In order to block United Command's tanks from crossing the bridges to attack the Majority, Zhang commanded the bombing of the bridges and the destruction of several public facilities.[16]

Having joined the armed struggles significantly changed Zhang's fate. When the conflicts ended in early August 1968, he was wounded and sent to the hospital. Following the subsequent defeat of Majority in early September, Zhang and other rebels were struggled against and then held in custody until February 1969. In March 1969, Zhang was labeled an active counterrevolutionary at an assembly convened by several departments, and later sent to a detention center. Decades later, Zhang recalled that he had been extremely depressed at this moment, because he had felt that his political life was over. In March 1973, Zhang was released, but also simultaneously stripped of both his Party membership and cadre status. According to Zhang, the reason was given as "having joined armed struggles and having committed the crime of bombarding bridges."[17]

Criticize Lin Biao and Confucius: A Second Cultural Revolution?

In early 1974, Mao Zedong launched the Criticize Lin Biao and Confucius campaign. Although the texts that accompanied the campaign were allegorical and indirect, in many regions, a wide array of local forces mobilized the obscure language of central directives to their advantage. In cities like Wuhan and Hangzhou, the campaign served as an offensive by resurgent rebels against civilian officials.[18] In Nanjing, however, civilian officials used the campaign to ensure their victory over military rivals.[19] The campaign in Guangxi shared characteristics with that in Wuhan and Hangzhou, but the political landscape was completely different. When the Guangxi Regional Revolutionary Committee was established at the end of August 1968, Wei Guoqing was appointed as its head. Army officers and members from United Command dominated the local leadership throughout the region. Nevertheless, Zhang and other former rebels, as well as the family members of victims killed during the earlier repression, sought to attack Wei Guoqing and the local leadership. They used two strategies to attack Wei and the leadership: the discourse of the Criticize Lin Biao and Confucius campaign and Wei's suppression of rivaling factions in 1968. Although the objective of the campaign was obscure, it did openly encourage criticism of leaders who allegedly opposed the aims of the Cultural Revolution and sought to restore the status quo ante.[20] The repression of rebel factions in 1968 had caused huge casualties, as exemplified in Guilin by the August 20 Action.

The August 20 Action was a continuation of a series of nationwide measures taken following a central document released on July 3, 1968, that contained a public notice targeting rebel factions.[21] Along with the subsequent July 23 Public Notice, this was an important document in curbing nationwide armed struggles.[22] After the July 3 Public Notice was issued, Guangxi local PLA units and United Command successively destroyed rebel faction strongholds. On the morning of August 20, 1968, more than 10,000 PLA soldiers and United Command militias from the twelve counties neighboring Guilin were "transformed" into Mao Zedong Thought Propaganda Teams and sent into areas previously controlled by the Majority.[23] Simultaneously, the Guilin Municipal Revolutionary Committee, Guilin Garrison Headquarters, and two other departments jointly released the "Notice Concerning Completely Implementing the July 3 Public Notice." The notice harshly denounced the Majority and the cadres that had persistently supported it. It also threatened to suppress those who dared to oppose the Mao Zedong Thought Propaganda Teams.[24] Subsequently, massive raids were conducted to locate and punish five groups of people: (1) big and small leaders of the Majority; (2) combatants (from the Majority); (3) cadres who had been in power but who had refused to support the United Command; (4) those classified as "landlords, rich peasants, counterrevolutionaries and bad elements," as well as "leftover GMD elements who had not been reformed completely;" and (5) supporters of the Majority who had bad family backgrounds or other historical problems.[25] As a result of these raids, 7,000 people were imprisoned.[26] Among the local leadership, nineteen of the twenty-two standing members from the Guilin Municipal Revolutionary Committee, who were also members of the Majority, were arrested.[27] Guilin's anti-Wei Guoqing Majority faction was thus organizationally dismantled. Numerous random killings by the local leadership occurred following these events. According to a later investigation, in Guilin and its neighboring Lingui County alone, 1,154 people were killed during the August 20 Action and its aftermath.[28]

Between April 1974 and early 1975, Zhang used big-character posters to openly criticize Wei Guoqing and the current leadership for their roles in the August 20 Action and its aftermath. Prior to openly criticizing Wei and the local leadership, because of his previous misfortunes, Zhang hesitated for a while. He recollected in March 2016:

> When beginning to write big-character posters, I was only planning to do some behind-the-scenes work. [The reason was that] prior to working at the Guilin Steel Works, I had been detained for four and a half years and stripped of my Party membership and official positions, [so I thought] it would be very dangerous for me to openly attack [*gongkai qu gan*].[29]

Although this may have truly been how he felt at the time, he changed his mind soon after when he heard that Hunan rebels had "turned the body" (*fanshen*).[30] Spurred by a situation favorable to the rebels, Zhang eventually wrote his own first big-character poster and displayed it a few days later.[31] In the poster he stated: "I am going to smash my own cooker, burn my own house in order to fight the executioner who slaughtered Guangxi's people." This was a clear accusation against Wei as having instrumentalized one of the massacres in Guangxi's Cultural Revolution. Zhang further argued that Wei should take the primary responsibility for the massacre. Zhang signed the poster with his real name.[32] In another poster, Zhang employed campaign language to label Wei Guoqing as "the general representative of the right-deviationist, regime-restoring force that reverses correct verdicts in order to suppress and destroy the newborn socialist force."[33] To substantiate his arguments, Zhang subsequently noted several killings conducted during the August 20 Action under the support and consent of the local leadership. He bluntly explained the strategy of his criticism against Wei Guoqing to one of his supporters: "Guangxi Regional Party Committee and Guilin Municipal Party Committee are definitely pursuing the revisionist line. We are going to remove Guilin Municipal Party Committee's lid by revealing [what happened during] the August 20 Action."[34]

After Zhang's first poster was made public, he became a symbol for a grassroots rights movement. Many family members of those killed as a result of the August 20 Action repression went to see Zhang and tell him their stories. Liu Chanrong was one of them. Her father, the former head of the People's Court of Lingui County, had been beaten to death at a struggle session because he supported the Majority. Her mother was killed during a summary execution with twenty other people. Her older brother, who had fled to the family hometown, was captured and killed by Lingui militia. She temporarily worked as a prostitute in order to feed her two younger brothers and sister.[35] For Liu and others, this was the first opportunity they had been given to share their stories. As one of them explained decades later, "only when the Zhang Xiongfei affair took place, could we [the family members of the dead] really get together. There was someone to help us speak, therefore we dared to speak [...] before that, we didn't dare speak out."[36] Zhang wrote a series of big-character posters based on materials about the killings he had received from family members of the dead. For example, the poster "Investigation Report on the Killing of Cadres and Masses through Lingui [County]'s Illegal Poor and Middle Peasants' Supreme Court" tells the story of how, with the support of the local militia, a so-called Poor and Middle Peasants' Supreme Court was established in Lingui County. This "court" was responsible for ordering the killing of 172 people in the aftermath of the August 20 Action, including the vice secretary of the Lingui Party Committee, the vice governor of Lingui, the president of the Lingui People's Court, and the vice president of the Lingui People's Procuratorate. Another poster, "A Bloody Murder in Guilin Gear Factory" described the execution of six cadres and workers at the factory in July 1968, while yet another told how a provincial cadre and his four family members were killed together by a United Command chief after the August 20 Action.[37] These accounts emphasized the brutality of the repression of the rebels and how victims and their family members were negatively affected. They also strongly condemned the killings and blamed the local leadership at various levels. Through the stories, Zhang attempted to connect Wei Guoqing and the local leadership he represented with the killings, repression, and persecution, in an effort to convince the CCP Center that Wei was responsible for the suppression of "revolutionary rebels" and needed to be purged.

In addition to using these big-character posters to criticize Wei and the local leadership, Zhang also established contacts with many former rebels from other places in Guangxi and other provinces during the Criticize Lin Biao and Confucius campaign. Through these contacts, Zhang tried to accomplish two things: to connect and prove that Wei was a follower of Lin Biao and thus should be purged, and to shore up more support from other rebels. On April 5, 1974, just a few days prior to his first big-character poster, Zhang implicitly labeled Wei Guoqing as a follower of Lin Biao. Commenting on a speech by Hunan rebel leader Tang Zhongfu, he stated that:

> From Tang's speech we can see that the Center is clear regarding the Guangxi issue. [Lin Biao's "supporters"] from Guizhou, Sichuan, Jiangxi, and Eastern China have [already] been struggled against [*jiu chulai*], that is why [Tang] brought up their names [in his speech]. Meanwhile Guangxi's XXX [referring to Wei Guoqing] has not been touched, so Tang didn't bring up his name...In the speeches made by Vice Chairman Wang [Hongwen] and comrade Mao Yuanxin, both stated that the problems of military force had been more severe than those of the local [leadership]. Meanwhile, the Center has struggled against the figures of the "Li Desheng and Tian Weixin black line;" is there no relation between Guangxi and this black line?[38]

From this we can see that although Zhang was very cautious and avoided using Wei's name, he considered Wei a follower of Lin. In a letter to Liuzhou rebels dated October 6, 1974, co-authored by Zhang and his supporters, Zhang explicitly pointed out that Wei Guoqing was a follower of Lin Biao:

> The crimes committed by [Wei and the local leadership] are too numerous to list here. Many facts prove that they are a capitalist restoration force of Liu Shaoqi and Lin Biao in Guangxi; they are time bombs buried in Guangxi by a counterrevolutionary black line. Comrades, although we live in Liuzhou and Guilin respectively, we have a common enemy; we are comrades-in-arms in the same trench. Through this contact, we hope that we can exchange information with each other, support each other, learn from each other, and turn two forces into one, making the revolutionary flames rage over the whole region.[39]

It is worth noting that in this letter from Zhang and his supporters he not only accused Wei Guoqing of being a follower of Lin Biao, but also eagerly desired to gain other rebels' support for reviving the long-repressed rebel force in Guangxi. Furthermore, in order to achieve this goal, Zhang sent his supporters to places where former rebel factions were very active during the Criticize Lin Biao and Confucius campaign—Guangzhou, Changsha, Wuhan, and even Beijing—in order to set up contact with local and central-level radical forces.[40] However, as previously mentioned, following the repression of 1968, Guangxi's political landscape was very different from other regions. Taking Guilin as an example, all members from the opposing factions had been prevented from partaking in the local leadership, while members from United Command and Wei's supporters had held onto key positions.[41] In short, factional politics continued to rule locally and Zhang was considered an opponent of the local leadership. It was impossible for Zhang to be rehabilitated like the Hunan rebels. Instead, his fate was sealed by his activities in the Criticize Lin Biao and Confucius campaign. In July 1975, with the approval of and instructions from the Guangxi Regional Party Committee, the Guilin Municipal Party Committee arrested Zhang.

Creating a "Gang of Four" Follower: Arrest, Sentencing, and Criticism

As Xu Lizhi argues in his chapter, the Cultural Revolution did not simply amount to a state of lawlessness. Rather, several key characteristics of the pre-Cultural Revolution legal system continued to exist. Xu even suggests that the Cultural Revolution strengthened some of its basic traits. As I will show below, the process of arresting, sentencing, and criticizing Zhang in the second half of the 1970s does indeed indicate that the legal procedures of the pre-Cultural Revolution had once again become the norm. However, at the same time, the local leadership's will and political intention played a crucial role in dealing with legal affairs. The establishment of a counterrevolutionary case against Zhang and the subsequent criticism of him were decided by Wei Guoqing. In addition, the case was motivated by the pro-Wei faction's political interest of dominating Guangxi's political landscape, while also serving as a tool for their pragmatic political need of following the national campaigns to criticize Deng Xiaoping and, later, the Gang of Four.

Arrest

When Zhang and his supporters started writing big-character posters, they attracted the attention of the local leadership. On April 20, 1974, the Guilin Revolutionary Committee held an emergency meeting to criticize what they described as distractions from the main purpose of the Criticize Lin Biao and Confucius campaign. The committee asked that all work units organize cadres and the masses to study the July 3 Public Notice.[42] In January 1975, the Guangxi Party Committee approved Guilin Party Committee's request to designate Zhang and his supporters' activities as counterrevolutionary. Soon thereafter, the Guangxi Party Committee took over direct management of the case. Wei Guoqing regarded it as a top priority in the ongoing class struggle in Guangxi and personally called for Zhang Xiongfei's arrest.[43] In April 1975, two supporters of Zhang were apprehended and by July 14, when Guilin police finally arrested him, twenty-three others had already been detained. Of those, nine were either former leaders of the Majority, or cadres who had been supporters of the Majority, but none had been linked to Zhang's activities. The arrest of these nine people indicates that Wei and the local leadership considered Zhang's activities as a continuation of the factional fights from the height of the Cultural Revolution, and they attempted to take this opportunity to suppress a potential challenge from the rival faction.

Sentencing

Zhang was not sentenced until one year later, at the height of the nationwide campaign to Criticize Deng Xiaoping and Beat Back the Right-Deviationist Wind to Reverse Correct Verdicts (hereafter, the Criticize Deng campaign). In June 1976, the Guangxi Department of Public Security and the Guangxi Higher People's Court co-organized three meetings to discuss the prison sentence of Zhang and his supporters. During and after these meetings, the standing committee of the Guangxi Party Committee held two separate meetings to discuss the issue. Following Wei Guoqing's transfer to Guangdong in October 1975, An Pingsheng, Wei's aide and first secretary of the Guangxi Party Committee, presided over these meetings. The first one confirmed the sentences against some of those who had been arrested. An Pingsheng proposed two further measures: to sentence eleven of them in two rounds, the first round including Zhang and three of his supporters; and to change one death sentence to a death sentence with reprieve.[44] The second meeting of the standing committee accepted both suggestions.[45] On July 26, Zhang Xiongfei and three others were struggled against in a public sentencing rally attended by the first secretary of the Guilin Party Committee. Zhang Xiongfei was declared an active counterrevolutionary and sentenced to life imprisonment.[46]

Criticism

Zhang was denounced publicly, with the charges against him varying according to the changes in the political environment and as a function of the wishes of the regional leadership. The various ways in which Zhang was criticized, in other words, reflected the instability and fluidity of the national political situation, but also served the local leadership's need to contribute to nationwide criticism campaigns. From July 1976 to March 1977, the Guangxi leadership organized two rounds of large-scale criticism. The initial round presented a set of evidence compiled by the Guilin Municipal Intermediate Court in July 1976. In these materials, Zhang and his supporters were linked to Deng Xiaoping and those deemed his followers:

> [T]his handful of counterrevolutionaries [Zhang and his supporters] is the social base and supportive force of Deng Xiaoping in restoring capitalist society. The objectives they attacked, their counterrevolutionary tricks and evil goals are the same as in the Tiananmen Square Counterrevolutionary Incident, [both are] produced by the class enemy.[47]

The second round of criticism followed the release of a second set of evidence and the appearance of a series of papers criticizing Zhang in the *Guangxi Daily* between January and March 1977. The evidence was provided by the Guilin Bureau of Public Security in January 1977, and then quickly transmitted by the Guangxi Party Committee throughout the region.⁴⁸ In this new set of material, although many charges from the first set remained, the framing of the evidence fundamentally changed. The former criticism of Zhang's relations with Deng completely disappeared. Now it was overwhelmingly related to the Gang of Four, the label given to the radical group around Jiang Qing following their arrest in October 1976 at the hands of Mao Zedong's successor Hua Guofeng. A national campaign to criticize the Gang of Four was launched in the weeks after the arrest. In this new material, Zhang and his supporters were subsequently linked to the purged radicals and designated as their followers. The preface of the material criticized the Gang of Four for having had close relations with Zhang, stating:

> Wang [Hongwen], Zhang [Chunqiao], Jiang [Qing], and Yao [Wenyuan], the Gang of Four Anti-Party Clique, has always deemed Guangxi's stability and unity and the great situation of production development as an obstacle to the usurpation of Party and state power […] A lot of hard evidence substantiates that the matters caused by Guilin's Gong XX [one of Zhang's supporters], Zhang Xiongfei, and several other counterrevolutionaries during the Criticize Lin Biao and Confucius campaign, was a severe incident of the Gang of Four intervening in Guangxi affairs, and a component part of their attempt at usurping Party and state power.⁴⁹

All the charges from the first set of criminal evidence were combined and merged into three sections in the second set, in an apparent attempt to imitate the look and feel of the evidence issued by the CCP Center in December 1976 on the Gang of Four. In the first and third sections, the charges were intentionally merged and connected to the criticism of the Gang of Four.⁵⁰ In section one, for example, the charges accuse Zhang Xiongfei and his supporters of having cooperated with the Gang of Four in usurping Party and state power, having frantically opposed and attacked the "great leader and teacher Chairman Mao," and having "shamelessly boosted and beautified the Wang-Zhang-Jiang-Yao Anti-Party Clique."⁵¹ In section three, the charges included accusations that Zhang and his supporters had colluded with the Gang of Four's followers in Hunan, delivered "black material," wrote "black letters," and brought "black lawsuits" to the Gang of Four.⁵²

Based on the tone of this material, the *Guangxi Daily* organized a series of articles criticizing Zhang and his supporters as followers of the Gang of Four. From January to March 1977, the newspaper included a regular column entitled "Study the documents and grasp the key link firmly, thoroughly expose and criticize 'the Gang of Four.'" Approximately twenty articles were published during this short time. The authors came from various work units, including a few large factories, government departments, military units from Guilin, and the newspaper itself. The content of these articles followed the charges made in the new set of material, and criticized Zhang's so-called relations with the Gang of Four from different angles. One article, entitled, "The iron verdict of August 20 cannot be reversed," came from Zhang's former work unit and criticized him and his supporters for having "relied on counterrevolutionary sensibilities"—referring to Zhang being acquainted with people who would be willing to participate in criticism of the Guangxi leadership—"to sense the evil wind from the Gang of Four's [plot] to plunge the whole country into chaos." It accused Zhang and his supporters of actively seeking contact with "the Gang of Four's black hands in other provinces" and "deliberately organizing a counterrevolutionary plot under the pretext of attacking the August 20 revolutionary measures."[53]

As the difference between the first and second set of material shows, the local leadership connected Zhang with ever-new charges dependent on the changes in the political climate, thus reassuring the continued rule of the pro-Wei faction within the leadership. By connecting Zhang with the current targets of national criticism, the local leadership distanced itself from potential criticism by the CCP Center, and managed to minimize or conceal their responsibility for involvement in the injustices and atrocities of the Cultural Revolution.

Reversal of Verdict: Appeal, Petition, and Review

In initiating reversals of unjust, false, and mistaken cases after the Third Plenary Session of the Eleventh Central Committee in December 1978, Guangxi was quite late compared to other provinces, given the comparative stability of its leadership following the repression of rivaling factions in 1968. Whereas most provinces and municipalities began the process of reversing cases now deemed unjust in 1979, it took several years before Guangxi followed suit. After Wei Guoqing was transferred to Guangdong in 1975—before taking over the General Political Department of the PLA, a post that he kept until his dismissal in 1982—his supporters continued to occupy local leadership positions at various levels until the CCP Center ordered the substitution of several senior cadres in the region in March 1983. Following this change in leadership, Guangxi's work of dealing with injustices from the Cultural Revolution finally began. Zhang's verdict was reversed on the eve of this event. A close look at the intricacies of his rehabilitation reveals the roles played by various parties in the process and can help us understand why the Guangxi leadership was so late in adopting the CCP Center's measures for case reversal.

Appeal

As Daniel Leese has noted, the possibility of filing appeals had been institutionalized at least since the demise of the military control committees in August 1972.[54] For Zhang and his family, appealing to people's courts and other political-legal departments at various levels was an important component of pursuing a revised verdict. From 1977 to January 1983, Zhang's family members appealed numerous times; his sister Zhang Wen alone filed over 200 appeals.[55] With the help of an acquaintance in Nanning, Zhang Wen submitted her first appeal as early as September 1976.[56] As time went on, she became skillful at writing appeals herself. However, before 1979, her appeals were largely ignored by the local leadership. Her appeals at this time reflect how skillfully petitioners would employ strategic communication and political language in this transitional period.

Zhang Wen's early appeals were based on charges found in the verdict against Zhang Xiongfei from July 1976. The verdict begins with the charge that Zhang is "extremely reactionary" and denounces his father as a GMD agent. Zhang is further found to have "maliciously slandered" Mao and Zhou Enlai as well as the July 3 Public Notice, and to have sought to reverse the just verdicts of the Cultural Revolution. Furthermore, it alleges that Zhang was trying to overturn the proletarian dictatorship and restore capitalism. It was on these grounds that Zhang had been sentenced to life imprisonment. The last part of this verdict states that Zhang has the right to appeal to the Guangxi Higher People's Court.[57]

In one of Zhang Wen's appeals, probably dated from the first half of 1979, she asserts that the Zhang Xiongfei case "is completely false and unjust!"[58] She requests that his case be given a re-trial as soon as possible and that the local leadership admit its error, acquit Zhang, and compensate the loss of wages that had been the result of years of persecution.[59] She continues by meticulously refuting the charges against her brother.

She rejects the use of their father's political problems against Zhang Xiongfei as a relic of the "bourgeois bloodline theory."[60] At the same time, she provides a list of historical facts to demonstrate that their father was in fact not a GMD agent, but rather a righteous CCP member.[61] Regarding the charge of "engaging in subversive activities without any restraint" during the Cultural Revolution, she justifies Zhang's bombing of a small bridge by claiming he did so in order to reduce unnecessary casualties. Furthermore, she stresses that all armed struggles should be attributed to Lin Biao and the Gang of Four.[62] As for the charges that her brother would have attacked the CCP Center and maliciously slandered Zhou Enlai as a "conservative," she argues these are simply "problems of ideological understanding" (*renshi wenti*). Concerning the charge of having attacked the July 3 Public Notice and its implementation through the August 20 Action, she defends Zhang's actions by claiming that they had not constituted an attack at all. In fact, he had put his life on the line to implement the notice's call to turn in weapons. Moreover, she asserts that her brother was correct to criticize the August 20 Action because of its "negative consequences"—the violent repression and killings.[63]

In short, Zhang Wen accepted some of the charges made in the verdict, but justified them in different ways, either according to the national political climate at the time or commonly held sentiments at the local level. In attributing her brother's attacks on central leaders to problems of ideological understanding, for example, she was most likely influenced by the policy of how to clearly distinguish between actual crimes and political errors.[64] Likewise, her attempts to exonerate her brother by blaming the Gang of Four and Lin Biao employed the vocabulary of contemporary propaganda, which designated them as the primary perpetrators responsible for the excesses of the Cultural Revolution.[65] Her criticism of the "bloodline theory" indicates that she had probably learned that the CCP Center had taken measures to remove similar class labels in January 1979.[66] Finally, she did not deny Zhang's attacks of the August 20 Action, but argued that he did so in order to call attention to its serious repercussions. In contrast to the other charges, which employed general references from the current political discourse, her justification here likely reflected a common feeling among many locals still distraught over the 1968 repression and spree of mass killings.

Petition

The historian Xiao Donglian has argued that, although policies related to reversing unjust, false, and mistaken cases were implemented after the Third Plenary Session of the Eleventh Central Committee in December 1978, most ordinary victims of Maoist period injustices still had to advocate their own cases by petitioning.[67] Zhang Wen and Li Heping, a supporter of Zhang Xiongfei who had also been detained in 1975 but was released in 1979, both took part in petitioning to reverse Zhang's verdict. Li spent most his time building contacts with personnel sent to Guangxi by the CCP Center, while Zhang Wen focused on petitioning the local leadership and central departments, as well as establishing contacts with several veteran cadres.

In late 1979, with the financial aid from Zhang's other supporters, Li traveled to Beijing. Li, with introduction letters from his well-connected uncle, was able to visit the Supreme People's Procuratorate and the Ministry of Public Security.[68] It seems that Li presented a convincing case and left a good impression during this brief visit, because both institutions asked him to submit a detailed report on Zhang's case. When he returned to Beijing in early 1980, he brought a set of materials compiled by Zhang's supporters called the "Report Concerning the Zhang Xiongfei Counterrevolutionary Clique Incident," which was then delivered to the Legislative Affairs Commission of the National People's Congress Standing Committee. The commission sent an investigation group to Guangxi in May 1980. This group, which consisted of personnel from the Supreme People's Procuratorate and the Ministry of Public Security, was led by the vice director of the Legislative Affairs Commission. During their investigation, Li was asked to cooperate in the investigation of Zhang's case. In April 1981, the CCP Center sent a Second Central Investigation Group (formally named the Central Commission for Discipline Inspection and Organization Department of the Central Committee Guangxi Investigation Group for Policy Fixing in Guangxi). A few members of this new group had also been part of the first investigation. Upon their arrival in Nanning, Li was once again asked to report on Zhang's case with the group.[69] It appears that Li's continued close contact with the Second Central Investigation Group pushed the Center to pay closer attention to and even directly influence Zhang's case, as will be discussed in the next section of the chapter.

Zhang Wen faced more difficulties in her petitioning efforts. Her experiences reflect both the inert and passive sides of the political-legal system as it began dealing with Maoist period injustices and the divergences that existed between the local leadership and the CCP Center on how to handle these. At the time, she was an ordinary worker without any financial support other than her own wages and her mother's.[70] Initially, she concentrated on writing appeals, but because others began petitioning in person in 1978, she decided to try this too. For the next five years she continued to petition her brother's case.[71] According to her recollections, her petitioning began with visits to departments in Guilin and Nanning, including the Guangxi Party Committee's Group for Petition Work, the Guangxi People's Procuratorate, the Guangxi Higher People's Court, and the Guangxi People's Government. In March 1983, she described these earlier attempts as a frustrating and unsuccessful experience:

> When I mentioned the Zhang Xiongfei case, they did not receive me, did not speak with me, only said that 'this case is not our business' or 'we don't handle this case.' Later, they would say, 'this case was handled by the Guangxi Party Committee and approved by Wei Guoqing, [so] we have no authority to administer this case'... I went to the Guilin Intermediate People's Court, [and] they said it was handled by the Guangxi Higher People's Court; when I went to the Guangxi Higher People's Court, they said it was handled by the Guangxi Party Committee. I went to the Guangxi Party Committee office [and] the guards did not even allow me to enter. They just passed the buck to one another [*laihui ti piqiu*] in this way. They did not accept this case, [and] if I kept talking, they would yell 'get out, get out!' [and] then [physically] push me out.[72]

In short, Zhang Wen visited all provincial political and legal departments, but her efforts were fruitless; she never received any satisfactory response concerning her brother's case. It was obvious that the local leadership had little interest or intention to review, let alone revise, the Zhang Xiongfei case. In 1979, she went on to take part in what would later become known as Beijing's "great petition tide."[73] She visited Beijing twice (see Figure 7.1) and considered these trips successful despite an intimidating experience in which four unidentified men in uniforms whipped her.[74] Reflecting on her visit to the Supreme People's Court, she said:

> Fan Ping's [a female worker for the Supreme People's Court in charge of criminal affairs from South and Central China] attitude was good, she said [to me]: "They handled [this case] wrongfully, we will correct it little by little. Don't be so sad, don't grieve, we will ask Guangxi to handle this case as soon as possible." She showed me so much sympathy.[75]

Zhang Wen's visit to Beijing had effect: a report produced in June 1979 mentioned her petitioning to the Supreme People's Court as the cause for review.[76] In mid-1979, Zhang Xiongfei's case was reviewed and, in November 1980, the verdict against him was changed for the first time.

Figure 7.1: Zhang Wen in Beijing to petition, April 1979. Courtesy of Zhang Xiongfei.

In addition to her official petitioning efforts, Zhang Wen also used private relations to petition. She had close contacts with at least three prominent veteran cadres in Guangxi. One of these was Xu Jiangping, Chen Yun's former secretary, who at the time was serving as vice secretary of the Guangxi Party Commission for Discipline Inspection. He helped Zhang's family members deliver appeal materials to Hu Qili, the person responsible for taking appeals at the CCP General Office. Another veteran, Wang Zujian, had been a colleague of Zhang's mother and was president of Guangxi Normal College at the time. Incidentally, Wang was the first to reveal acts of cannibalism that occurred in Guangxi during the Cultural Revolution.[77] In 1982, Wang delivered a letter written by Zhang Xiongfei, who was at this time still in prison, to Hu Yaobang.[78] The third veteran cadre was Zhang's uncle. Through him, Zhang Wen was able to contact Jiang Hua, then president of the Supreme People's Court. As a result, Jiang Hua closely examined the Zhang Xiongfei case during his inspection of Guangxi's court work in February 1982.

In sum, we can see through Zhang Wen and Li's petitioning activities how little the local administration contributed to the review of Zhang Xiongfei's case. In fact, they preferred to avoid the case altogether by stalling the process. By contrast, it was the central leadership and several veteran cadres who, through the active efforts of Zhang's family and supporters, made use of their personal connections to push for a reversal of the case.

Review and Rehabilitation

On December 29, 1978, a week after the end of the Third Plenum, the CCP Center circulated a report from the Supreme People's Court about accelerating the process to review and correct unjust, false, and mistaken cases.[79] In this context, faced both with direct pressure from the Supreme People's Court and Zhang Wen's constant petitioning, the Guilin Municipal Review Group made the decision to review the Zhang Xiongfei case in June 1979. The group's opinion was consistent with the first court verdict in reaffirming the charges against Zhang Xiongfei, but recommended removing certain phrases (e.g., "malicious slandering" and "reversing the verdict of the Cultural Revolution and settling the account of the Cultural Revolution").[80] It also suggested reconsidering the length of Zhang's prison sentence and removing the charges related to his father from any new verdict.[81]

It took nearly one and a half years before the court revised Zhang's verdict. On November 25, 1980, Guilin Intermediate People's Court issued a second verdict in the case. This new verdict revoked the original verdict and lowered Zhang's sentence from life imprisonment to twelve years. It also completely dropped the original charges of malicious slander of Mao and other central leaders, the Cultural

Revolution, as well as of the July 3 Public Notice and the August 20 Action.[82] Any mentioning of his father's background was also removed, as family background was no longer considered relevant to the matter. Zhang's main charge in the new verdict was that he had used the pretext of the Criticize Lin campaign to "incite chaos and seize power" (*luan zhong duoquan*) by setting up secret liaison points and an illegal Workers and Peasants Association for Executing and Upholding the New Constitution that "instigated the masses and manufactured public opinion" (*shandong qunzhong, zhizao yulun*).[83] Thus, although the court dropped some charges considered outdated in 1980, his activities in the Criticize Lin Biao and Confucius campaign were still deemed counterrevolutionary. When he received this verdict, Zhang immediately appealed to the Guangxi Higher People's Court, but his appeal was rejected in February 1981.

Zhang's sister and his supporters continued to petition. As a result of the active petitioning, the Zhang Xiongfei case already had the attention of the central departments when they took action to intervene directly by sending the investigation group. Upon the group's return to Beijing in July 1981, they immediately submitted a detailed "Investigation Report for Policy Fixing in Guangxi," which amounted to a comprehensive summary of Cultural Revolution injustices and atrocities in Guangxi. In one of the attachments to this report, the investigation group singled out Zhang's case as a typical counterrevolutionary case permeated by numerous problems. The attachment harshly criticized the local leadership:

> [T]his case was a completely unjust case. The reasons why it has not been corrected and reversed up to now lie in certain responsible members from provincial-level Party and administration organs deviating from Party principles and the people's interests, resisting the political line, guiding principles, and policies laid down since the Third Plenary Session, and [instead choosing to] serve their factional political interests.[84]

Despite such a severe tone, the local leadership in Guangxi largely ignored the report. In February 1982, the president of the Supreme People's Court, Jiang Hua, began his inspection of court work in Guangxi. He focused in particular on Zhang's case. Jiang saw it as typical of cases that needed to be reopened. At a conference with leaders from provincial political and legal departments, Jiang stated that courts should rigorously distinguish between committing errors and committing crimes. He explicitly pointed out that Zhang's problems during the Criticize Lin campaign were the result of factional activities (i.e., errors), and thus could not constitute counterrevolutionary crimes.[85] One week later, Guangxi Higher People's Court submitted a report to the Guangxi Party Committee suggesting that the second verdict against Zhang Xiongfei be revoked and that he be declared innocent. However, the Guangxi Party Committee refused to approve this report, choosing instead to temporarily defer any decision.[86] Nine months later, on November 29, 1982, the court submitted another report to the Party committee concerning Zhang's case. This time, however, the report criticized the first report's suggestion of pronouncing Zhang not guilty and instead advised simply revising Zhang's prison sentence down to eight years.[87] There was no response from the Party committee.

Instead, just a month and a half later, the Guangxi local leadership suddenly decided to reverse Zhang's case. On January 19, 1983, the Guangxi Higher People's Court acquitted Zhang and he was released from prison.[88] In March, the Guilin Party Committee rehabilitated him.[89] This seemingly dramatic about-turn was in all likelihood the result of a major political change that had just taken place in Guangxi. On December 17, 1982, under pressure from the CCP Center and victims of the Cultural Revolution, the Guangxi Party Committee submitted a report to the CCP Center claiming that it would thoroughly deal with past injustices. The CCP Center quickly commented and approved this report on January 2, 1983.[90] In March, the CCP Center adjusted the leadership of the Guangxi Party Committee by transferring some of its members to other provinces or forcing them into early retirement. The reversal of Zhang's verdict shows how, despite the decisions made at the Third Plenum, decisions on individual cases were contingent on the attitude of the local leadership. In places like Guangxi, it was impossible to move forward on case reversals before there had been a change of leadership and policy at the local level.

In February 1984, the Guangxi Party Committee announced that the previous designation of Zhang's activities during the Criticize Lin and Confucius campaign as counterrevolutionary and the criticism of him were wrong. It decided to rehabilitate all of those who had been implicated in Zhang's case. Zhang's case was thereby officially settled.[91]

Thirty years later, however, Zhang continues to complain that he was cheated in terms of his meager compensation and low rank. When Zhang describes his release from prison in February 1983, he narrates himself as a triumphant hero by proudly pointing to the lively parade held for him by his supporters (see Figure 7.2). He marched at the front of this parade holding a placard with the slogans, "Wei Guoqing owes much blood debt" and "Resolutely reverse all unjust cases that occurred during Guangxi's ten years of Cultural Revolution."[92] In fact, regardless of the time period he is describing, Zhang portrays himself in heroic terms. In describing his July 1975 arrest, for example, he made sure to tell the author that he used Fidel Castro's motto against the police: "Remember my words, history will absolve me!"[93] Nevertheless, he admits that he never knew how hard it would be to obtain a reversal of his case, nor had he predicted that his rebel stigma would continue to prevent his chances of promotion. In the 1980s and 1990s, he continued to work as a cadre of the lowest rank in the Guilin Song and Dance Troupe. Today he lives in retirement in Guilin with his family. Although his

7 The Floating Fate of a Rebel Leader in Guangxi, 1966–1984 — 193

Figure 7.2: Zhang Xiongfei and his supporters parading on the street in Guilin, February 1983. The man in the middle holding a placard is Zhang Xiongfei. Courtesy of Zhang Xiongfei.

online blog has been blocked for a several years, he still seeks to tell his story of having fought Wei Guoqing.[94]

Conclusion

This chapter has traced Zhang Xiongfei's fate from the beginning of the Cultural Revolution until 1984. Over the course of these eighteen years, Zhang rebelled, was detained, released, imprisoned, and rehabilitated. As an individual with a strong sense of character, Zhang wanted to control his own fate—that is, his political status and trajectory—but was ultimately unable to do so. Instead, his efforts to change his fate were constrained by the political environment and it was the local administration that had the power to determine his future. Zhang's participation in the call to rebel and oppose Wei Guoqing in the early Cultural Revolution resulted in his first arrest. When he used the campaign to Criticize Lin and Confucius to publicly reveal and denounce widespread killings, holding Wei Guoqing responsible, he was once again imprisoned. In the aftermath of the Cultural

Revolution, the local leadership still tightly controlled Zhang's fate in spite of his and his family members' constant appeals. Not until eight years later, following a change of the political environment, was he acquitted and fully rehabilitated. From the perspective of the Guangxi leadership, the Zhang Xiongfei case became a valuable political prop that could be used to denounce its opponents. As this chapter has shown, the fluid labels used to describe Zhang's crimes shifted over the course of a few months as allegations that he was a follower of Deng Xiaoping turned into charges of supporting the Gang of Four. The swift change in labeling reflected the instability and fluidity of the political situation in the late stages of the Cultural Revolution and its immediate aftermath.

Zhang's case also sheds some light on the process of dealing with Maoist era injustices and atrocities in early reform era China. The Chinese leadership is unique both in having distanced itself from the past injustices and having re-affirmed the authority of the Party through selected measures. Its efforts to "bring order out of chaos" (*boluan fanzheng*) included putting the Gang of Four and their followers on trial, providing (limited) compensation to victims, and reversing vast numbers of "unjust, false, and mistaken" cases. However, the grand narrative fails to address how the local context was affected as the CCP began dealing with the past injustices committed under its rule. As this chapter shows, the reversal of Zhang Xiongfei's case was not immediate due to the local leadership's resistance to the Center's reconciliatory policies. Rather, it entailed years of fighting with the system and outmaneuvering the local leadership's constant obstructions.[95] Furthermore, in Zhang's case, the central leadership and departments, along with Zhang and his family, were actively working to have his case revised, notwithstanding the obstacles resulting from ongoing factional rivalries. Despite the policies to end the Cultural Revolution, the divergence between the two rivaling factions in Guangxi has continued right through to the present. The possibility of reconciliation between them remains difficult.

Notes

1   Guilin shi gonganju, "Guilin jige fangeming fenzi de zuizheng ziliao" [Reference Materials with Criminal Evidence on Several Counterrevolutionaries from Guilin], January 1977, 72. Courtesy of Zhang Xiongfei.
2   Yang Su, *Collective Killings in Rural China during the Cultural Revolution* (New York: Cambridge University Press, 2011). Yan Fei, "Zhengzhi yundong zhong de jiti baoli: 'Fei zhengchang siwang' zai huigu" [Collective Violence within Political Movements: Unnatural Deaths during the Cultural Revolution (1966–1976)], *Er shi yi shiji*, no. 155 (June 2016): 61–66. Song Guoqing and Dong Guoqiang, "Guangxi wenge fei zhengchang siwang

yanjiu" [A Research on the Unnatural Deaths in Guangxi during the Cultural Revolution], *Lingdao zhe*, no. 68 (February 2016): 154–62.
3   Zhang Xiongfei, "Wo yijiuliuba nian zhi yijiuqisi nian de dazhi jingli" [My General Experiences from 1968 to 1974], unpublished manuscript, 2016. Courtesy of Zhang Xiongfei.
4   See Alexander C. Cook, *The Cultural Revolution on Trial: Mao and the Gang of Four* (London: Cambridge University Press, 2016).
5   Zhonggong zhongyang, "Zhongyang pizhuan Zhonggong zui gao renmin fayuan dangzu, 'Guanyu zhuajin fucha jiuzheng yuan, jia, cuo an renzhen luoshi dang de zhengce de qingshi baogao'" [CCP Center Comments and Circulates the Supreme People's Court Party Group's "Request for Instructions Regarding the Urgent Review and Correction of Unjust, False, and Mistaken Cases and the Conscientious Fixing of Party Policies"], *Zhongfa* (1978) no. 78, December 29, 1978, in *Ganshen gongzuo zhengce wenjian xuanbian* [Selection of Policy Documents on the Work of Cadre Investigation], ed. Zhonggong zhongyang zuzhibu ganshenju, vol. 1 (Beijing: Dangjian duwu chubanshe, 1993), 799–804. Text available in the Maoist Legacy Database (MLD), item no. 73.
6   See Pamela Lubell, *The Chinese Communist Party and the Cultural Revolution: The Case of the Sixty-One Renegades* (New York: Palgrave Macmillan, 2002) and Dai Huang, *Hu Yaobang yu pingfan yuan jia cuo an* [Hu Yaobang and the Reversal of Unjust, False, and Mistaken Cases] (Beijing: Zhongguo gongren chubanshe, 2004).
7   Susan Trevaskes, "People's Justice and Injustice: Courts and the Redressing of Cultural Revolution Cases," *China Information* 16, no. 2 (2002): 1–26 and Daniel Leese, "Revising Political Verdicts in Post-Mao China: The Case of Beijing's Fengtai District," in *Maoism at the Grassroots: Everyday Life in China's Era of High Socialism*, ed. Jeremy Brown and Matthew D. Johnson (Cambridge, MA: Harvard University Press, 2015), 102–28.
8   See Wang Yuhua, "Wang Yuhua zizhuan" [Wang Yuhua's Autobiography], 1968. Courtesy of Zhang Xiongfei. Wang was Zhang's mother; she joined the Party during the "suppression of bandits." She was later named head of the Women's Federation in Liucheng County, Guangxi.
9   Huang Wanqiu played the leading role in the eponymous feature film *Liu San Jie* (Third Sister Liu) in 1960, after which he became well known throughout the country.
10 Guangxi wenge dashi nianbiao bianxie xiaozu, ed., *Guangxi wenge dashi nianbiao* [Chronological Record of Major Events in the Cultural Revolution in Guangxi] (Nanning: Guangxi renmin chubanshe, 1990), 2.
11 Interview with Zhang Xiongfei, 2016.
12 Xiao Ming, "Wo zai Guilin dang laoduo" [I was a member of *Laoduo* in Guilin], *Zuotian*, no. 33 (April 30, 2014): 3–27.
13 Guangxi wenge dashi nianbiao bianxie xiaozu, *Guangxi wenge*, 38.
14 Zhang Xiongfei, "Wenhua da geming zhong de qushi" [Stories from the Cultural Revolution], unpublished manuscript, 2005. Courtesy of Zhang Xiongfei.
15 Song Yongyi, ed., *Secret Archives about the Cultural Revolution in Guangxi, Classified Documents*, vol. 21 (New York: Guoshi chubanshe, 2016), 146–55.
16 See Zhang Xiongfei, "Yuzhong shangsu zhuang" [Appeals from Prison], December 9, 1980 and Guilin shi fucha xiaozu, "Guanyu Zhang Xiongfei xianxing fangeming an de fucha baogao" [Review Report concerning the Active Counterrevolutionary Case of Zhang Xiongfei], June 27, 1979. Courtesy of Zhang Xiongfei.
17 Zhang, "Wo yijiuliuba nian."

18. Wang Shaoguang, *Failure of Charisma: The Cultural Revolution in Wuhan* (Oxford: Oxford University Press, 1995), 228–51. Keith Forster, *Rebellion and Factionalism in a Chinese Province: Zhejiang, 1966–1976* (London: Routledge, 1990), 131–76.
19. Dong Guoqiang and Andrew G. Walder, "Nanjing's 'Second Cultural Revolution' of 1974," *The China Quarterly*, vol. 212 (December 2012): 893–918.
20. Ibid., 894.
21. Full text in Song, *Classified Documents*, vol. 36, 104–5.
22. Daniel Leese, *Mao Cult: Rhetoric and Ritual in China's Cultural Revolution* (New York: Cambridge University Press, 2011), 219.
23. See Song, *Classified Documents*, vol. 11, 178. This was a common practice copied from Beijing for stabilizing social order in the aftermath of the armed struggles.
24. Ibid.
25. Ibid.
26. Zhongjiwei, zhongzubu luoshi zhengce Guangxi diaochazu, "Guilin ba er ling shijian de qingkuang diaocha" [Investigation of the Situation of Guilin's August 20 Incident], July 6, 1981. Courtesy of informant no. 20.
27. Song, *Classified Documents*, vol. 11, 179.
28. Zhongjiwei and zhongzubu luoshi zhengce Guangxi diaochazu, "Guilin ba er ling shijian."
29. Zhang, "Wo yijiuliuba nian."
30. *Fanshen*, during the Cultural Revolution, was a metaphor often used by the rebels to refer to political rehabilitation.
31. Interview with Zhang Xiongfei, 2016.
32. Zhang, "Wo yijiuliuba nian."
33. Guilin shi gonganju, "Guilin jige fangeming," 36.
34. Ibid., 32.
35. Zhongjiwei and zhongzubu luoshi zhengce Guangxi diaochazu, "Guilin ba er ling shijian."
36. Interview with informant no. 24, 2017.
37. Zhang Xiongfei, "Yijiuqisi nian Zhang Xiongfei deng jielu ba er ling shijian de bufen wenzhang neirong" [Partial Content of Zhang Xiongfei's Papers on Revealing the August 20 Action in 1974], unpublished manuscript, 2017. Courtesy of Zhang Xiongfei.
38. Guilin shi gonganju, "Guilin jige fangeming," 46.
39. Ibid., 57.
40. Interview with informant no. 23, 2017; Zhang Xiongfei, "Lüe lun 'Guilin jige fangeming fenzi' yu 'Guilin laoduo' zhi butong" [Brief discussion of the Differences between the "Several Counterrevolutionaries of Guilin" and "the Majority in Guilin"], unpublished manuscript, 2010. Courtesy of Zhang Xiongfei.
41. In Song, *Classified Documents*, vol. 11, 179.
42. Ibid., vol. 11, 184–85.
43. Zhang Xiongfei, "Zheyang da de yuan'an weishenme bu gan xie? San jie Guilin Wanbao huibi, waiqu, niezao Guilin wenge lishi" [Why not Dare to Write about such a Major Unjust Case? A Third Exposure of the Guilin Evening News' Avoidance, Distortion, and Fabrication of Guilin's Cultural Revolution History], unpublished manuscript, 2009. Courtesy of Zhang Xiongfei.
44. "Xiang qu dangwei huibao qi si anjian jielu" [Minutes of the Report on the July Fourth Case to the Guangxi Regional Party Committee], June 8, 1976. Courtesy of Zhang Xiongfei.
45. Ibid.
46. Ibid.

47 Guilin shi zhongji renmin fayuan, "Jianjue zhenya fangeming jiaqiang wuchanjieji zhuanzheng: xianxing fangeming fenzi Gong XX, Zhang Xiongfei, Xu XX, Huang XX de zuixing cailiao" [Resolutely Suppress Counterrevolution and Strengthen the Dictatorship of the Proletariat: Documentation of the Crimes of Active Counterrevolutionaries Gong XX, Zhang Xiongfei, Xu XX, and Huang XX], July 12, 1976, 1. Courtesy of Zhang Xiongfei.
48 Guangxi qu dangwei, "Guanyu zhuanfa Guilin shiwei 'Guanyu wei suowei Guilin jige fangeming fenzi pingfan de jueding' de tongzhi" [Notice about Transmitting the Guilin Municipal Party Committee's Decision on Rehabilitating the so-called "Several Counterrevolutionaries of Guilin"], February 22, 1984. Courtesy of Zhang Xiongfei.
49 Guilin shi gonganju, "Guilin jige fangeming," preface.
50 Zhonggong zhongyang, "Zhonggong zhongyang tongzhi" [CCP Center Notice], *Zhongfa* (1976) no. 24, December 10, 1976. Available in MLD, item no. 1869.
51 Guilin shi gonganju, "Guilin jige fangeming," 1–25.
52 Ibid., 42–74.
53 Guilin Gangchang da pipanzu, "Ba er ling tie'an fan bu le" [The Iron Verdict of August 20 Can Not be Reversed], *Guangxi ribao*, February 17, 1977, 1.
54 Leese: "Revising Political Verdicts," 111.
55 Zhang Xiongfei, "Meimei wei wo shensu" [My Younger Sister Appealed for Me], unpublished manuscript, 2017. Courtesy of Zhang Xiongfei.
56 Zhang Xiongfei's interview with Zhang Wen, 1983.
57 Guilin shi renmin fayuan, "Guilin shi renmin fayuan xingshi panjueshu" [Criminal Verdict by the Guilin Municipal People's Court] (76), *Xingpanzi* 67, July 26, 1976. Courtesy of Zhang Xiongfei.
58 Zhang Wen, "Shensushu" [Letter of Appeal], 1979. Courtesy of Zhang Xiongfei.
59 Ibid.
60 "The bloodline theory" (*xuetong lun*) was a hotly debated interpretation of the issue of class during the early Cultural Revolution, because it claimed that China should be run only by those who had the finest revolutionary family pedigree. It encountered harsh criticism from both those who had bad family backgrounds and the Party Center. See Yiching Wu, *The Cultural Revolution at the Margins: Chinese Socialism in Crisis* (Cambridge and London: Harvard University Press, 2014), 53–94.
61 Zhang, "Shensu shu."
62 Ibid.
63 Ibid.
64 This point had been clearly explained in the document *Zhongfa* (1978) no. 78.
65 Daniel Leese notes that this practice of dropping the charges of "malicious slandering" by designating them as "problems of ideological understanding" had been generally used in the procedure of review and rehabilitation in the Fengtai case. See Leese, "Revising Political Verdicts," 114–18.
66 Zhonggong zhongyang, "Zhongyang guanyu dizhu, funong fenzi zhaimao wenti he di, fu zinü chengfen wenti de jueding" [CCP Center's Decision Regarding the Problem of Removing Political Labels for Landlords and Rich Peasants and of Determining the Social Status of their Children], *Zhongfa* (1979) no. 5, January 11, 1979, in *Ganshen gongzuo zhengce wenjian xuanbian*, vol. 2, 1777–78. Available in MLD, item no. 16.
67 Xiao Donglian, *Lishi de zhuanzhe: cong boluan fanzheng dao gaige kaifang (1979–1981)* [Turning Point in History: From Bringing Order Out of Chaos to Reform and Opening Up] (Hong Kong: Chinese University Press, 2008), 107.

68 See Li Heping, "Li Heping tan wenge jingli" [Li Heping Talks about His Experience in the Cultural Revolution], unpublished manuscript, 2012. Courtesy of Zhang Xiongfei.
69 Ibid.
70 Her mother was a county-level veteran cadre; she was rehabilitated and compensated after the Cultural Revolution.
71 Zhang Xiongfei's interview with Zhang Wen, 1983.
72 Ibid.
73 Xiao, *Lishi de zhuanzhe*, 107–10.
74 Zhang Xiongfei's interview with Zhang Wen, 1983.
75 Ibid.
76 Guilin shi fucha xiaozu, "Guanyu Zhang Xiongfei xianxing fangeming an."
77 Zheng Yi, *Scarlet Memorial: Tales of Cannibalism in Modern China* (Boulder: Westview Press, 1996).
78 In the winter of 1982, Zhang's letter in which she sought help was smuggled out by a prison doctor, through whom this letter was sent to Wang, and finally delivered to Hu Yaobang, Zhang Xiongfei, "Zhang Xiongfei fangeming jituan an de fan'an lichen jiqi lishi zuoyong" [The Reversal Process of the Case of the Zhang Xiongfei Counterrevolutionary Clique and Its Historical Significance], unpublished manuscript, 2010. Courtesy of Zhang Xiongfei.
79 See *Zhongfa* (1978) no. 78.
80 Guilin shi fucha xiaozu, "Guanyu Zhang Xiongfei xianxing fangeming an."
81 Ibid.
82 Guilin shi renmin fayuan, "Guilin shi renmin fayuan xingshi panjueshu" [The Criminal Verdict by the Guilin Municipal Intermediate Court], November 25, 1980. Courtesy of Zhang Xiongfei.
83 Ibid.
84 Zhongjiwei, zhongzubu luoshi zhengce Guangxi diaochazu, "Guangxi wenge qijian panchu fangeming anjian cunzai de yixie wenti" [A Few Problems in Adjudicating Counter-revolutionary Cases in Guangxi during the Cultural Revolution], July 1981. Courtesy of informant no. 20.
85 Zhonggong qu gaoji renmin fayuan dangzu, "Jiang Hua yuanzhang tingqu huibao Zhang Xiongfei fangeming an shi de jianghua" [Talk by President Jiang Hua at the Debriefing on the Zhang Xiongfei Counterrevolutionary Case], February 24, 1982. Also see Jiang Hua zhuan bianshen weiyuanhui, ed., *Jiang Hua zhuan* [Biography of Jiang Hua] (Beijing: Zhonggong dangshi chubanshe, 2007), 379–80.
86 Guangxi qu gaoji renmin fayuan dangzu, "Guanyu chuli Zhang Xiongfei, Wang Zhancheng liang'an de qingshi baogao" [Report Asking for Instructions on Dealing with the Cases of Zhang Xiongfei and Wang Zhancheng], November 29, 1982.
87 Ibid.
88 Guangxi Zhuangzu zizhiqu gaoji renmin fayuan, "Guangxi Zhuangzu zizhiqu gaoji renmin fayuan xingshi panjueshu" [Criminal Verdict by the Guangxi Zhuang Autonomous Region Higher People's Court], January 19, 1983.
89 Zhonggong Guilin shiwei, "Guanyu wei Zhang Xiongfei deng tongzhi pingfan de jueding" [Decision on Rehabilitating Zhang Xiongfei and other Comrades], March 10, 1983.
90 See Song, *Classified Documents*, vol. 1, 42.
91 Guangxi qu dangwei, "Guanyu zhuanfa Guilin shiwei 'Guanyu wei suowei Guilin jige fangeming fenzi pingfan de jueding' de tongzhi" [Notice about Transmitting the Guilin

Municipal Party Committee's 'Decision to Rehabilitate the so-called several Counterrevolutionaries of Guilin'"], February 22, 1984.
92 Zhang Xiongfei, "Zhang Xiongfei riji" [Diary of Zhang Xiongfei], unpublished manuscript, 1984. Courtesy of Zhang Xiongfei.
93 Zhang Xiongfei, "Lishi jiang xuanpan wo wuzui" [History will Absolve Me], unpublished manuscript, 2014. Courtesy of Zhang Xiongfei.
94 Since 2009, Zhang has published many papers through Sina Blog, most of them about his experiences in the Cultural Revolution. His blog was blocked around 2014 and is no longer accessible.
95- Another prominent case is the Dao County massacre, which was not dealt with until 1984, Tan Hecheng, *The Killing Wind: A Chinese County's Descent into Madness during the Cultural Revolution*, trans. by Stacy Mosher and Guo Jian (Oxford: Oxford University Press, 2017).

Contributors

Jeremy Brown is Associate Professor of History at Simon Fraser University in Burnaby, British Columbia, Canada. He is the co-editor, with Paul Pickowicz, of *Dilemmas of Victory: The Early Years of the People's Republic of China* (2010) and, with Matthew Johnson, of *Maoism at the Grassroots: Everyday Life in China's Era of High Socialism* (2015). Among his many publications on the social and grassroots history of the PRC is *City versus Countryside in Mao's China: Negotiating the Divide* (2012).

Puck Engman is a Ph.D. candidate at the University of Freiburg, Germany, and a core member of the ERC project "The Maoist Legacy: Party Dictatorship, Transitional Justice and the Politics of Truth." His dissertation interrogates the nexus between property and identity in the PRC.

Daniel Leese is Professor of Sinology at the University of Freiburg and principal investigator of the ERC project "The Maoist Legacy: Party Dictatorship, Transitional Justice and the Politics of Truth." He is the author of *Mao Cult: Rhetoric and Ritual during the Cultural Revolution* (2011) and *Die Chinesische Kulturrevolution* (2016), as well as the editor-in-chief of *Brill's Encyclopedia of China* (2009).

Michael Schoenhals is Professor of Chinese in the Centre for Languages and Literature, Lund University. He has by now spent the better part of an only moderately productive academic life trying, he claims, often in vain, to understand the socio-political history of the PRC. His publications include *Spying for the People: Mao's Secret Agents, 1949–1967* (2013), "The Global War on Terrorism as Meta-Narrative: An Alternative Reading of Recent Chinese History" (2008), and *Doing Things with Words in Chinese Politics: Five Studies* (1992).

Song Guoqing is completing his Ph.D. at the University of Freiburg. His doctoral research on the social and political reactions to the killings in Guangxi during the Cultural Revolution is a key part of the ERC project on legacies of the Maoist era. He is the co-author, with Dong Guoqiang, of "Guangxi wenge qijian fei zhengchang siwang yanjiu" (2016) and has contributed to the compilation of *Nanjing tongshi*.

Wang Haiguang is Professor Emeritus of Party History at the Central Party School, Beijing. He is the author of many books and articles on the socio-political history of the PRC, including "Cong chedi fouding dao chedi fansi: wenge de jiyi yu sikao" (2016), *Shi guo jing wei qian: Zhongguo dangdai shi caiwei* (2014), *Zhe ji chen sha Wendu'erhan* (2012).

Xu Lizhi is Professor Emeritus at the Chinese Academy of Social Sciences, Institute of Law, Beijing. His work covers many aspects of Chinese legal history, from late imperial times to the present. Notably, he is the author of the chapter on law in the Cultural Revolution in *Zhonghua renmin gongheguo fazhi tongshi* (1998), edited by Han Yanlong.

Zhang Man is a Ph.D. candidate at the University of Freiburg and a core member of the ERC Maoist legacy project. In her dissertation, she is exploring questions of culpability and identity following the Cultural Revolution in Jiangsu Province. She has contributed to the compilation of *Nanjing tongshi*.

Index

Archives 6–7

Big-character posters 15, 81, 176, 179–180

Capitalists 101, 105–107, 109, 115–116
– differentiation work (*qubie gongzuo*) 116
Case examination groups 38, 41, 87
– Central Case Examination Group 111
Cases 52
– review of 14, 91, 112, 141, 162, 190
– terminological complication 52
– *zhuan'an* 52–53
Chinese Communist Party (CCP) 1, 16, 28, 101–102, 119
– CCP Central Organization Department 103, 111, 141
– Central Group of Ten 53–54, 68
– leadership of 28, 31
– Third Plenum of the Eleventh Central Committee 14, 159, 175, 190, 192
– united front 55, 98, 115–116
Class status 11–12, 77–79, 82, 101, 105–107, 109, 115
Confessions 11, 105
– confessional scripts 7, 151–152
– forced confessions 91, 155
– self-criticism 7, 158
Counterrevolutionaries 35, 89, 191
– active counterrevolutionaries 86, 177
Courts 1–2, 11, 36, 183, 191
– adjudication committees (*shenpan weiyuanhui*) 36
– appeals to 186, 191
– as instruments of campaign justice 13
– Organic Law of the People's Courts 29
– organization of 4, 40
– people's tribunals 38
– Supreme People's Court 1–2, 4, 33, 141, 175, 190
Crime
– crime rate 42
– economic crimes 32
– ordinary crime 16, 42

Criminal justice 144
– criminal law 3, 11
– criminal procedure 2, 4, 11, 36
– during the Cultural Revolution 128
Cultural Revolution 75–76, 80, 93–94, 118–119, 133–134, 144, 152, 176
– law in the 9–10
– lawlessness of the 8, 25, 41
– rebels 152–153, 176–177

Deng Xiaoping 14, 16
Dong Biwu 3, 13–14

Files 7
– case files 7, 69, 76
– "file-selves" 7
– personnel dossiers 7, 117
Four Types elements (*si lei fenzi*) 40, 75, 78–80, 94, 139
– bad elements 11, 15, 127–128, 135–140
– landlords 76

Gang of Four 8, 150, 184–185
Guangxi 55, 174, 177–182, 187–189, 192, 194

Historical problems 102–104, 113, 137
Hu Yaobang 141, 189

Integrity 98–102, 104, 118–119
Interrogation 88–89, 154–156, 158, 163
Investigation
– external investigation 62, 64
– security risk assessment 53–54

Jia Qian 1–3
Judiciary 4, 38
– judicial system 35–38
– public security organs, procuratorates, and courts (*gong-jian-fa*) 9, 37, 38
– smashing of 30
Justice 134
– administrative justice 8
– campaign justice 8

Kang Sheng 113

Labor reform 89, 141
Law 5–6, 8–11, 13, 17, 93
- "administrating justice independently," 1
- "bourgeois" law 3, 10
- class struggle and 3
- codified law 3, 9, 12
- law-and-society perspective 6
- politics and 2–3, 5–6, 17
- practice of 5–6, 8
- "rule of man" vs. "rule of law," 25–26
Legal debate 5
Legal nihilism 3, 5, 26
Legal principles 28
- Mao Zedong Thought 3, 28, 30, 113
- two types of contradictions 29, 32
Legal sources 32–34
- hierarchical relation of 33
Legal system 5, 26–28, 42–43, 75, 94, 182
- destruction of 26
- dictatorship (*zhuanzheng*) 13, 26, 29–31
- Socialist legality 4, 8
Li Yizhe 9, 25
Liu Shaoqi 33, 111

Mao Zedong 33, 84, 108, 111, 135
- death of 14, 102, 115, 141
- destroying portraits of 76, 82–83, 87–88
- as source of contradictory authority 10
- views on the relation of law and politics 4, 32

Old society 99, 101, 109, 118

Petitioning 15, 138–140, 187–190
Political campaigns 2–3, 12, 157
- Anti-Rightist campaign 1, 3–5, 29
- campaign time 101
- Cleansing of the Class Ranks 83
- Criticize Lin Biao and Confucius 178, 180–182
- Four Cleanups 108–111
- Great Leap Forward 37, 107–108
- Internal Elimination of Counterrevolution (*neibu sufan*) 53–54, 68

- One Strike, Three Antis 42, 87, 89, 93, 156, 158
Procuratorates 5, 36, 40
- Organic Law of the People's Procuratorates 29
- Supreme People's Procuratorate 131, 187, 188
Public security 67–69, 135, 138, 141
- Ministry of 52–54, 60, 62, 65, 68, 131–133, 188
- Six Articles 31, 34–35, 93–94
Punishment 11, 16, 32, 41, 78, 89, 128, 133–134, 150
- death sentences 2, 33, 39, 42, 183
- deportation 11, 80, 89, 127, 136, 138, 142, 145
- disciplinary 16
- exemption from 114, 165
- *guanzhi* 78, 86

Rape 130–132, 143–145
- allegations of 144
- investigation of 133
- national statistics 132
- of sent-down youth 139
Reform through labor 135
Rehabilitation (*pingfan*) 1, 8, 13–15, 90–92, 175, 190–192
- revision (*jiuzheng*) 13
Retroactive justice 14–15
Rightists 1, 107

Shanghai 14, 150, 152
Soviet Union 4, 13, 106
Stalin, Joseph 3, 4
- death of 14
Study classes 81, 151, 155–157
Suicide 155–156, 159–161, 163–167

Testimonies 11, 86–89, 103, 110, 113, 151, 162
- reliance on 104, 117
Tewu 54, 56–59, 65–67, 69
Three Types of People 150, 164–165
Tianjin 127, 129, 133–134, 136

Unjust, false, and mistaken cases 14, 41, 92, 102, 127, 175, 190

Vetting 98–99, 117
Violence 12

– during the Cultural Revolution 75
– killings 75, 174, 179–180, 187, 193
Vyshinsky, Andrey 3, 4

Wei Guoqing 16, 174, 177–183